CORAL REEFS

Cities of the Ocean

CORAL REEFS

Cities of the Ocean

MARIS WICKS

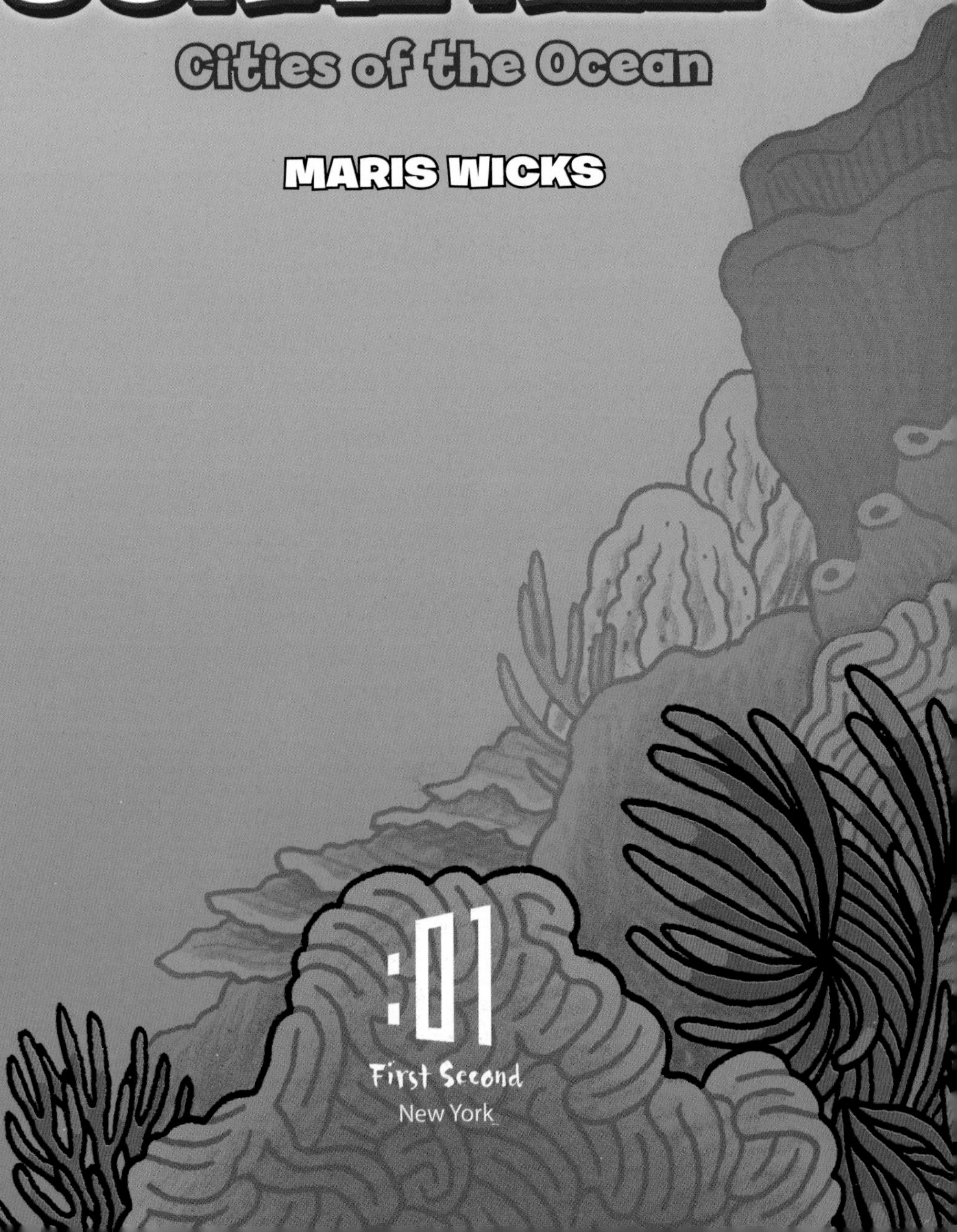

:01
First Second
New York

for D.C.

First Second

Drawn with a Staedtler HB pencil on Strathmore Bristol Smooth, inked with Uni Pin Pro 03 and 01 pens, and digitally colored in Photoshop. Lettered in Comicrazy.

Published by First Second
First Second is an imprint of Roaring Brook Press,
a division of Holtzbrinck Publishing Holdings Limited Partnership
175 Fifth Avenue, New York, NY 10010

Cataloging-in-Publication Data is on file at the Library of Congress.

Paperback ISBN 978-1-62672-145-6
Hardcover ISBN 978-1-62672-146-3

Our books may be purchased in bulk for promotional, educational, or business use. Please contact your local bookseller or the Macmillan Corporate and Premium Sales Department at (800) 221-7945 ext. 5442 or by e-mail at MacmillanSpecialMarkets@macmillan.com.

First edition 2016
Book design by John Green

Printed in China by Toppan Leefung Printing Ltd., Dongguan City, Guandong Province
Paperback: 10 9 8 7 6 5
Hardcover: 10 9 8 7 6 5 4

If you were a superhero what would your superpower be? Invisibility? Invincibility? Super strength? I'd choose the power of flight. Soaring over forests, cities, mountains, and oceans on a sunny day with a warm wind. Sounds pretty good, doesn't it?

As much as I've flapped my arms, I haven't taken off yet. But here's a secret: I can fly underwater—as a scuba diver! With just a mask, fins, and a snorkel, anyone can free-dive. And when you add on scuba gear, well, then you get to fly through those amazing underwater cities—coral reefs—for a whole hour at a time.

I have been studying coral reefs for about fifteen years, and every time I'm underwater I still feel like I'm flying. I work upside down, my head in the corals and my feet toward the sky. When I'm on a reef I look at coral animals to determine if they are healthy, measure how big they are, and observe other important details. It's a very slow task, but it's a lot of fun. I'm often so busy looking at the corals that I miss the amazing reef fish and sharks swimming over my head! I once finished measuring a coral and looked up to see about eighteen spotted eagle rays in a big group swimming right next to me. These are huge animals—each eagle ray has at least a three-foot wingspan. They're black with white spots and have great big eyes in their cute faces. If I hadn't looked up at that exact moment I would have missed them. But with my head in the corals, I get to see tiny critters that most people don't see: seahorses

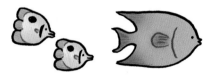

and pipefish, sponges of all shapes and colors, and the tiniest little shrimp and crabs hiding inside coral branches. I love spotting the wavy arm of a brittle star poking out from a crevice or seeing a nocturnal basket star curled up into a little ball on a giant sea fan. My favorites are the nudibranchs— beautiful little shell-less snails.

As a marine scientist I've traveled to some of the most remote places on our beautiful planet, searching for healthy coral reefs. They are increasingly hard to find. As you will read in chapter 5, coral reefs are in trouble. Their problems are complicated. Just like each human is unique and can get sick from different diseases or react to illness in different ways, each reef is unique and can suffer from different problems, with different potential solutions. Luckily, there are lots of ways to help coral reefs. (Chapter 5 is full of great suggestions!) And best of all, the things that we need to do to help corals also help other organisms and ecosystems that we love: Polar bears! Rain forests! Whales! Elephants! Aye-ayes! To ensure the survival of all of these creatures, we need to preserve their habitats and keep them clean and safe. We need to protect biodiversity to maintain food sources, symbioses, habitat, and so on. In addition, we need to prevent those animals from being harvested, poached, or otherwise removed.

But what can you do if you've never even seen a coral reef? There are so many ways to help, and all of them make a difference. For example, if you

live in North America, plant a milkweed. Really! It might sound weird, but let's consider it. Milkweed gives monarch butterflies a breeding habitat and a food source for their caterpillars. At the same time, milkweed plants also prevent runoff, provide a nectar source for insects, take up space that might otherwise be occupied by an invasive species, and connect people to nature. But wait a minute…can planting milkweed actually save coral reefs? Not exactly. But it's still a positive choice for our planet. Every choice you make matters. Recycling your water bottles is a good choice. Better yet, avoid all single-use plastics. Buy second-hand clothing and toys. Turn lights off when not in use. If you get into the habit of making choices with the environment in mind, you will be making our planet a better place. You make choices that impact the environment with every dollar you spend, every action you take, and every vote that you cast. A few good choices can make a huge difference. Just imagine if all of the seven billion people on earth made three positive environmental choices every day.

I hope you can get underwater and "fly" around a coral reef sometime—it's pretty amazing. But if you can't, learning about corals in this awesome comic book will help you to see just how amazing the corals and reefs that we're trying to protect are. And if you make great choices to support the environment you won't need to fly—you'll already be a superhero.

—Randi Rotjan, Ph.D.
Associate Research Scientist, New England Aquarium

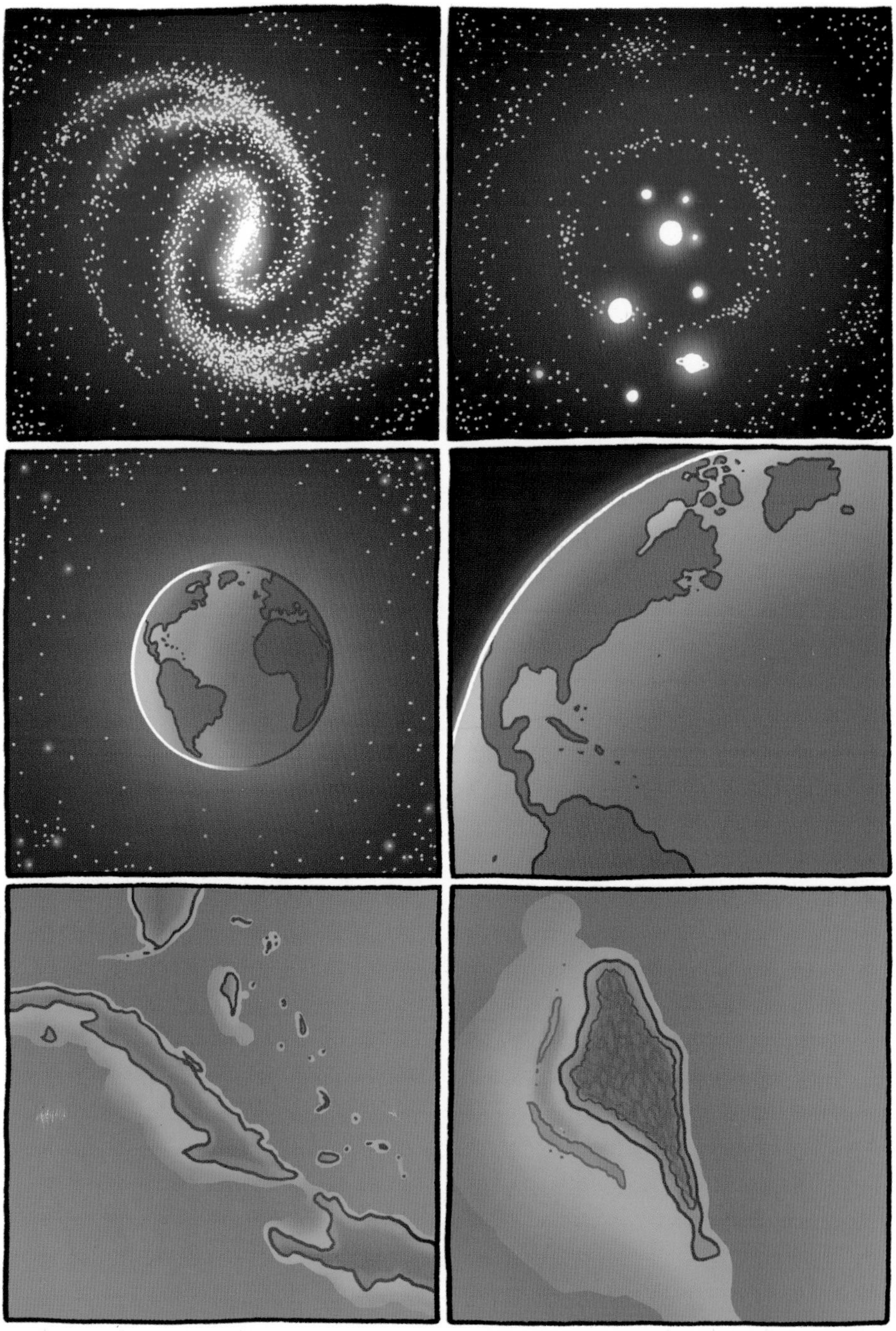

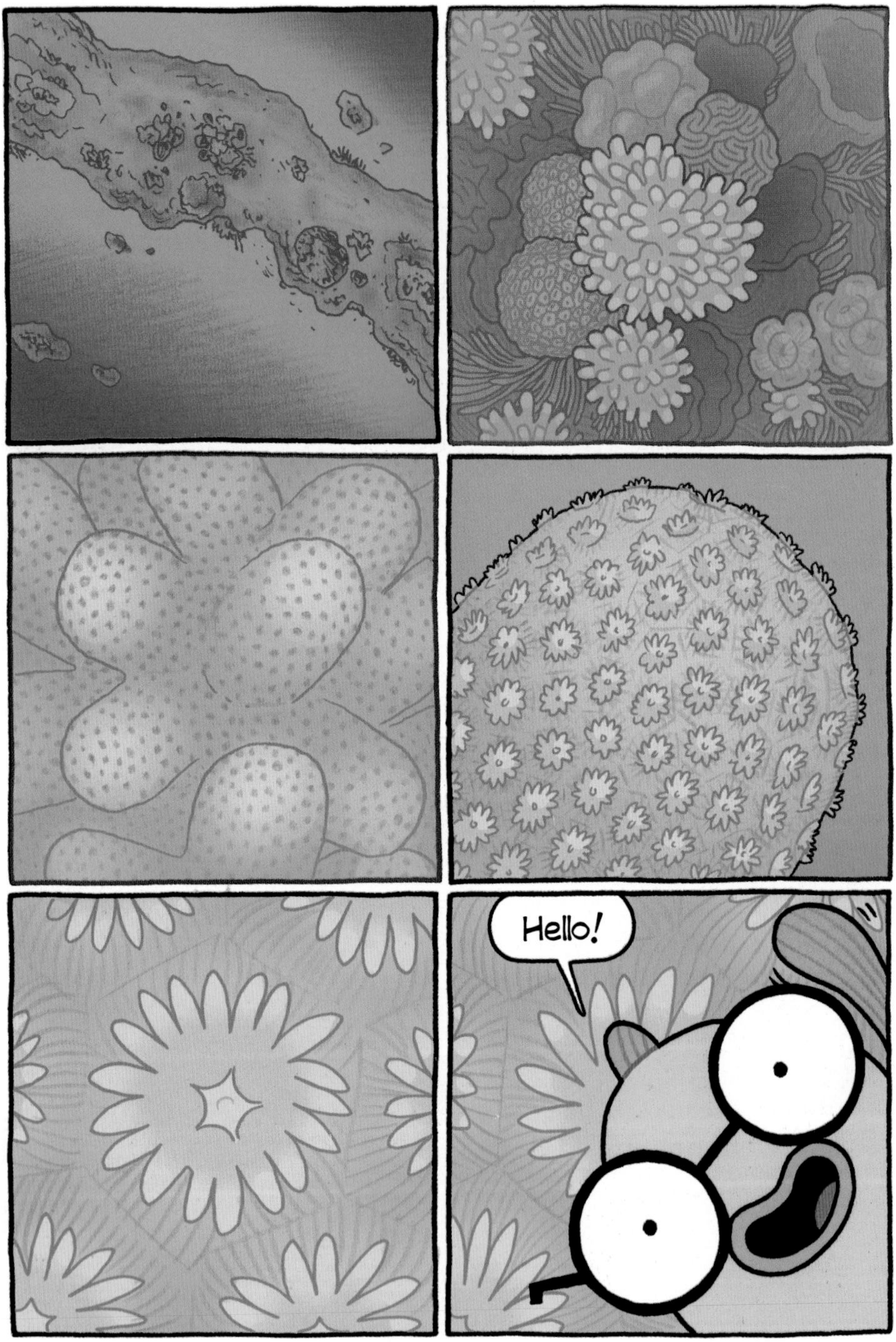
Hello!

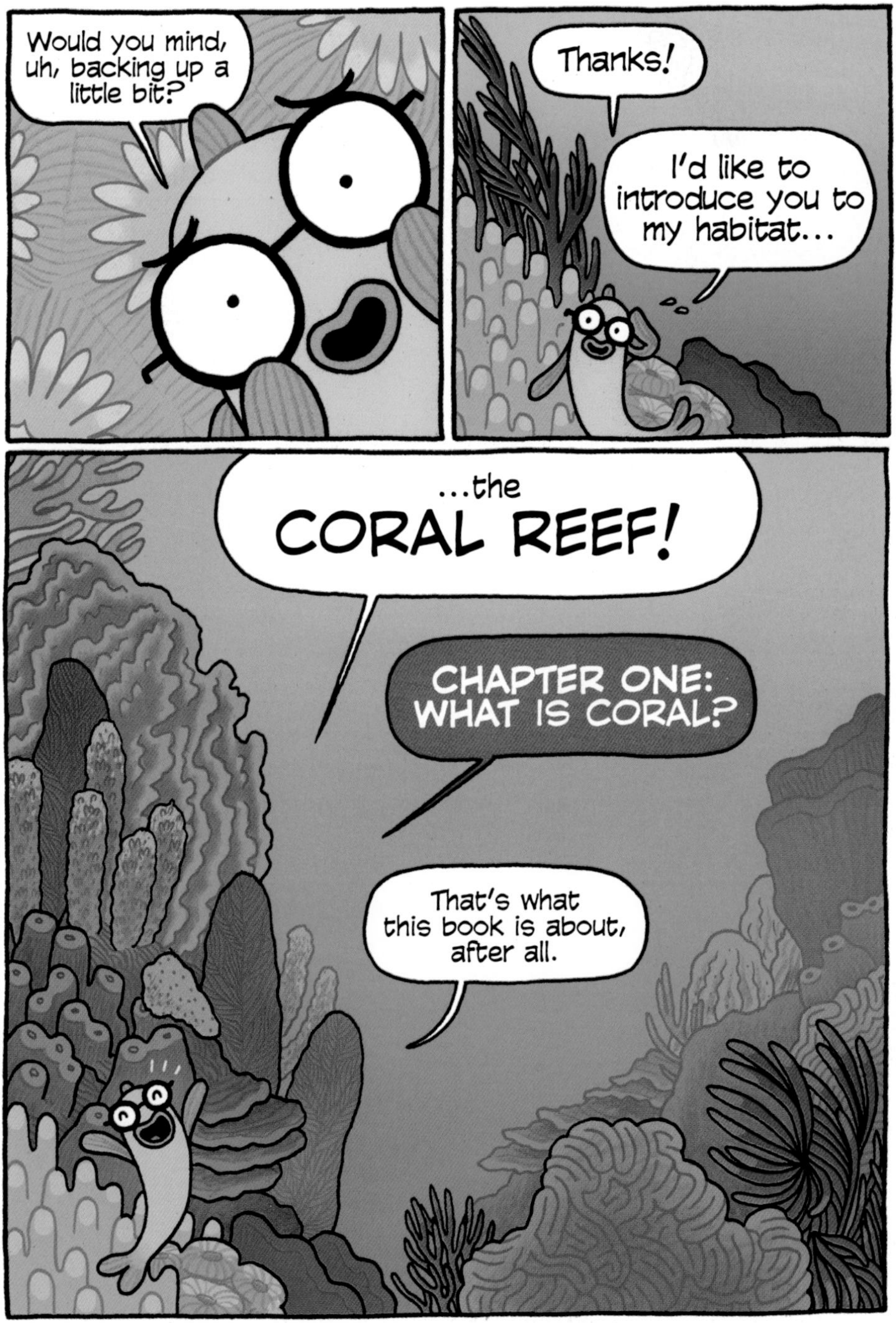
Would you mind, uh, backing up a little bit?
Thanks!
I'd like to introduce you to my habitat...
...the CORAL REEF!
CHAPTER ONE: WHAT IS CORAL?
That's what this book is about, after all.

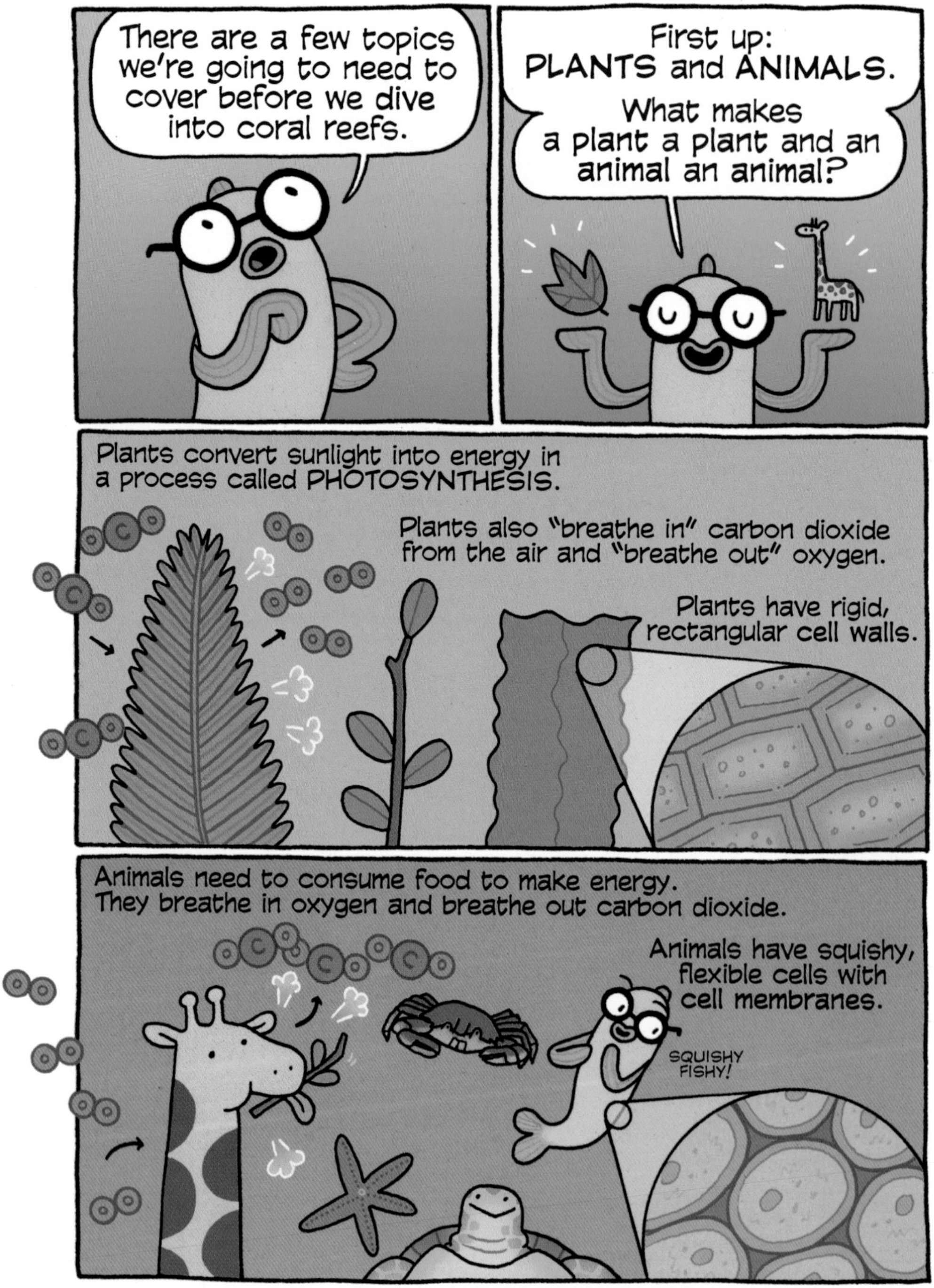
There are a few topics we're going to need to cover before we dive into coral reefs.
First up: PLANTS and ANIMALS.
What makes a plant a plant and an animal an animal?
Plants convert sunlight into energy in a process called PHOTOSYNTHESIS.
Plants also "breathe in" carbon dioxide from the air and "breathe out" oxygen.
Plants have rigid, rectangular cell walls.
Animals need to consume food to make energy. They breathe in oxygen and breathe out carbon dioxide.
Animals have squishy, flexible cells with cell membranes.
SQUISHY FISHY!

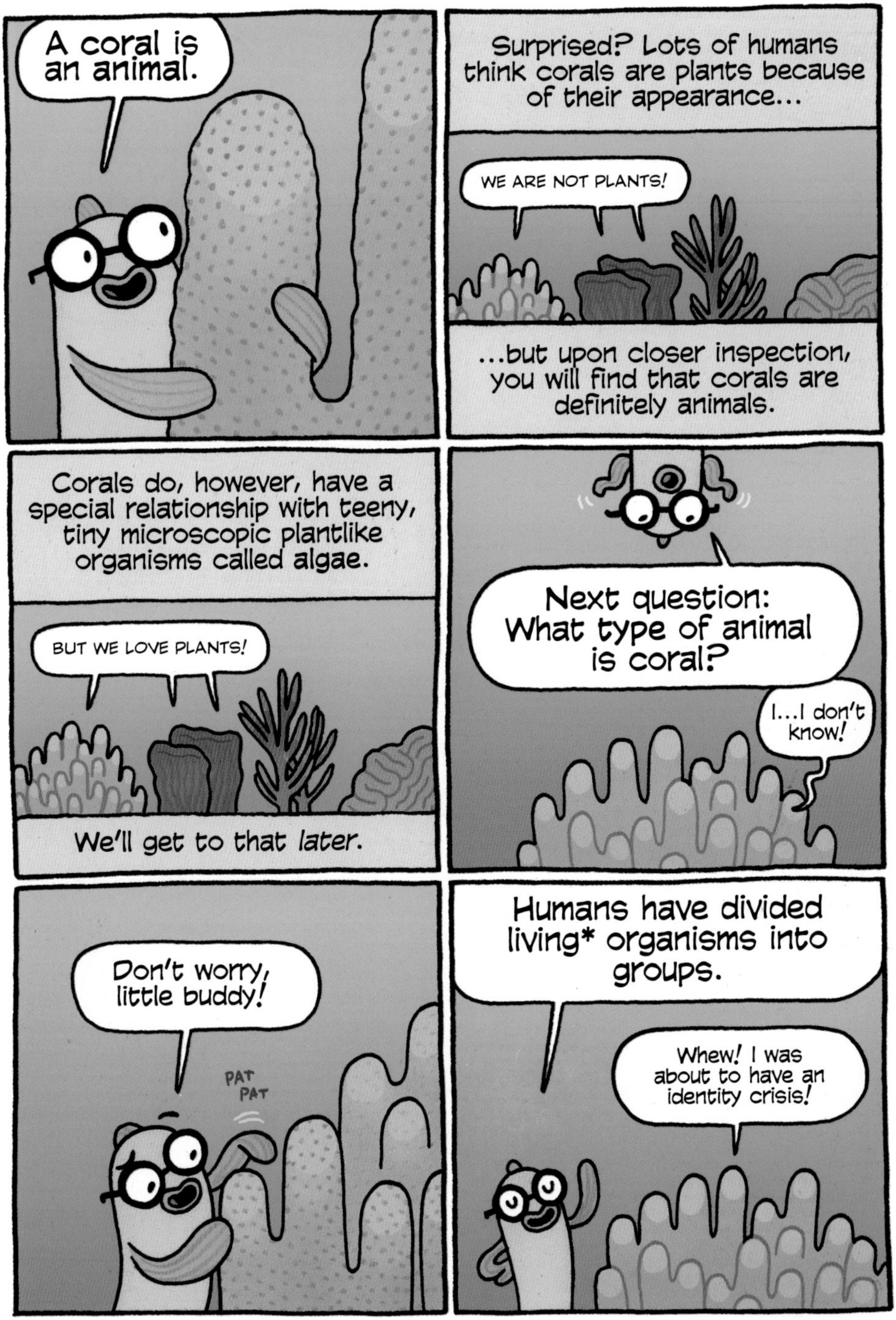
A coral is an animal.
Surprised? Lots of humans think corals are plants because of their appearance...
WE ARE NOT PLANTS!
...but upon closer inspection, you will find that corals are definitely animals.
Corals do, however, have a special relationship with teeny, tiny microscopic plantlike organisms called algae.
BUT WE LOVE PLANTS!
We'll get to that *later*.
Next question: What type of animal is coral?
I...I don't know!
Don't worry, little buddy!
PAT PAT
Humans have divided living* organisms into groups.
Whew! I was about to have an identity crisis!

*And nonliving (like the dinosaurs) too!

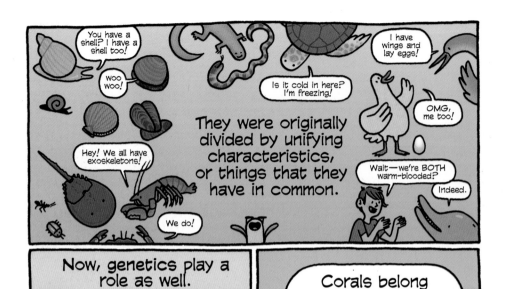

You have a shell? I have a shell too!
Woo woo!
Is it cold in here? I'm freezing!
I have wings and lay eggs!
OMG, me too!
They were originally divided by unifying characteristics, or things that they have in common.
Hey! We all have exoskeletons!
We do!
Wait—we're BOTH warm-blooded?
Indeed.
Now, genetics play a role as well.
Turns out that I'm more related to spiders and scorpions!
Corals belong to a large group of animals called invertebrates.
Invertebrates are animals that have no backbone or spinal cord—and they are EVERYWHERE!

That's the author up there, talking to a dolphin.

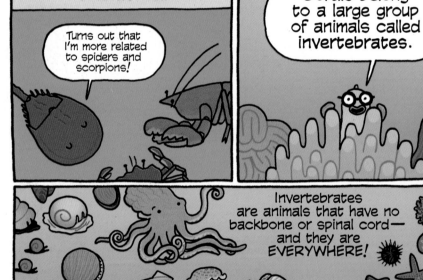

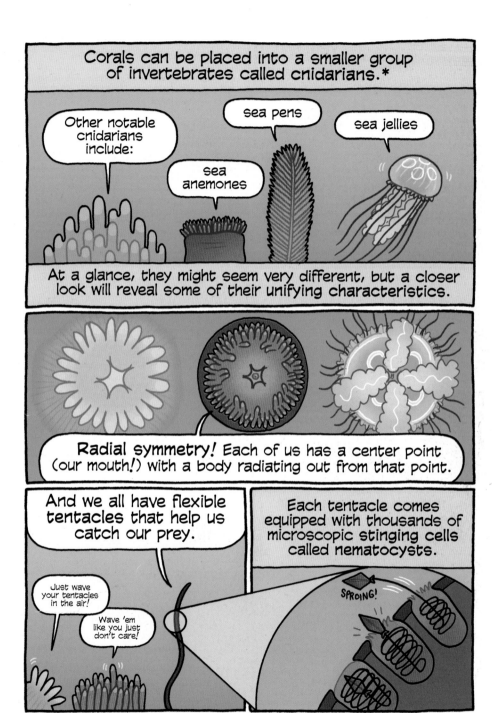

Corals can be placed into a smaller group of invertebrates called cnidarians.*

Other notable cnidarians include:

sea pens

sea jellies

sea anemones

At a glance, they might seem very different, but a closer look will reveal some of their unifying characteristics.

Radial symmetry! Each of us has a center point (our mouth!) with a body radiating out from that point.

And we all have flexible tentacles that help us catch our prey.

Each tentacle comes equipped with thousands of microscopic stinging cells called nematocysts.

Just wave your tentacles in the air!

Wave 'em like you just don't care!

SPROING!

*Pronounced "NIE-darians"; the "C" is silent!

7

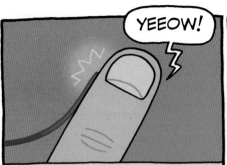

YEEOW!

When a tentacle comes in contact with another living thing, its nematocysts automatically eject.

Cnidarians use this adaptation to stun or kill prey before bringing it to their mouths.

YEEOW!

YEEOW!

Don't worry—cnidarians are not your nemesis.

The stinging action is involuntary; cnidarians cannot control it.

Ooops! I thought you were food!

FOOD!

The only time they will not sting is if they touch another jelly of the same species.

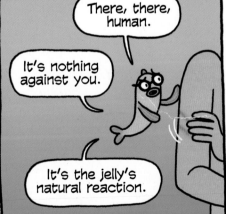

There, there, human.

It's nothing against you.

It's the jelly's natural reaction.

*Cnidarians don't have eyes or teeth. Actually, some of them have very primitive eyes, called eye spots or ocelli.

The last characteristic has to do with each cnidarian's life cycle:

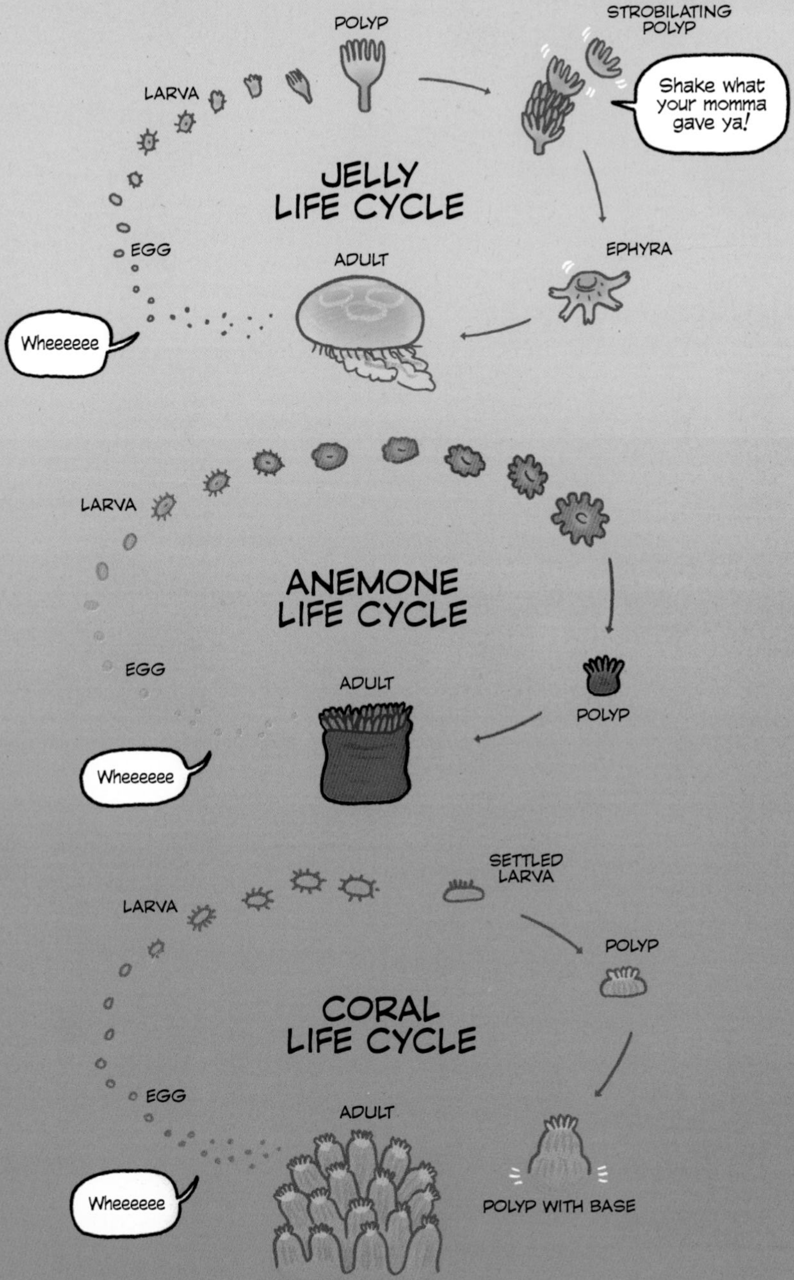
POLYP
STROBILATING POLYP
Shake what your momma gave ya!
LARVA
JELLY LIFE CYCLE
EGG
EPHYRA
ADULT
Wheeeeee
LARVA
ANEMONE LIFE CYCLE
EGG
ADULT
POLYP
Wheeeeee
SETTLED LARVA
LARVA
POLYP
CORAL LIFE CYCLE
EGG
ADULT
Wheeeeee
POLYP WITH BASE

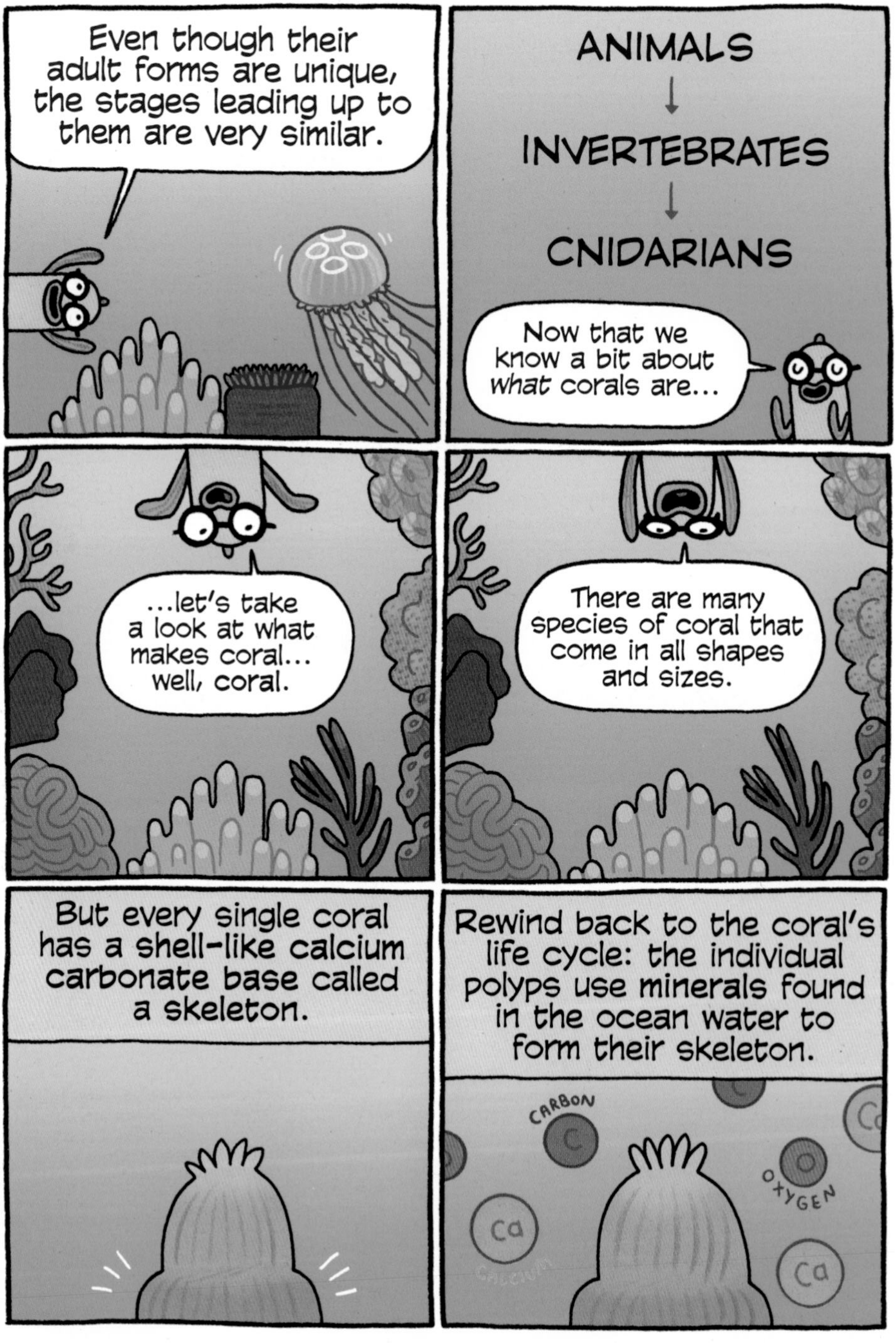
Even though their adult forms are unique, the stages leading up to them are very similar.
ANIMALS
INVERTEBRATES
CNIDARIANS
Now that we know a bit about *what* corals are...
...let's take a look at what makes coral... well, coral.
There are many species of coral that come in all shapes and sizes.
But every single coral has a shell-like calcium carbonate base called a skeleton.
Rewind back to the coral's life cycle: the individual polyps use minerals found in the ocean water to form their skeleton.
CARBON
C
O
OXYGEN
Ca
Ca
Ca

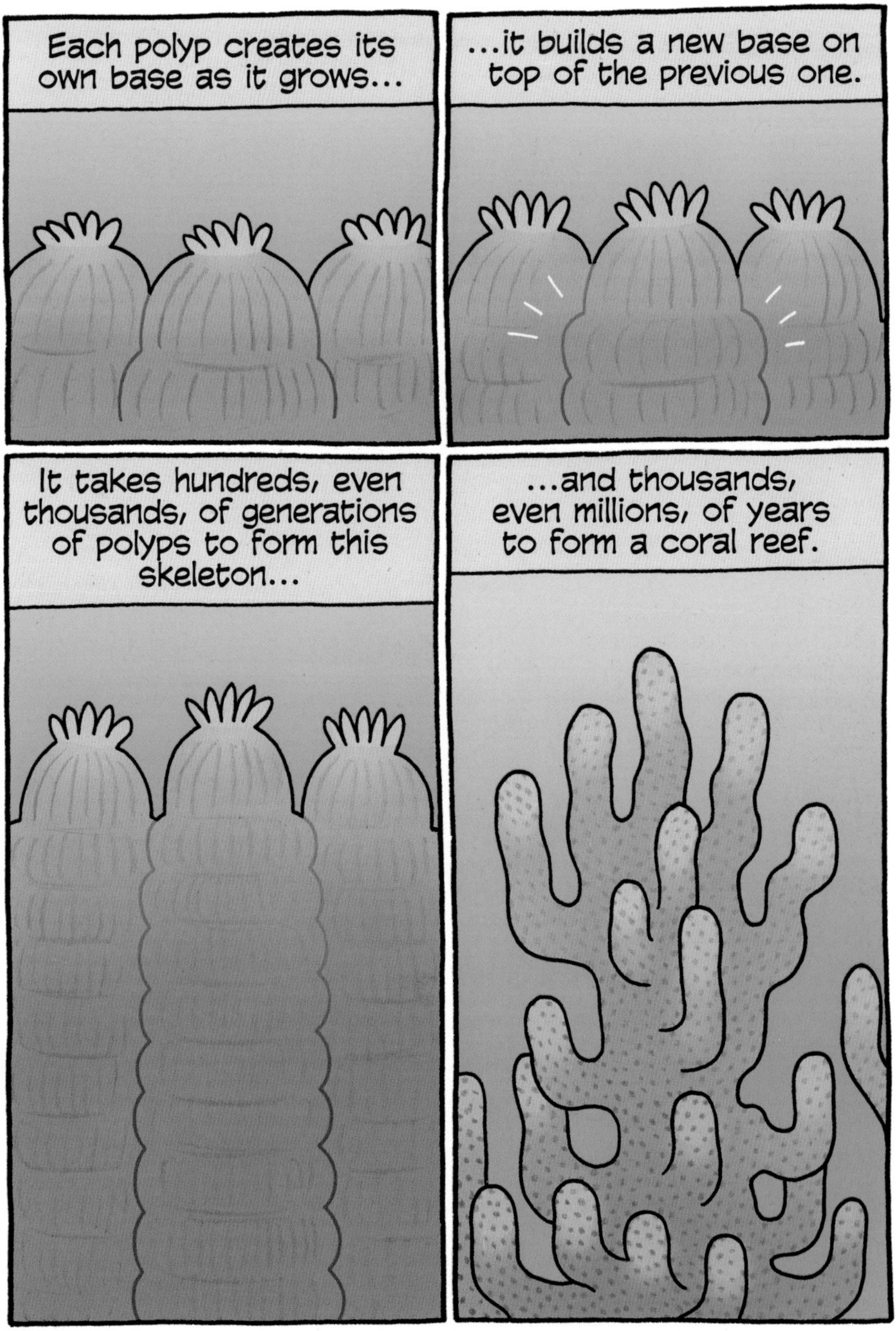
Each polyp creates its own base as it grows...
...it builds a new base on top of the previous one.
It takes hundreds, even thousands, of generations of polyps to form this skeleton...
...and thousands, even millions, of years to form a coral reef.

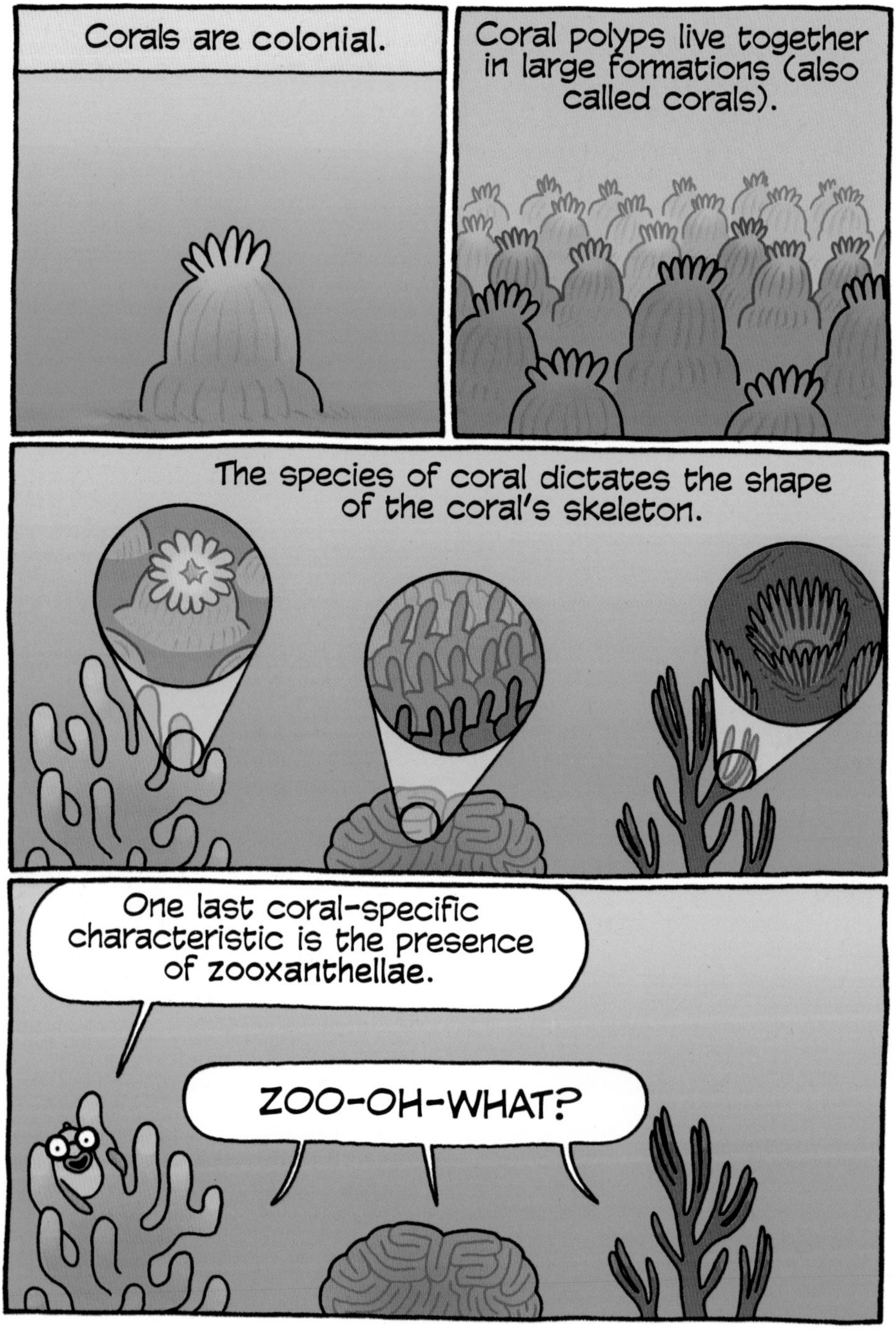
Corals are colonial.
Coral polyps live together in large formations (also called corals).
The species of coral dictates the shape of the coral's skeleton.
One last coral-specific characteristic is the presence of zooxanthellae.
ZOO-OH-WHAT?

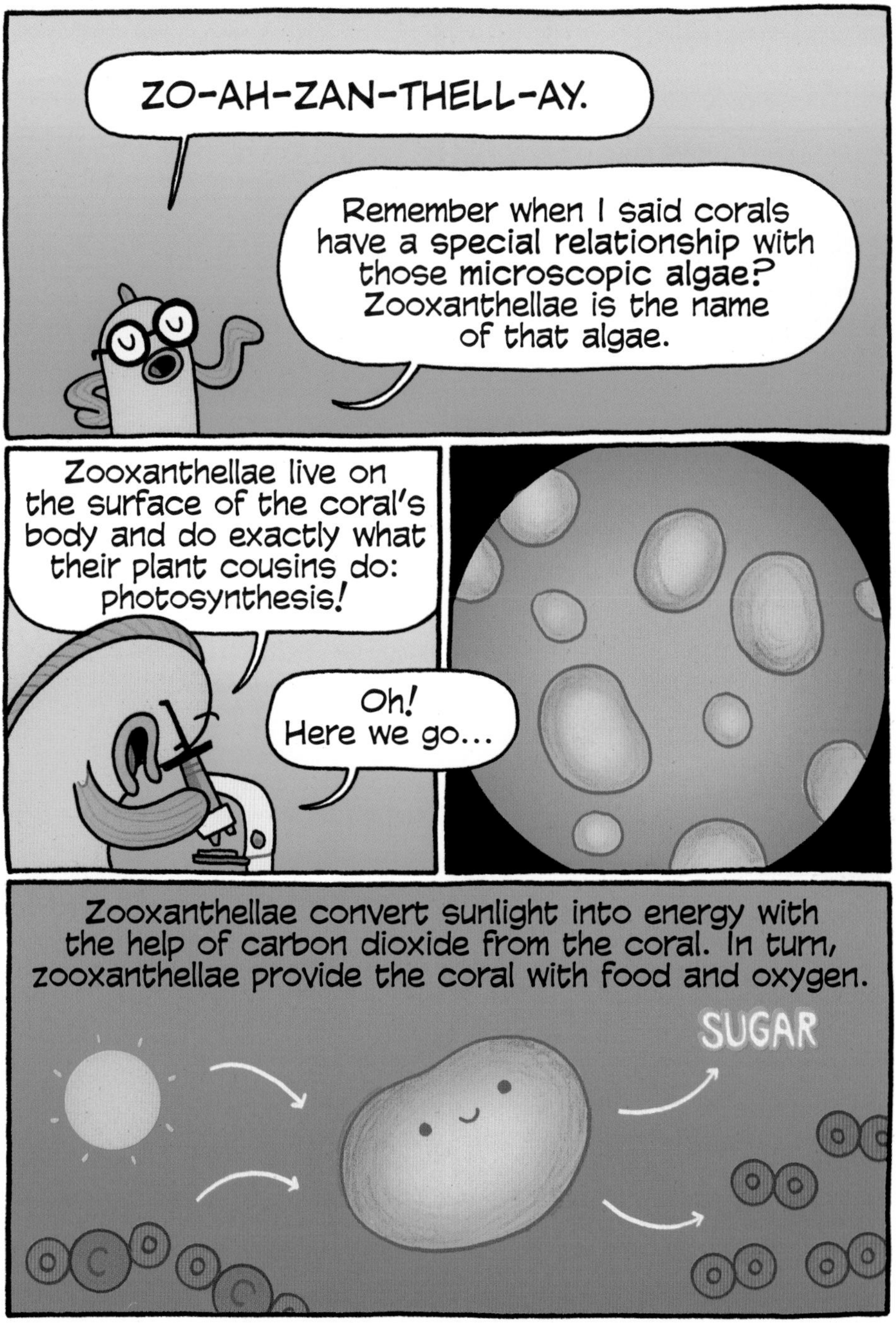
ZO-AH-ZAN-THELL-AY.
Remember when I said corals have a special relationship with those microscopic algae? Zooxanthellae is the name of that algae.
Zooxanthellae live on the surface of the coral's body and do exactly what their plant cousins do: photosynthesis!
Oh! Here we go...
Zooxanthellae convert sunlight into energy with the help of carbon dioxide from the coral. In turn, zooxanthellae provide the coral with food and oxygen.
SUGAR

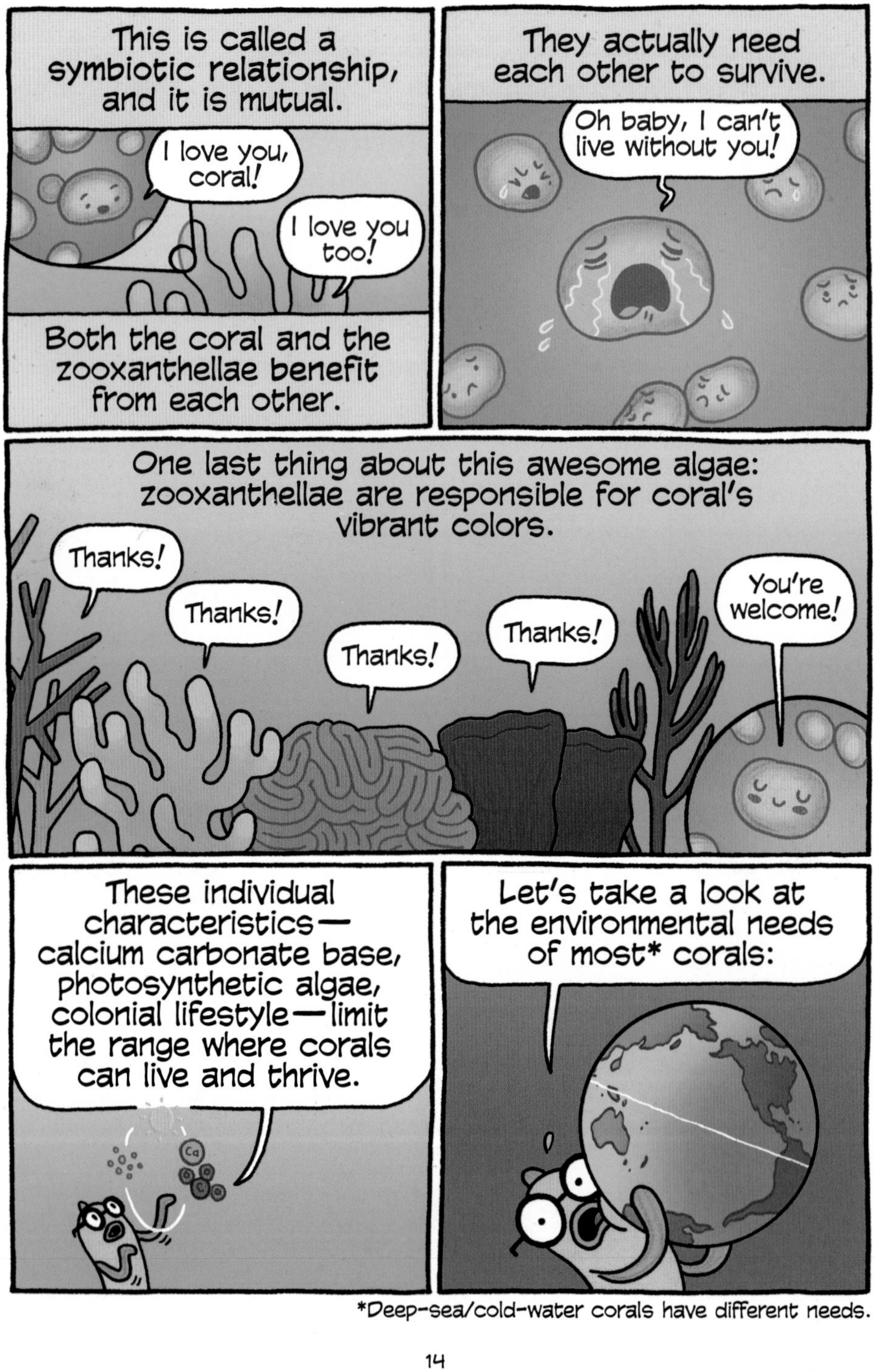
This is called a symbiotic relationship, and it is mutual.
I love you, coral!
I love you too!
Both the coral and the zooxanthellae benefit from each other.
They actually need each other to survive.
Oh baby, I can't live without you!
One last thing about this awesome algae: zooxanthellae are responsible for coral's vibrant colors.
Thanks!
Thanks!
Thanks!
Thanks!
You're welcome!
These individual characteristics—calcium carbonate base, photosynthetic algae, colonial lifestyle—limit the range where corals can live and thrive.
Let's take a look at the environmental needs of most* corals:
*Deep-sea/cold-water corals have different needs.

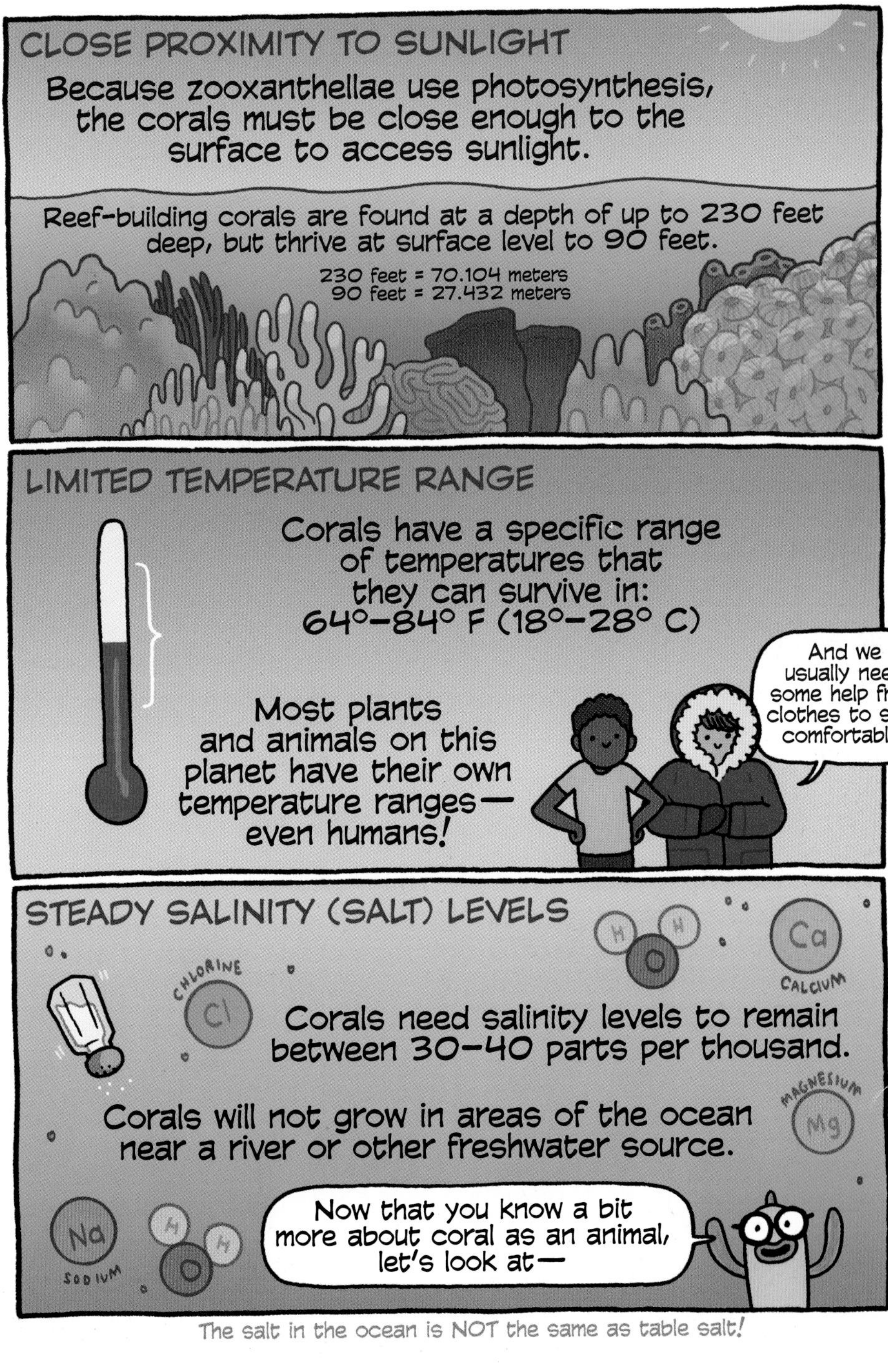
CLOSE PROXIMITY TO SUNLIGHT
Because zooxanthellae use photosynthesis, the corals must be close enough to the surface to access sunlight.
Reef-building corals are found at a depth of up to 230 feet deep, but thrive at surface level to 90 feet.
230 feet = 70.104 meters
90 feet = 27.432 meters
LIMITED TEMPERATURE RANGE
Corals have a specific range of temperatures that they can survive in: 64°-84° F (18°-28° C)
Most plants and animals on this planet have their own temperature ranges— even humans!
And we usually need some help from clothes to stay comfortable.
STEADY SALINITY (SALT) LEVELS
H
H
O
Ca
CALCIUM
CHLORINE
Cl
Corals need salinity levels to remain between 30-40 parts per thousand.
MAGNESIUM
Mg
Corals will not grow in areas of the ocean near a river or other freshwater source.
Na
SODIUM
H
H
O
Now that you know a bit more about coral as an animal, let's look at—

The salt in the ocean is NOT the same as table salt!

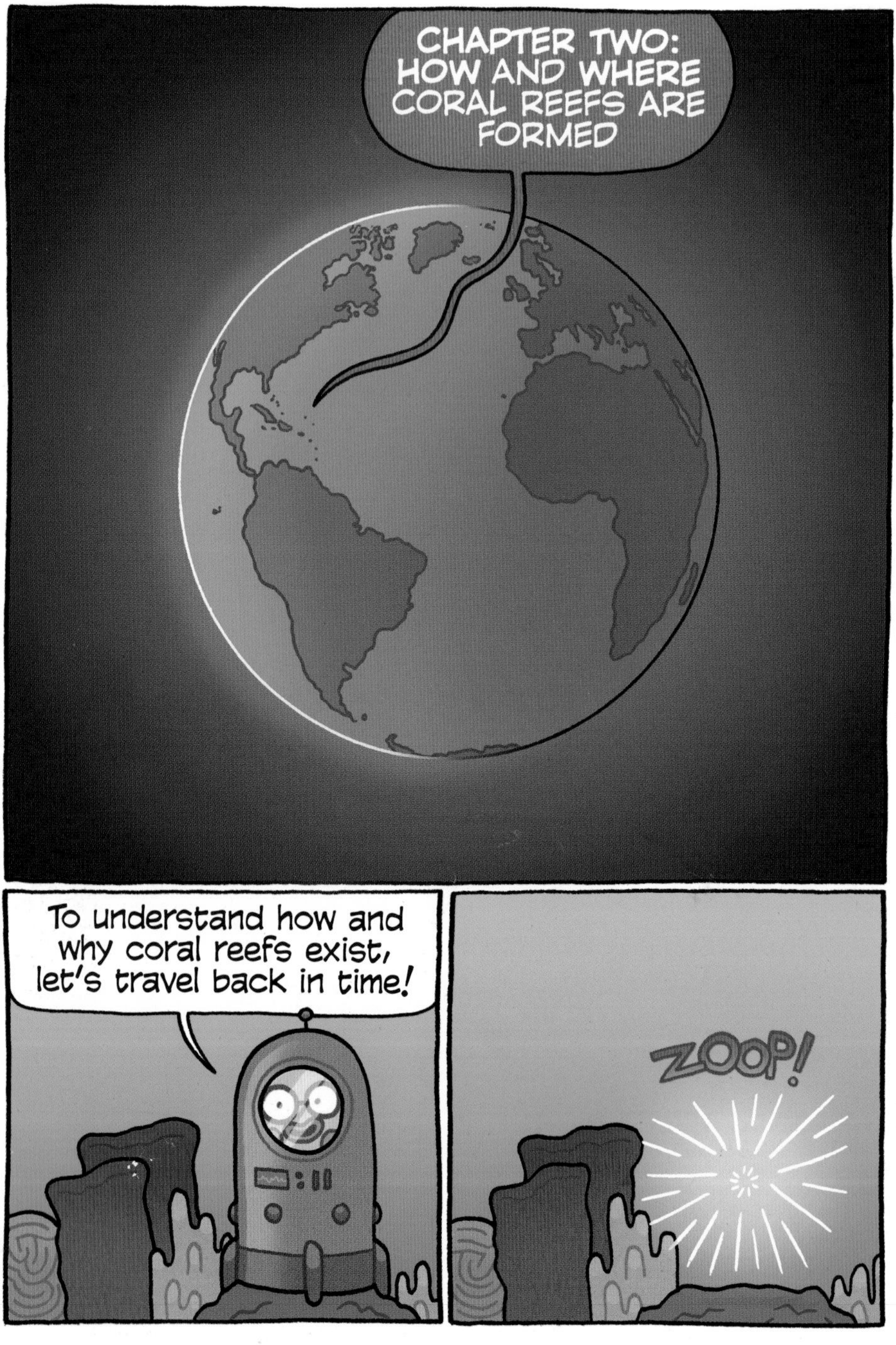
CHAPTER TWO:
HOW AND WHERE CORAL REEFS ARE FORMED
To understand how and why coral reefs exist, let's travel back in time!
ZOOP!

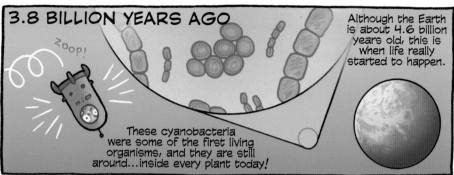

3.8 BILLION YEARS AGO

ZOOP!

These cyanobacteria were some of the first living organisms, and they are still around...inside every plant today!

Although the Earth is about 4.6 billion years old, this is when life really started to happen.

400 MILLION YEARS AGO

First corals appear! All that we have left of them today is fossils— and their modern-day descendants.

ZOOP!

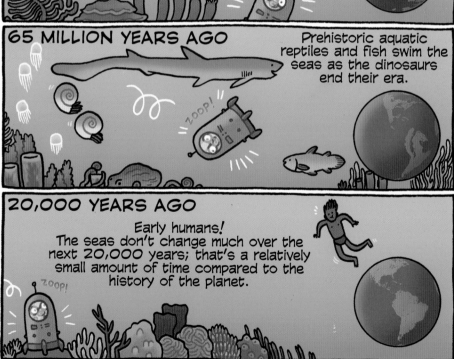

65 MILLION YEARS AGO

ZOOP!!

Prehistoric aquatic reptiles and fish swim the seas as the dinosaurs end their era.

20,000 YEARS AGO

Early humans!
The seas don't change much over the next 20,000 years; that's a relatively small amount of time compared to the history of the planet.

ZOOP!

PRESENT DAY

Yup, everything is pretty much the same. The reef has grown a bit, though!

That and humans have changed— all the way from loincloths to wetsuits!

ZOOP!

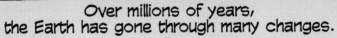

Over millions of years, the Earth has gone through many changes.

Drastic changes in the atmosphere...

Ugh. Excuse me.

poot!

PBBBT

FFFt!

AAH! HOT!

...volcanoes and tectonic plates...

...and meteorites.

OOF!

AW YEAH

The Earth has survived all these changes, but its residents are not always so lucky...

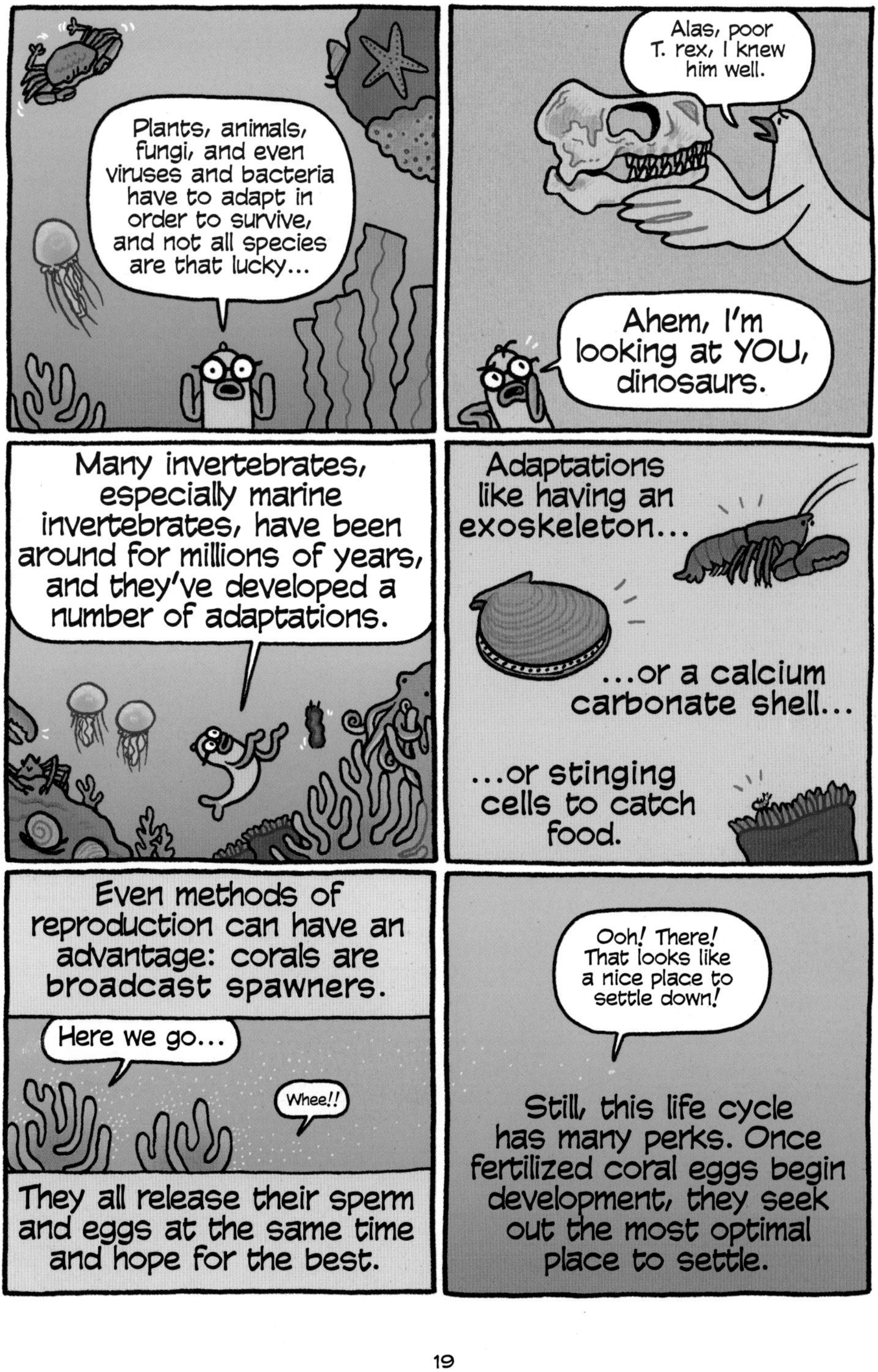

Plants, animals, fungi, and even viruses and bacteria have to adapt in order to survive, and not all species are that lucky...
Alas, poor T. rex, I knew him well.
Ahem, I'm looking at YOU, dinosaurs.
Many invertebrates, especially marine invertebrates, have been around for millions of years, and they've developed a number of adaptations.
Adaptations like having an exoskeleton...
...or a calcium carbonate shell...
...or stinging cells to catch food.
Even methods of reproduction can have an advantage: corals are broadcast spawners.
Here we go...
Whee!!
They all release their sperm and eggs at the same time and hope for the best.
Ooh! There! That looks like a nice place to settle down!
Still, this life cycle has many perks. Once fertilized coral eggs begin development, they seek out the most optimal place to settle.

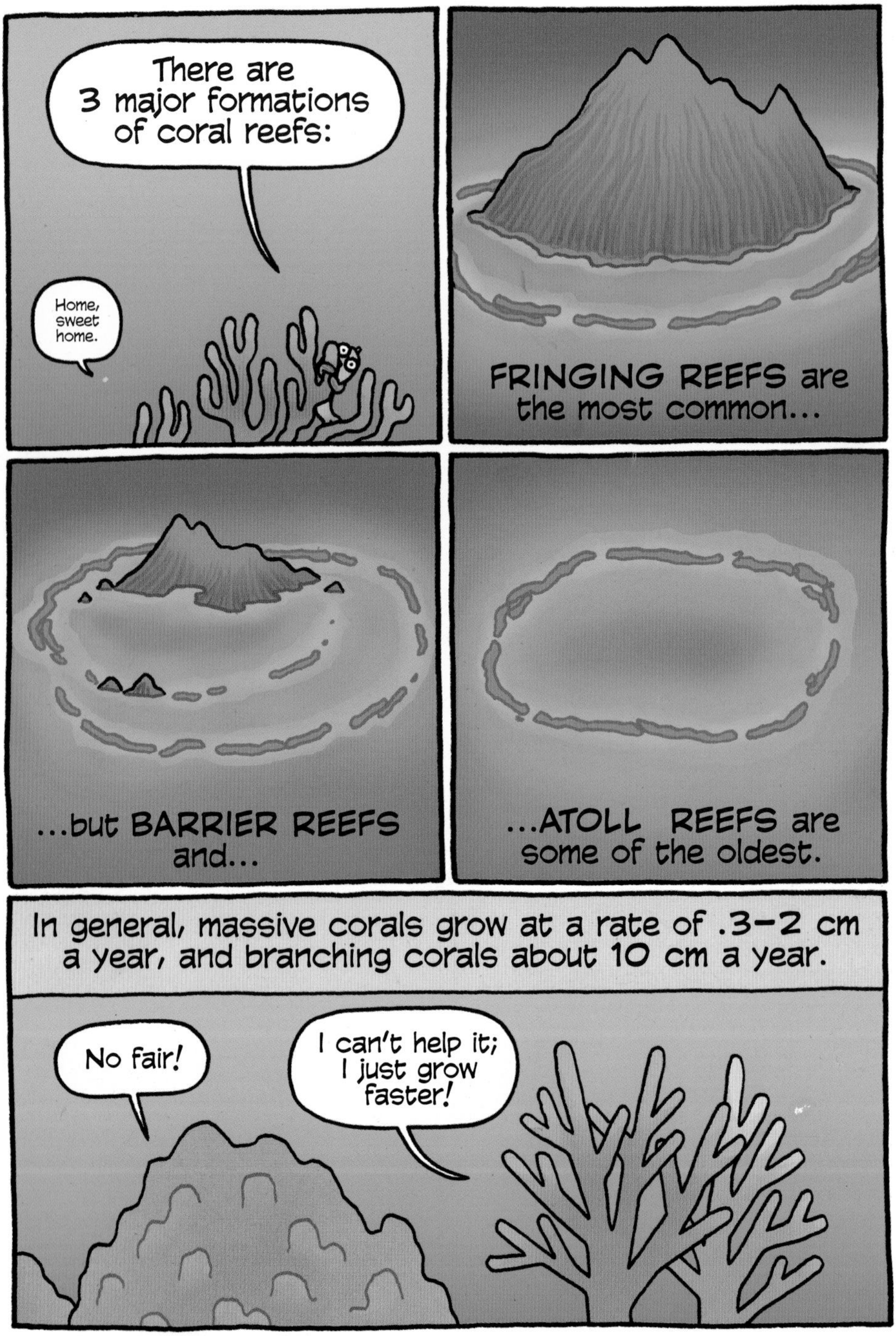

There are 3 major formations of coral reefs:
Home, sweet home.
FRINGING REEFS are the most common...
...but BARRIER REEFS and...
...ATOLL REEFS are some of the oldest.
In general, massive corals grow at a rate of .3–2 cm a year, and branching corals about 10 cm a year.
No fair!
I can't help it; I just grow faster!

Fringing reefs take over 10,000 years to form...

...while barrier and atoll reefs take anywhere from 100,000 to 30 million years to form.

We're young and hip!

Shush, you young whippersnappers!

Here is the current location and distribution of coral reefs on Earth:

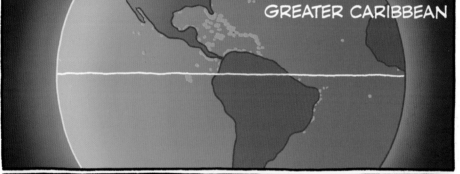

GREATER CARIBBEAN

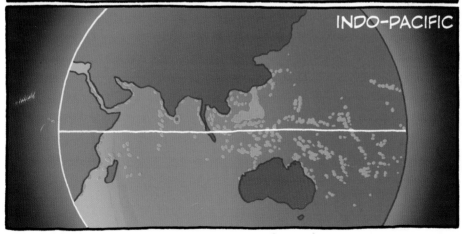

INDO-PACIFIC

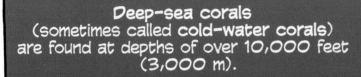

All of the corals we've focused on so far have been reef-building corals. Here are some "rule breakers":
Deep-sea corals (sometimes called cold-water corals) are found at depths of over 10,000 feet (3,000 m).
They lack the algae zooxanthellae and do not need sunlight to survive. Instead, they trap and eat tiny plankton.
I can't see 'em, but I can taste 'em.
Mmmmm...plankton!
But a large majority of corals are the reef-building variety, found in the tropics. Due to their specific environmental needs, as well as their evolutionary history...

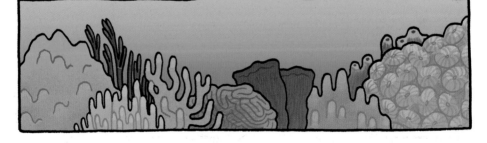

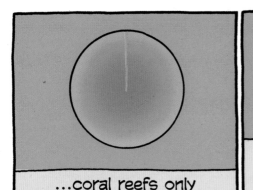

...coral reefs only occupy about .1% of the planet's surface.

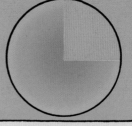

Despite this small area of coverage, coral reefs are home to **25%** of all the animals found in the ocean.

Of the 35 major animal groups (called phyla), 32 can be found in coral reefs (versus only 9 in a rain forest*). Coral reefs are some of the greatest examples of biodiversity found on Earth.

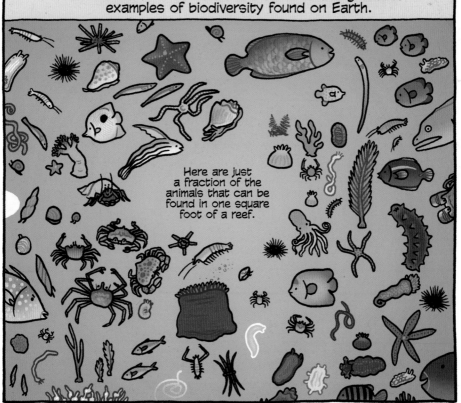

Here are just a fraction of the animals that can be found in one square foot of a reef.

*To be fair, oceans have been around waaaaaaaaaaaaaay longer than rain forests, like BILLIONS of years longer.

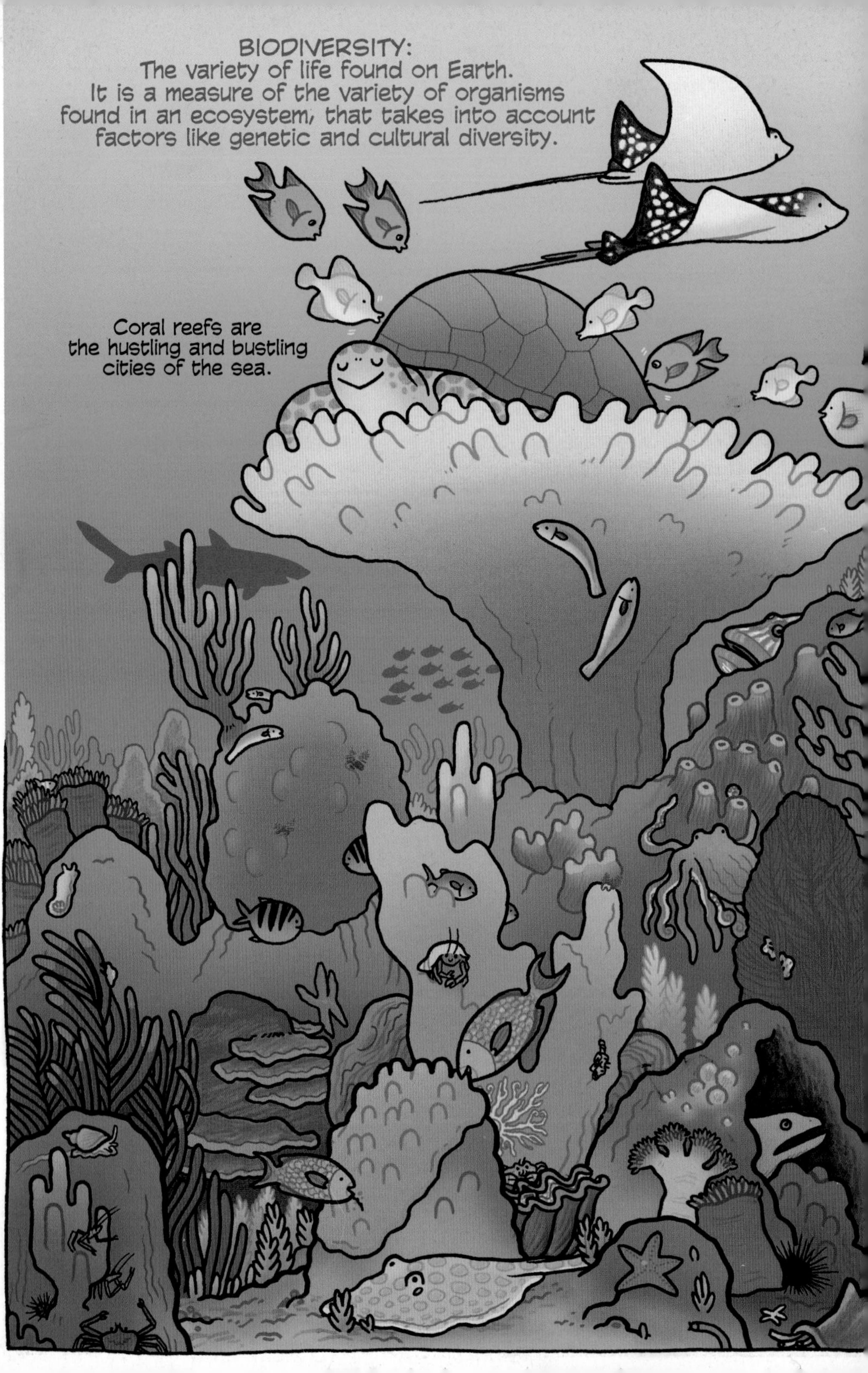
BIODIVERSITY:
The variety of life found on Earth.
It is a measure of the variety of organisms found in an ecosystem, that takes into account factors like genetic and cultural diversity.
Coral reefs are the hustling and bustling cities of the sea.

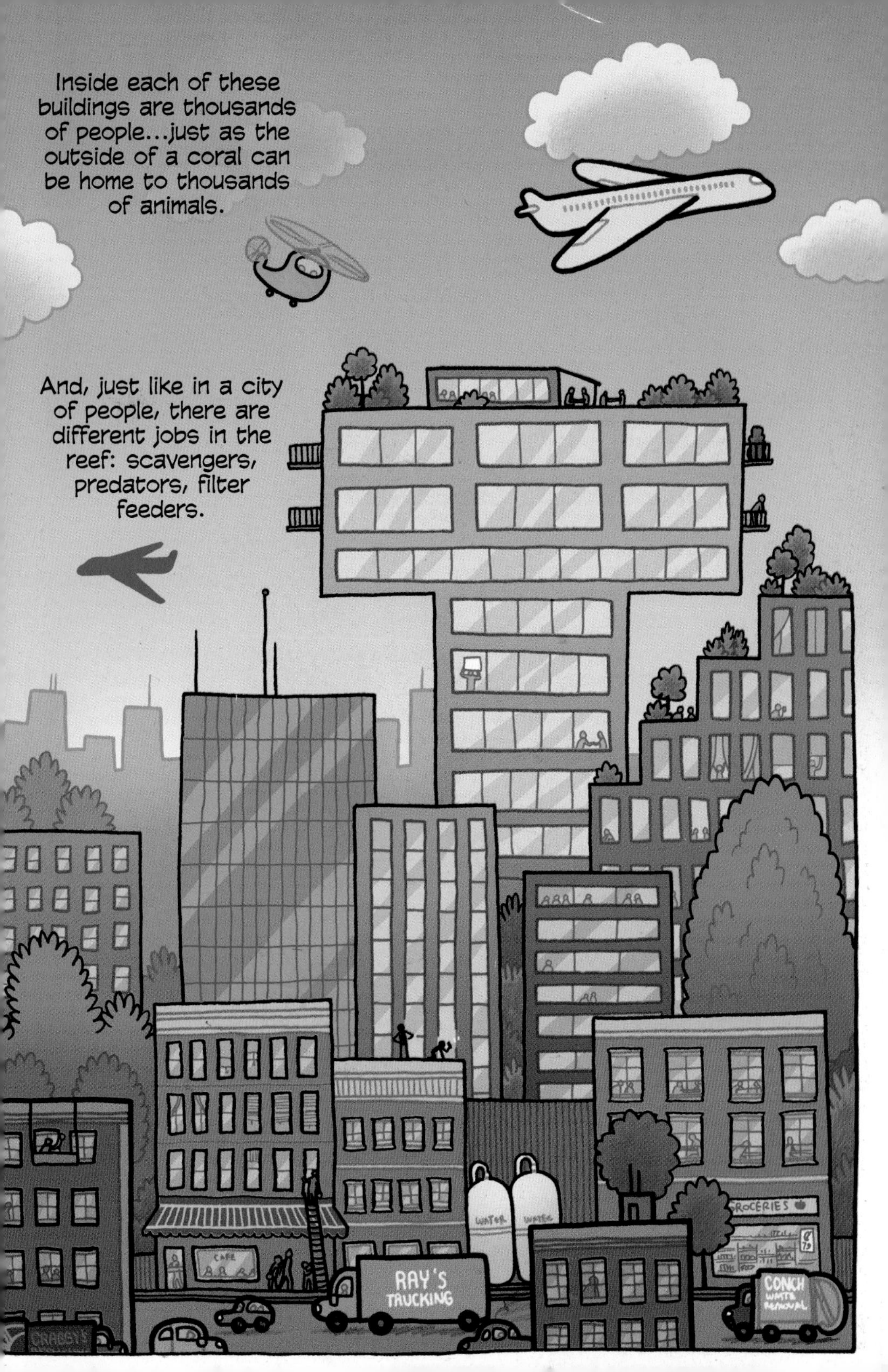
Inside each of these buildings are thousands of people...just as the outside of a coral can be home to thousands of animals.
And, just like in a city of people, there are different jobs in the reef: scavengers, predators, filter feeders.
CAFE
GROCERIES
WATER
WATER
RAY'S TRUCKING
CONCH WASTE REMOVAL

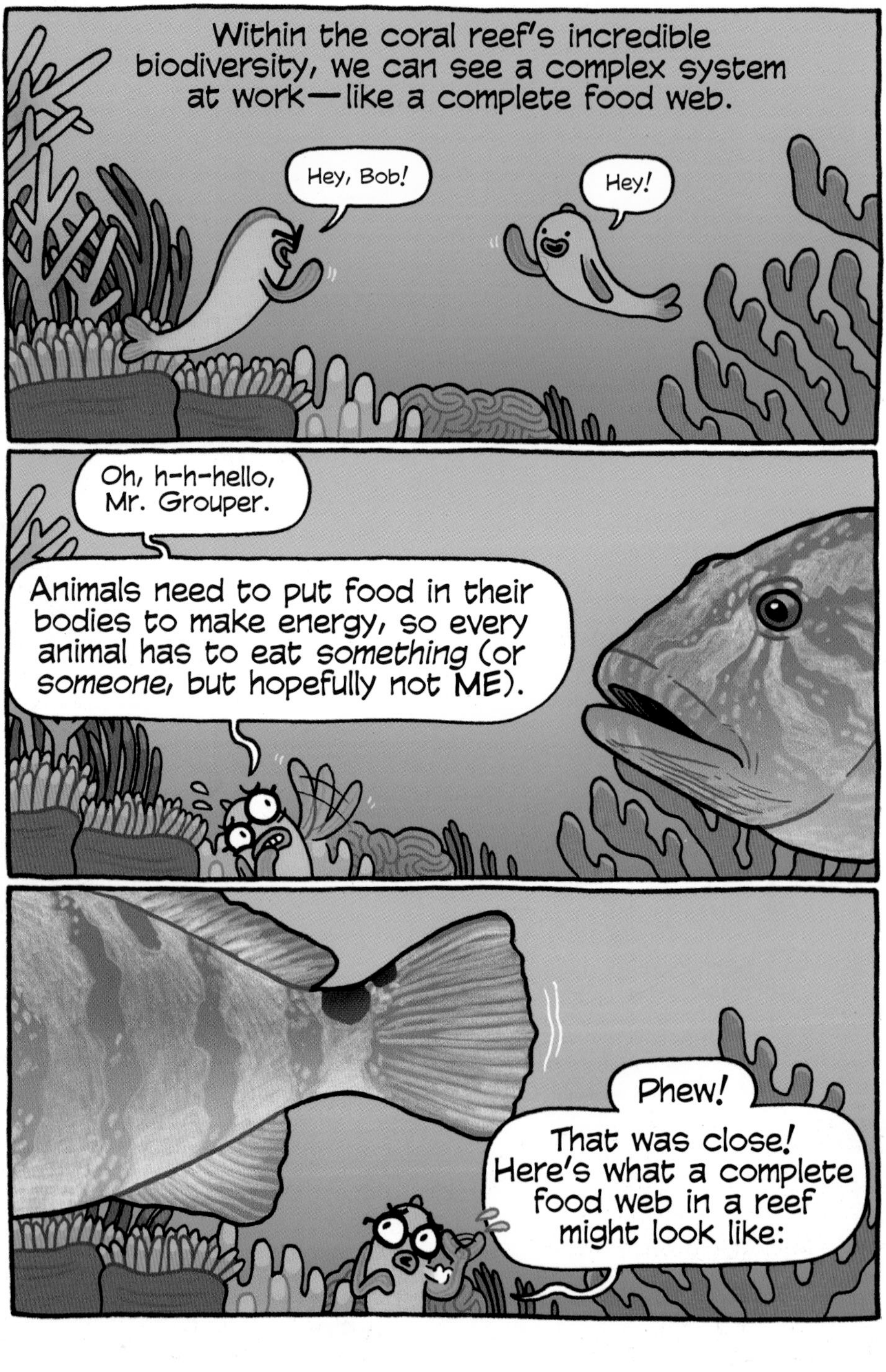
Within the coral reef's incredible biodiversity, we can see a complex system at work—like a complete food web.
Hey, Bob!
Hey!
Oh, h-h-hello, Mr. Grouper.
Animals need to put food in their bodies to make energy, so every animal has to eat *something* (or *someone*, but hopefully not ME).
Phew!
That was close! Here's what a complete food web in a reef might look like:

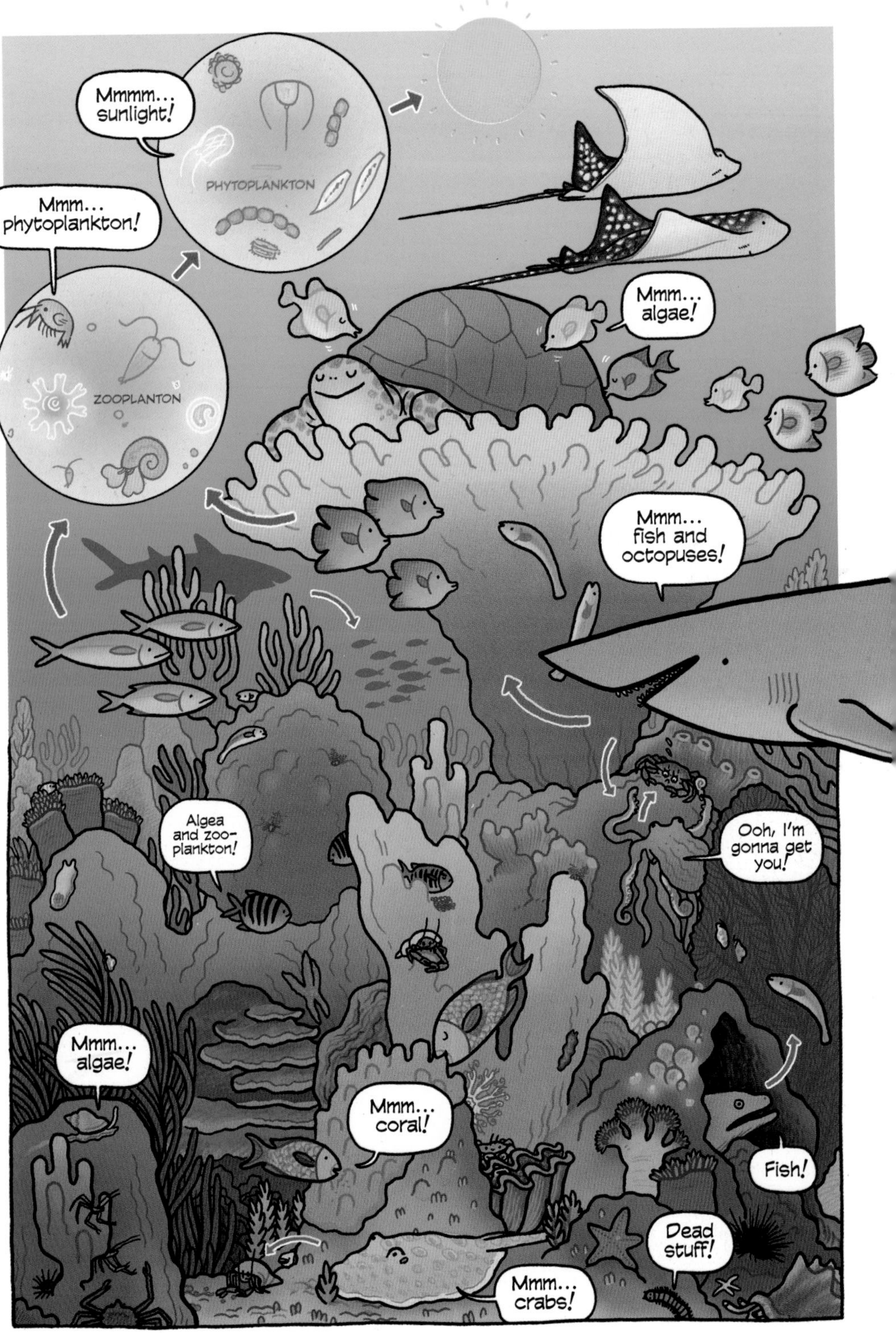
Mmmm... sunlight!
PHYTOPLANKTON
Mmm... phytoplankton!
ZOOPLANTON
Mmm... algae!
Mmm... fish and octopuses!
Algea and zoo-plankton!
Ooh, I'm gonna get you!
Mmm... algae!
Mmm... coral!
Fish!
Dead stuff!
Mmm... crabs!

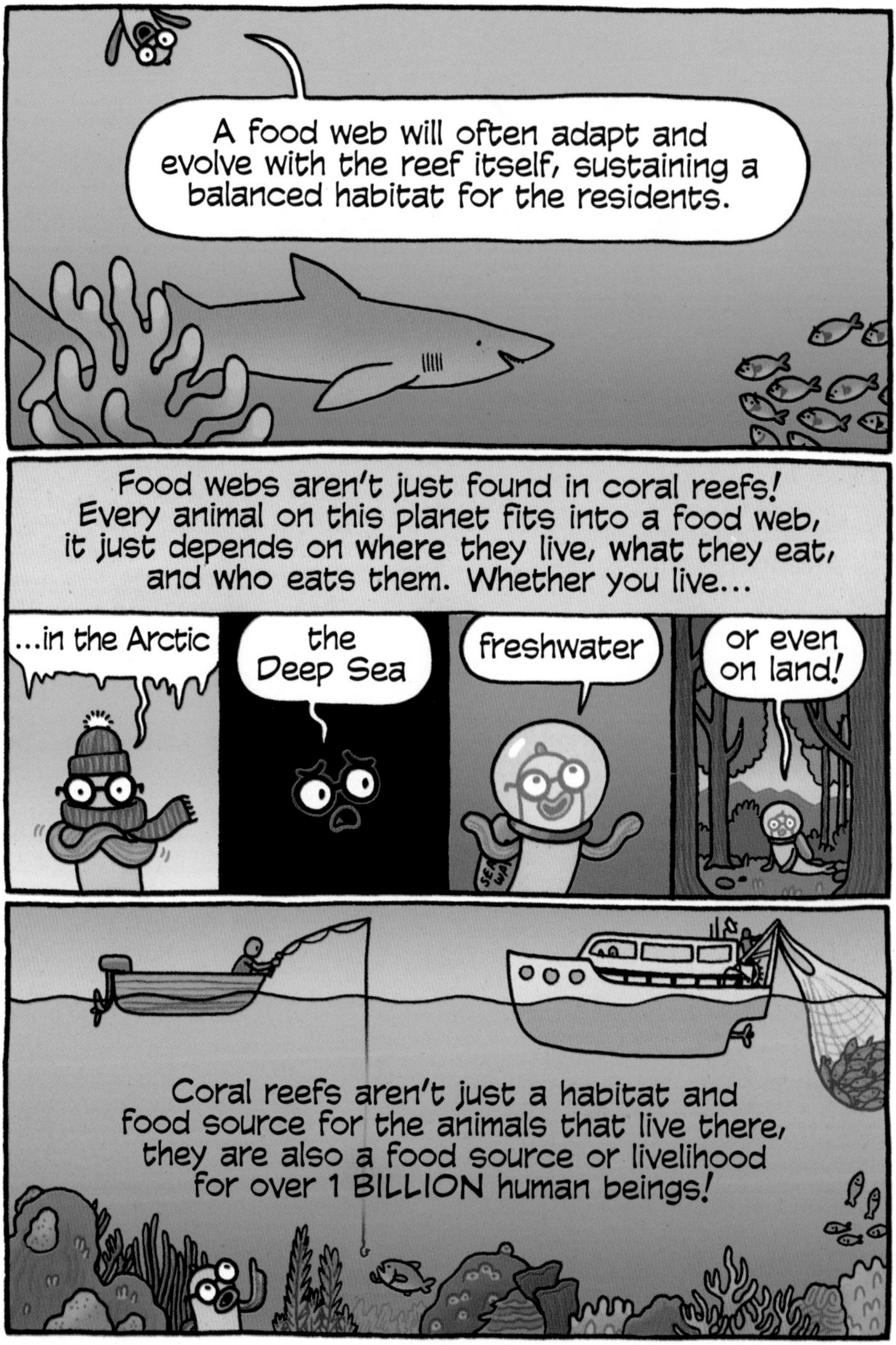
A food web will often adapt and evolve with the reef itself, sustaining a balanced habitat for the residents.
Food webs aren't just found in coral reefs! Every animal on this planet fits into a food web, it just depends on where they live, what they eat, and who eats them. Whether you live...
...in the Arctic
the Deep Sea
freshwater
or even on land!
Coral reefs aren't just a habitat and food source for the animals that live there, they are also a food source or livelihood for over 1 BILLION human beings!

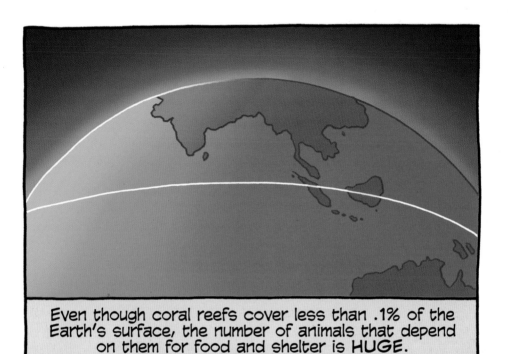

Even though coral reefs cover less than .1% of the Earth's surface, the number of animals that depend on them for food and shelter is **HUGE**.

Coral reefs play a large role in global ocean health.

But first let's get up close and personal with some of their inhabitants...

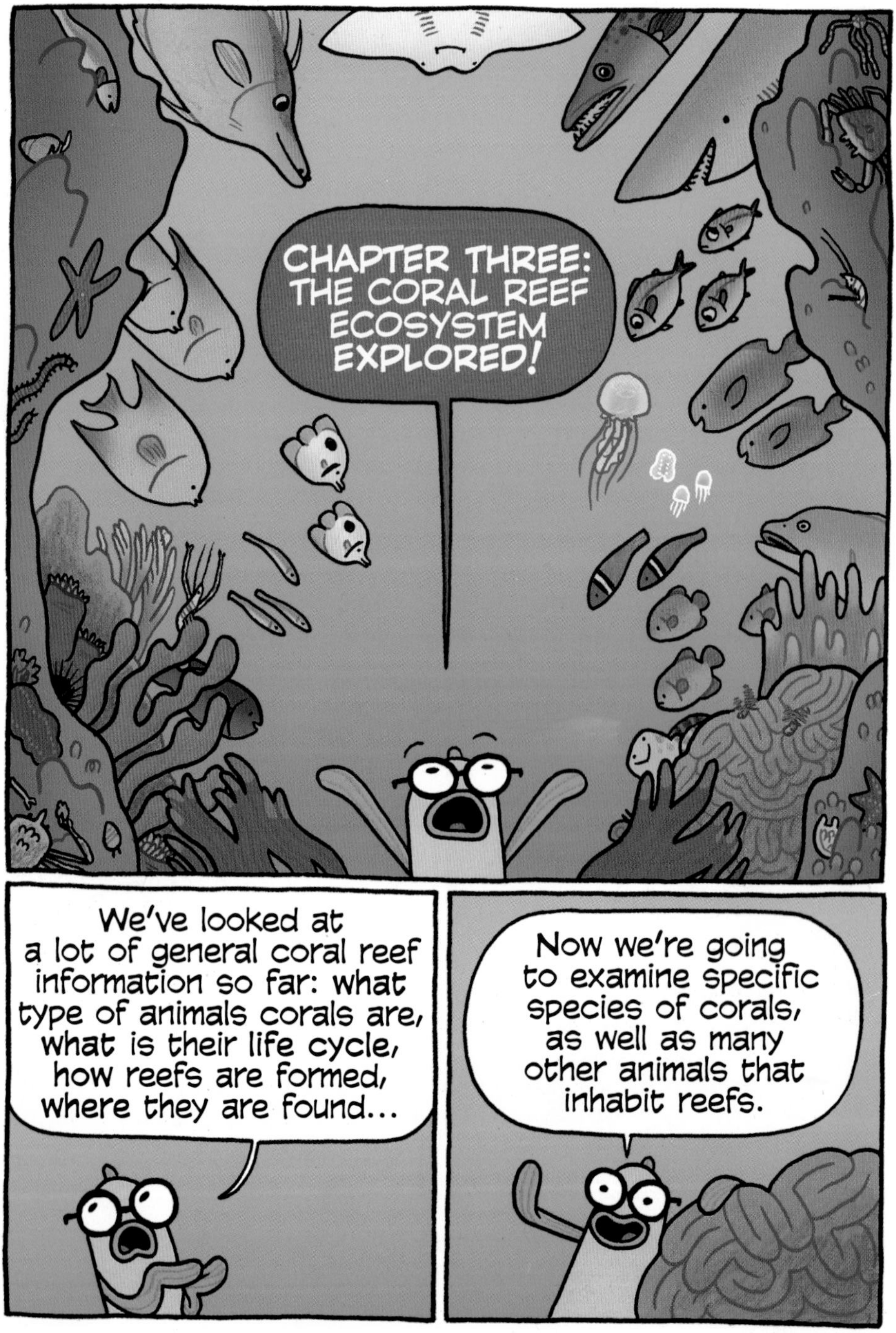
CHAPTER THREE: THE CORAL REEF ECOSYSTEM EXPLORED!
We've looked at a lot of general coral reef information so far: what type of animals corals are, what is their life cycle, how reefs are formed, where they are found...
Now we're going to examine specific species of corals, as well as many other animals that inhabit reefs.

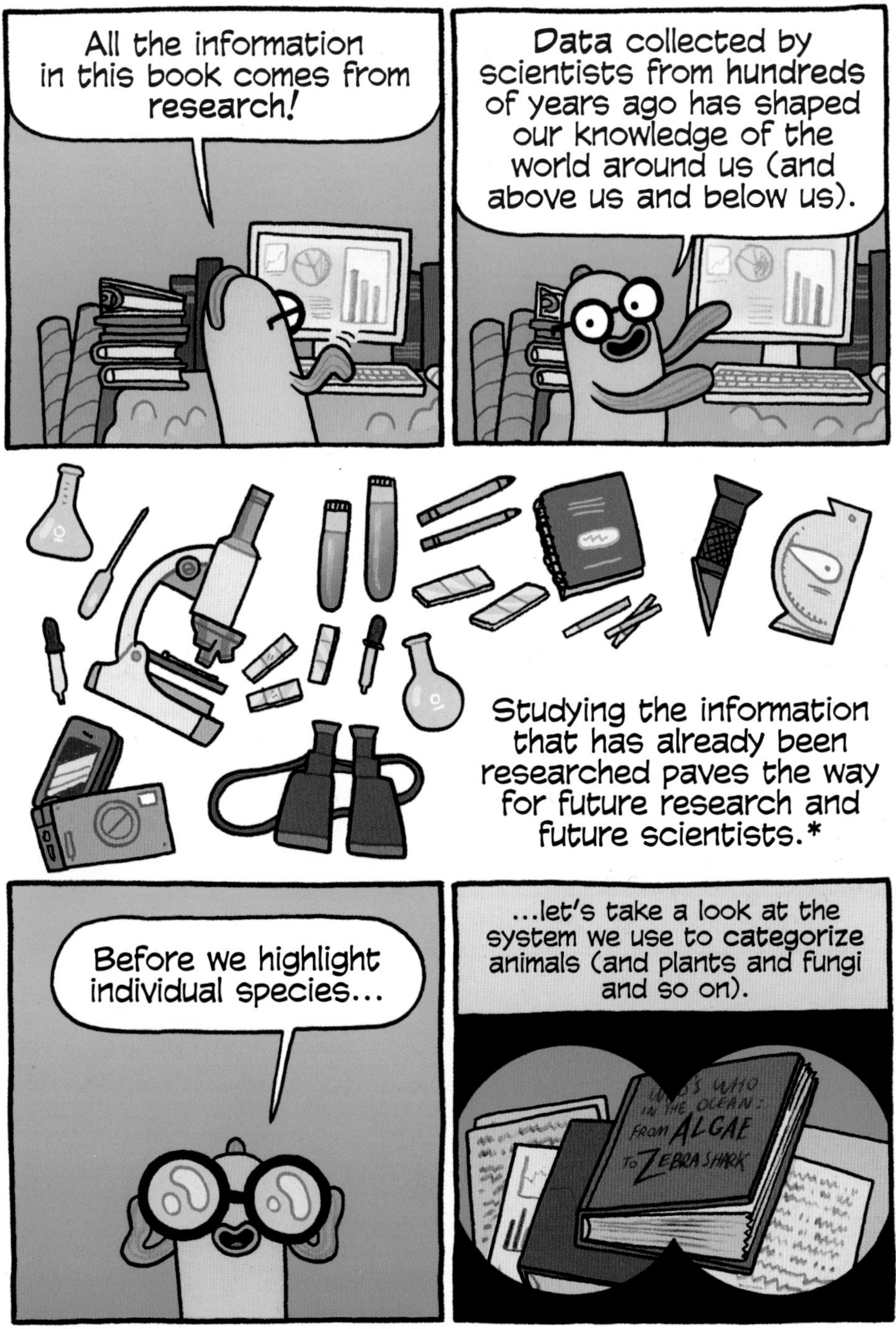

All the information in this book comes from research!
Data collected by scientists from hundreds of years ago has shaped our knowledge of the world around us (and above us and below us).
Studying the information that has already been researched paves the way for future research and future scientists.*
Before we highlight individual species...
...let's take a look at the system we use to categorize animals (and plants and fungi and so on).
IN THE OCEAN:
FROM ALGAE TO ZEBRA SHARK

*Like you! YOU may be a future scientist!

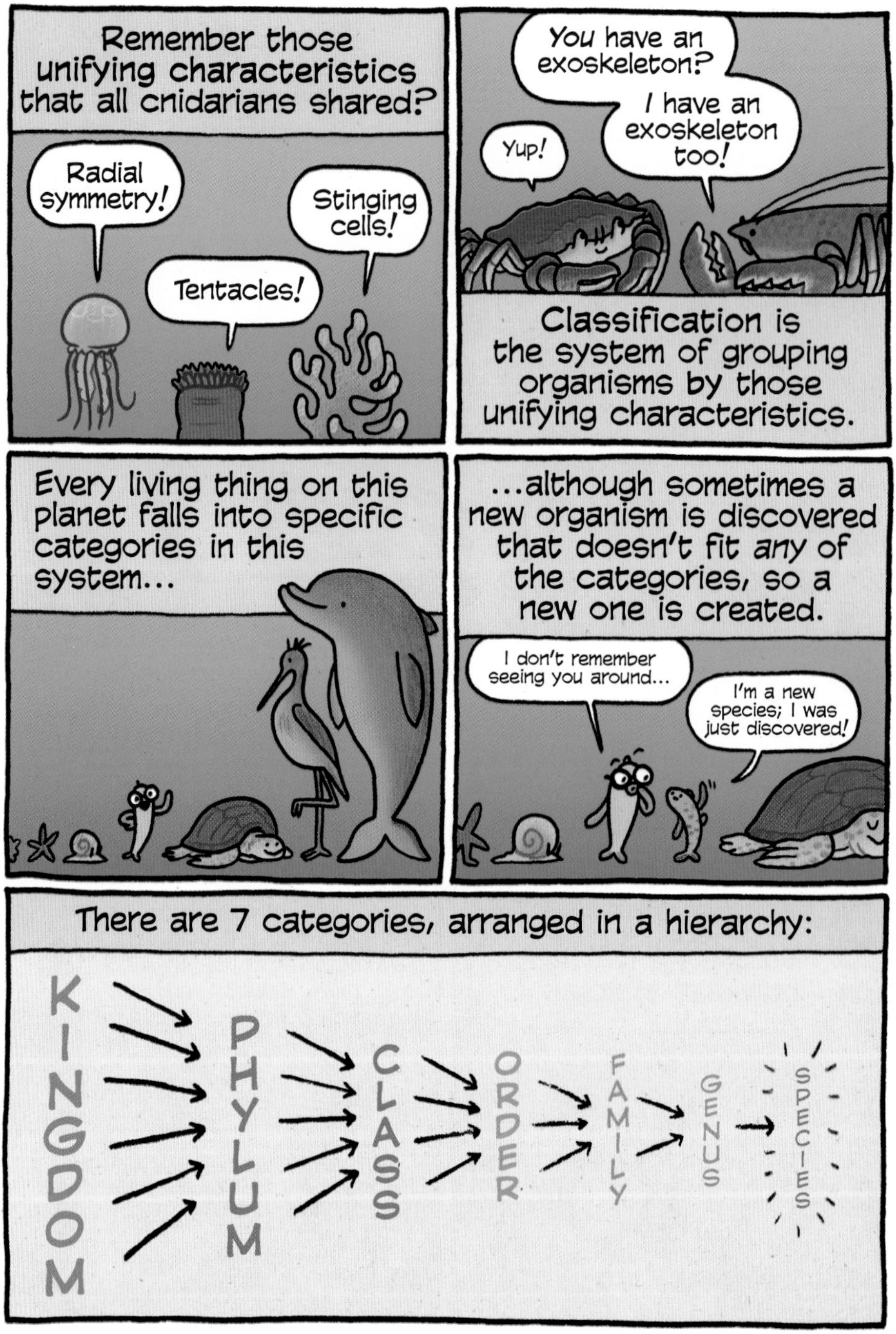
Remember those unifying characteristics that all cnidarians shared?
Radial symmetry!
Tentacles!
Stinging cells!
You have an exoskeleton?
Yup!
I have an exoskeleton too!
Classification is the system of grouping organisms by those unifying characteristics.
Every living thing on this planet falls into specific categories in this system...
...although sometimes a new organism is discovered that doesn't fit *any* of the categories, so a new one is created.
I don't remember seeing you around...
I'm a new species; I was just discovered!
There are 7 categories, arranged in a hierarchy:
KINGDOM
PHYLUM
CLASS
ORDER
FAMILY
GENUS
SPECIES

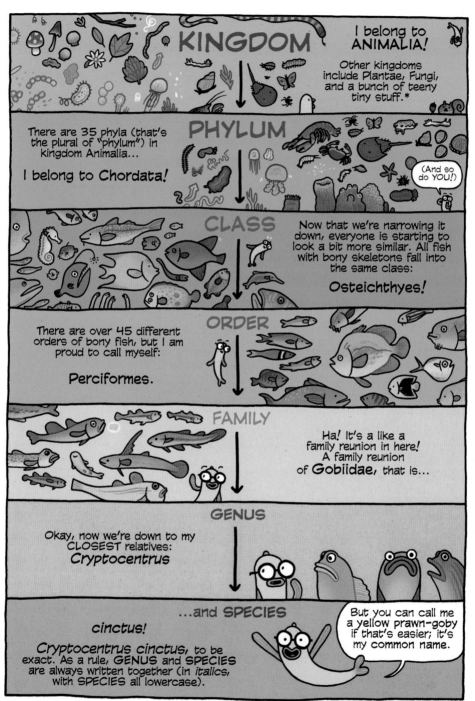

KINGDOM

I belong to ANIMALIA!

Other kingdoms include Plantae, Fungi, and a bunch of teeny tiny stuff.*

PHYLUM

There are 35 phyla (that's the plural of "phylum") in kingdom Animalia...

I belong to Chordata!

(And so do YOU!)

CLASS

Now that we're narrowing it down, everyone is starting to look a bit more similar. All fish with bony skeletons fall into the same class:

Osteichthyes!

ORDER

There are over 45 different orders of bony fish, but I am proud to call myself:

Perciformes.

FAMILY

Ha! It's a like a family reunion in here! A family reunion of **Gobiidae**, that is...

GENUS

Okay, now we're down to my CLOSEST relatives:
Cryptocentrus

...and SPECIES

cinctus!

Cryptocentrus cinctus, to be exact. As a rule, GENUS and SPECIES are always written together (in *italics*, with SPECIES all lowercase).

But you can call me a yellow prawn-goby if that's easier; it's my common name.

*Bacteria, Archaea, and Protista—and, despite their teeny tininess, they are all very important!

Just because two animals have a similar trait, it does not mean that they are closely related.

WINGS!

(mammal)

WINGS!

(bird)

DORSAL FIN!

(mammal)

DORSAL FIN!

(fish)

You know *my* classification, but let's compare some other animals:

HUMAN BEING

PILLAR CORAL

COMMON NAME: HUMAN BEING
(aka "PERSON," aka "THE AUTHOR")

KINGDOM: Animalia

PHYLUM: Chordata

CLASS: Mammalia

ORDER: Primates

FAMILY: Hominidae

GENUS: *Homo*
SPECIES: *sapiens*

COMMON NAME: PILLAR CORAL

KINGDOM: Animalia

PHYLUM: Cnidaria

CLASS: Anthozoa

ORDER: Scleractinia

FAMILY: Meandrinidae

GENUS: *Dendrogyra*
SPECIES: *cylindrus*

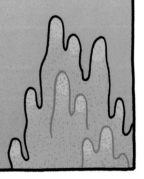

34

Whew! That's a lot of words!

| KINGDOM |
| PHYLUM |
| CLASS |
| ORDER |
| FAMILY |
| GENUS |
| SPECIES |

COMMON NAME

We are mostly going to focus on kingdom: Animalia...

...different phyla, individual species, and common names.

This system was not created to make your science tests more complicated.

Classification offers a language and order that can be used by scientists worldwide.

Anthozoa!

Having a universal system makes sharing data easier among the scientific community.

Anthozoa!

Anthozoa!

Anthozoa!

Anthozoa!

Anthozoa!

"Rolly Polly"

"Pill Bug"

"Sow Bug"

Personally, I prefer "Armadillidiidae."

"Potato Bug"

"Wood Louse"

While common names are often easy to remember, they vary from language to language, country to country, even state to state!

So...back to corals.
Let's apply what we know about classification to our cnidarian friends.
We're going to take a look at some of the major groups of corals. Each profile will feature:
species name
DIPLORIA LABYRINTHIFORMIS
common name
BRAIN CORAL
additional information
polyp
location
skeleton shape
This way, you'll get to know some of the individual reef builders...
...and how they relate to other organisms in the coral reef ecosystem.

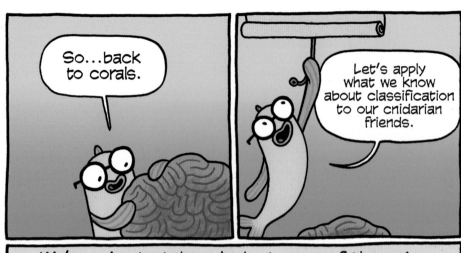

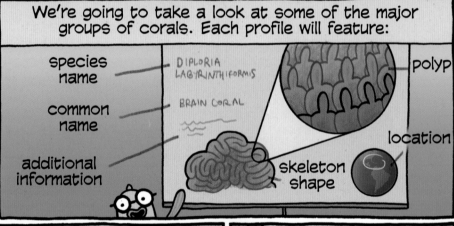

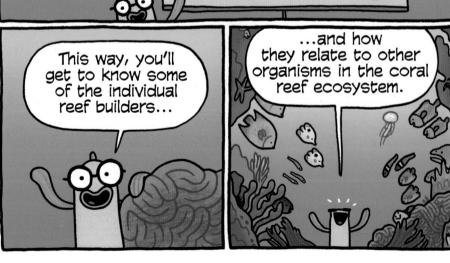

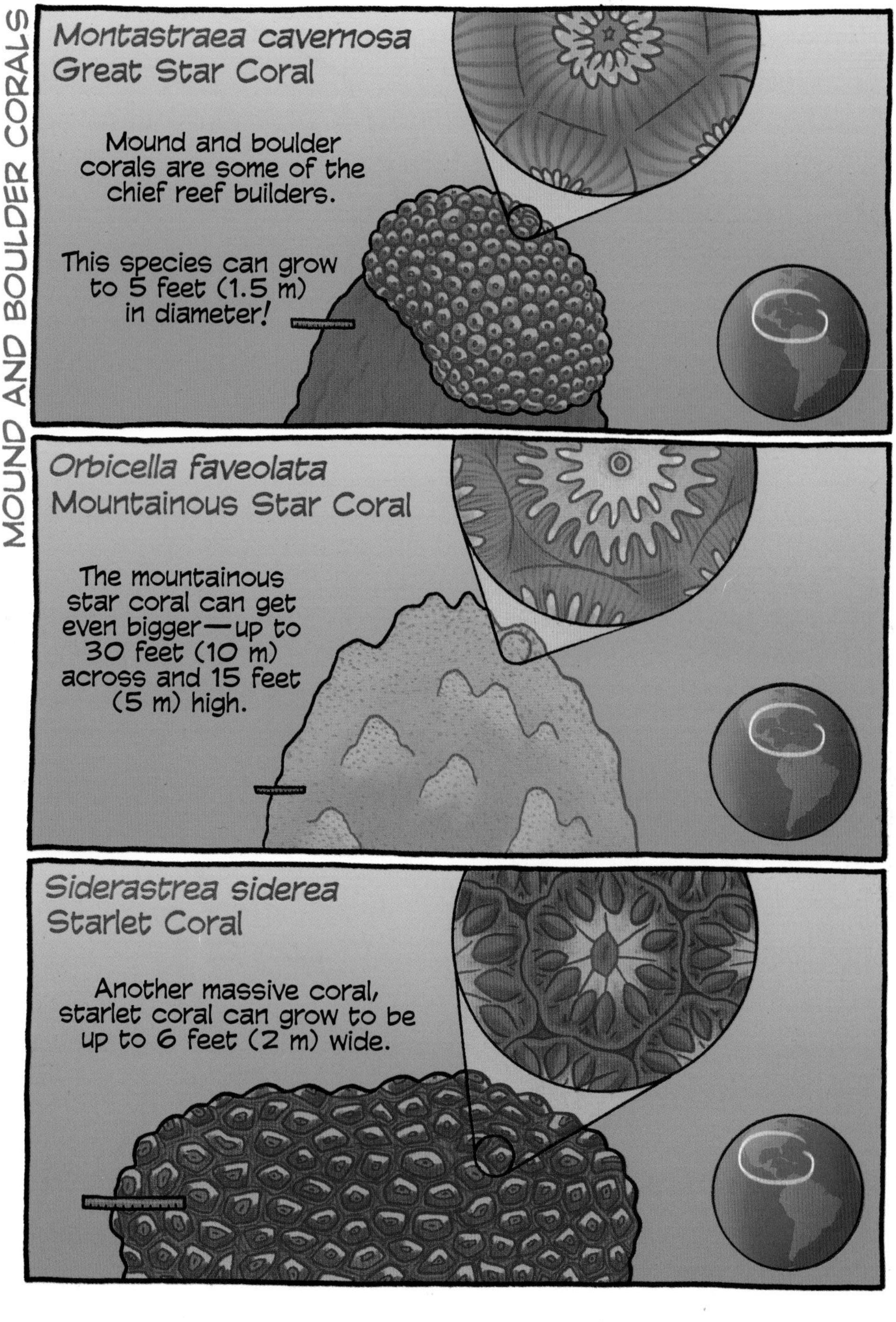
MOUND AND BOULDER CORALS
Montastraea cavernosa
Great Star Coral
Mound and boulder corals are some of the chief reef builders.
This species can grow to 5 feet (1.5 m) in diameter!
Orbicella faveolata
Mountainous Star Coral
The mountainous star coral can get even bigger—up to 30 feet (10 m) across and 15 feet (5 m) high.
Siderastrea siderea
Starlet Coral
Another massive coral, starlet coral can grow to be up to 6 feet (2 m) wide.

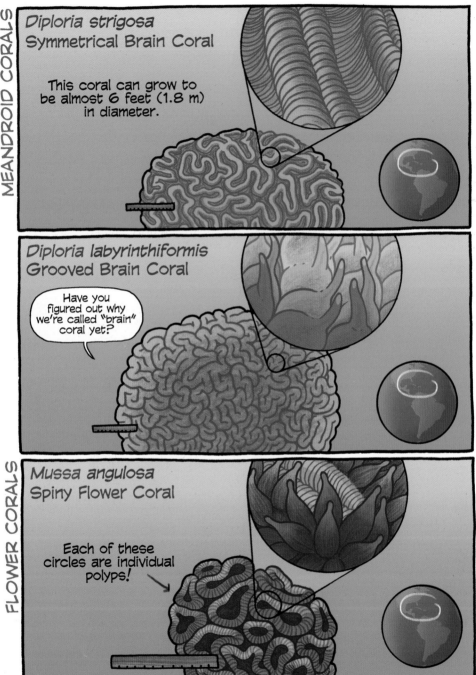

Diploria strigosa
Symmetrical Brain Coral

This coral can grow to be almost 6 feet (1.8 m) in diameter.

Diploria labyrinthiformis
Grooved Brain Coral

Have you figured out why we're called "brain" coral yet?

FLOWER CORALS

Mussa angulosa
Spiny Flower Coral

Each of these circles are individual polyps!

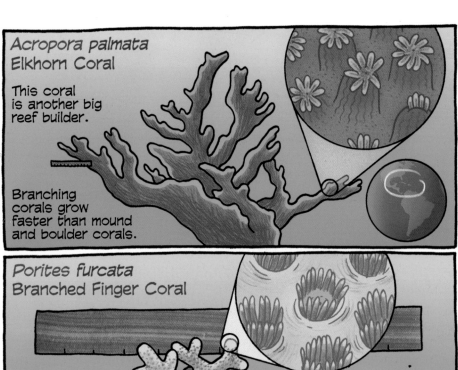

Acropora palmata
Elkhorn Coral

This coral is another big reef builder.

Branching corals grow faster than mound and boulder corals.

Porites furcata
Branched Finger Coral

Sadly, there is no "Toe Coral."

Madracis mirabilis
Yellow Pencil Coral

While the short branches are small, the whole colony of this coral can reach several feet (or meters) in diameter.

Pencil Coral is not to be used as a writing utensil.

39

AGARICIIDAE (CRUSTS AND PLATES)

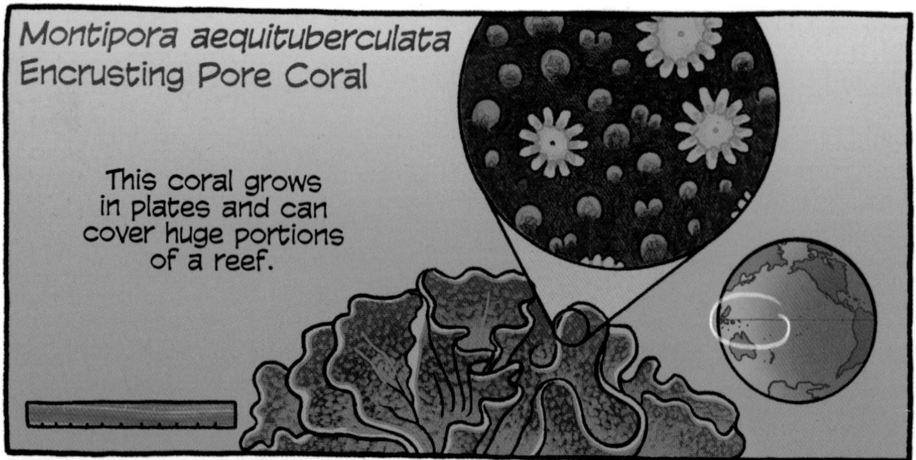

Montipora aequituberculata
Encrusting Pore Coral
This coral grows in plates and can cover huge portions of a reef.

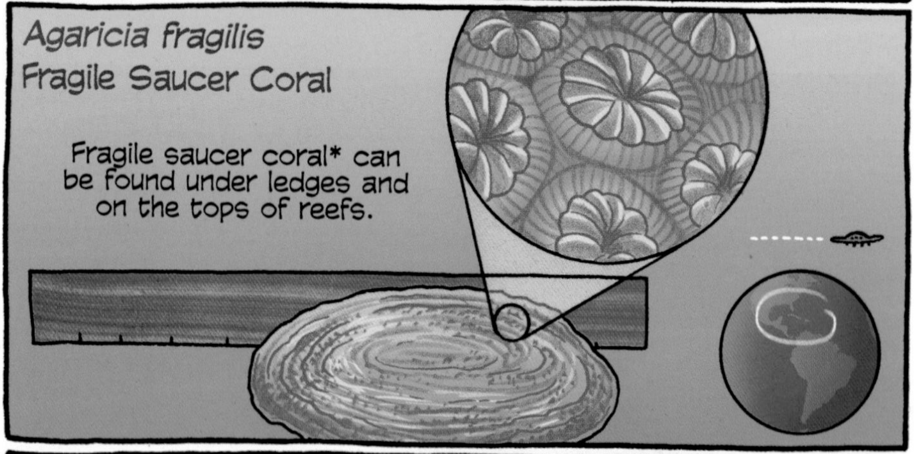

Agaricia fragilis
Fragile Saucer Coral
Fragile saucer coral* can be found under ledges and on the tops of reefs.

CUP CORALS

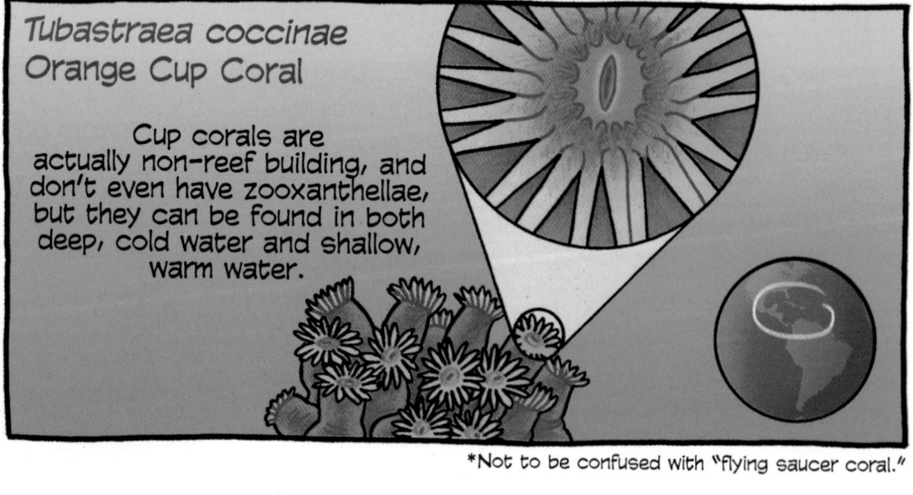

Tubastraea coccinae
Orange Cup Coral
Cup corals are actually non-reef building, and don't even have zooxanthellae, but they can be found in both deep, cold water and shallow, warm water.

*Not to be confused with "flying saucer coral."

SOLITARY CORALS

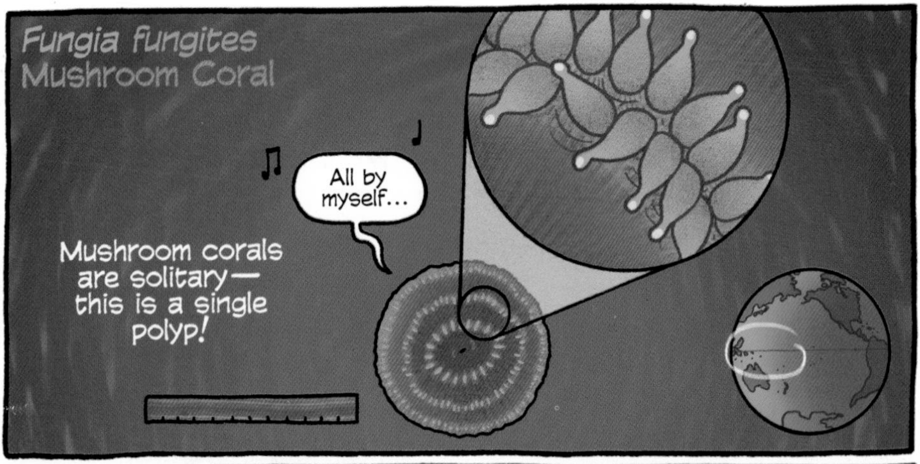
Fungia fungites
Mushroom Coral
All by myself...
Mushroom corals are solitary—this is a single polyp!

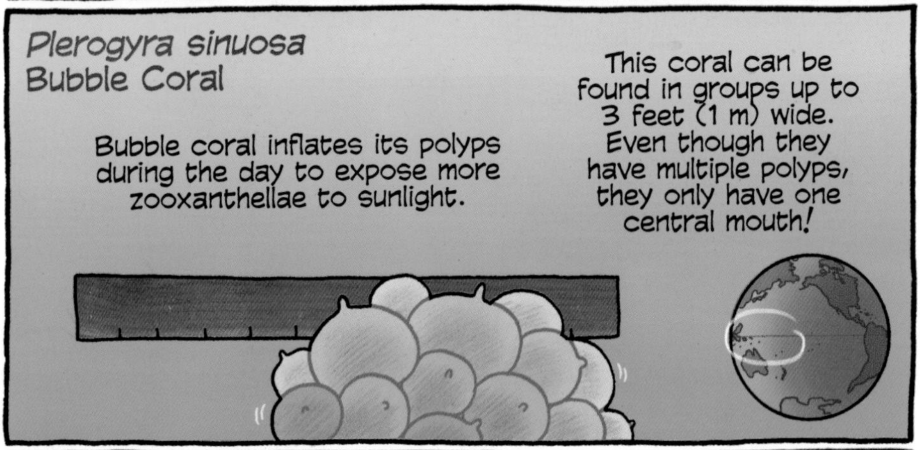
Plerogyra sinuosa
Bubble Coral
Bubble coral inflates its polyps during the day to expose more zooxanthellae to sunlight.
This coral can be found in groups up to 3 feet (1 m) wide. Even though they have multiple polyps, they only have one central mouth!

SOFT CORALS

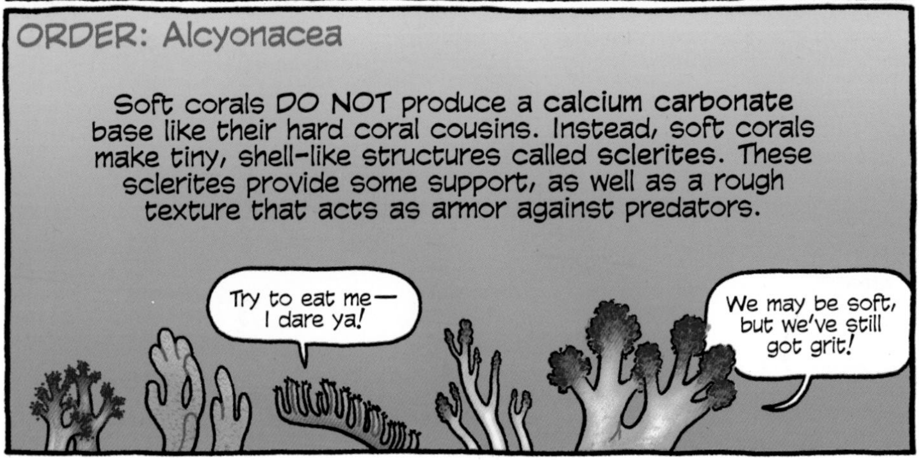
ORDER: Alcyonacea
Soft corals DO NOT produce a calcium carbonate base like their hard coral cousins. Instead, soft corals make tiny, shell-like structures called sclerites. These sclerites provide some support, as well as a rough texture that acts as armor against predators.
Try to eat me—I dare ya!
We may be soft, but we've still got grit!

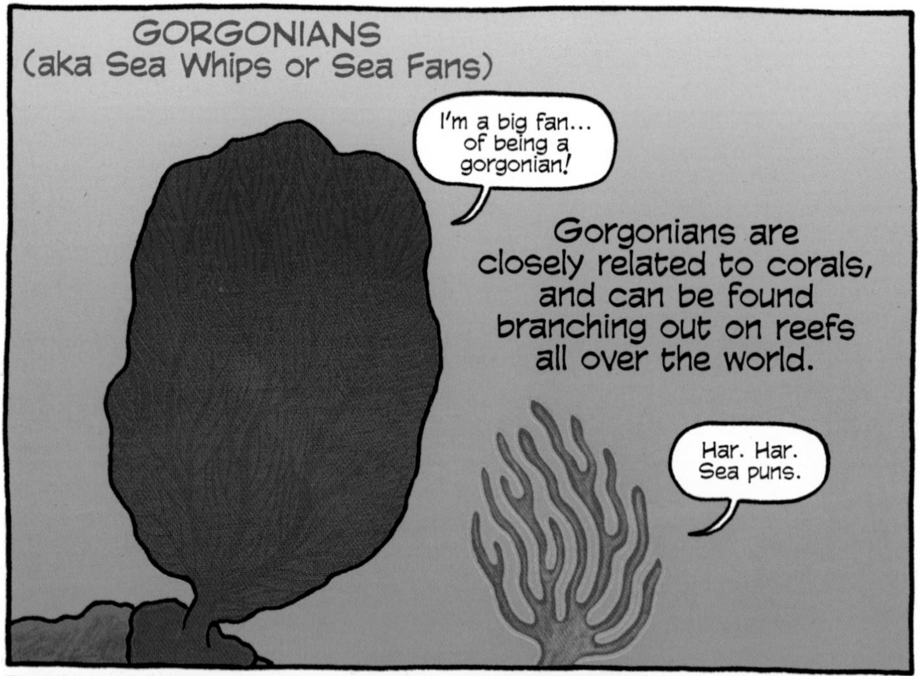
GORGONIANS
(aka Sea Whips or Sea Fans)
I'm a big fan... of being a gorgonian!
Gorgonians are closely related to corals, and can be found branching out on reefs all over the world.
Har. Har. Sea puns.

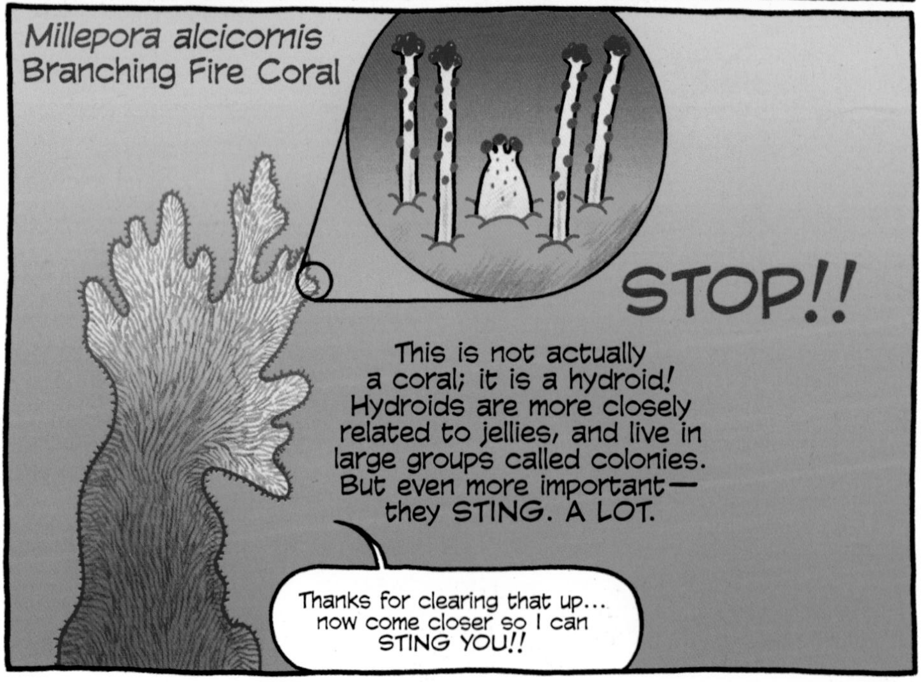
Millepora alcicornis
Branching Fire Coral
STOP!!
This is not actually a coral; it is a hydroid! Hydroids are more closely related to jellies, and live in large groups called colonies. But even more important— they STING. A LOT.
Thanks for clearing that up... now come closer so I can STING YOU!!

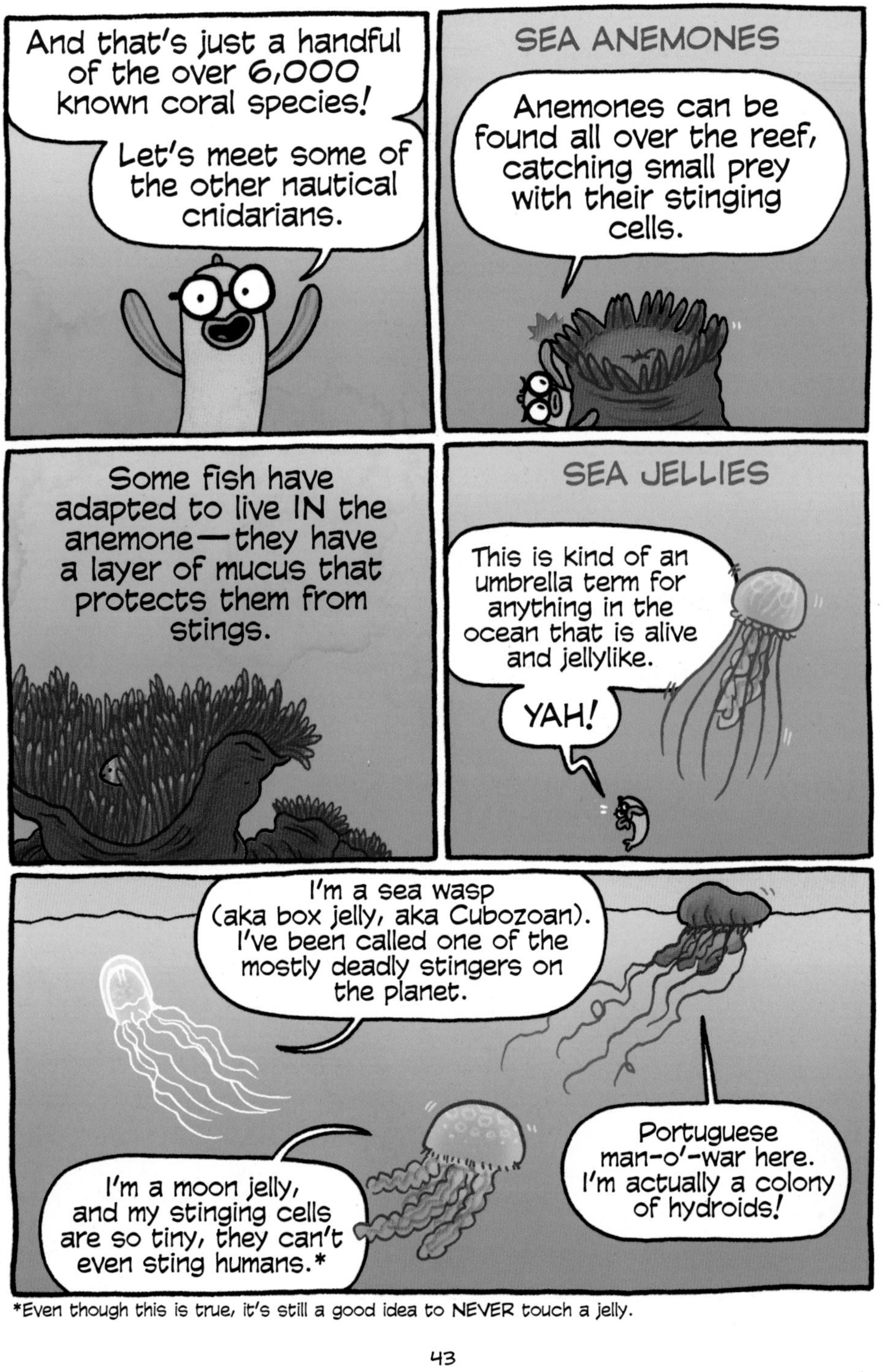
And that's just a handful of the over 6,000 known coral species!
Let's meet some of the other nautical cnidarians.
SEA ANEMONES
Anemones can be found all over the reef, catching small prey with their stinging cells.
Some fish have adapted to live IN the anemone—they have a layer of mucus that protects them from stings.
SEA JELLIES
This is kind of an umbrella term for anything in the ocean that is alive and jellylike.
YAH!
I'm a sea wasp (aka box jelly, aka Cubozoan). I've been called one of the mostly deadly stingers on the planet.
I'm a moon jelly, and my stinging cells are so tiny, they can't even sting humans.*
Portuguese man-o'-war here. I'm actually a colony of hydroids!

*Even though this is true, it's still a good idea to NEVER touch a jelly.

But let's not stop at cnidarians; there are countless other invertebrates that inhabit reefs:

Annelidae!

Platyhelminthes!

Echinodermata!

Arthropoda!

Porifera!

Mollusca!

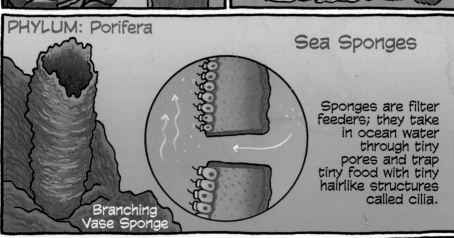

PHYLUM: Porifera

Sea Sponges

Sponges are filter feeders; they take in ocean water through tiny pores and trap tiny food with tiny hairlike structures called cilia.

Branching Vase Sponge

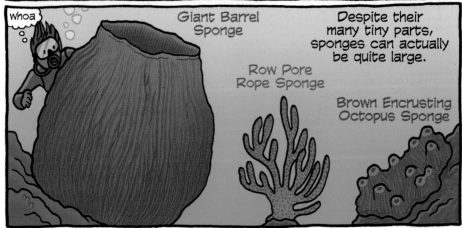

whoa

Giant Barrel Sponge

Row Pore Rope Sponge

Brown Encrusting Octopus Sponge

Despite their many tiny parts, sponges can actually be quite large.

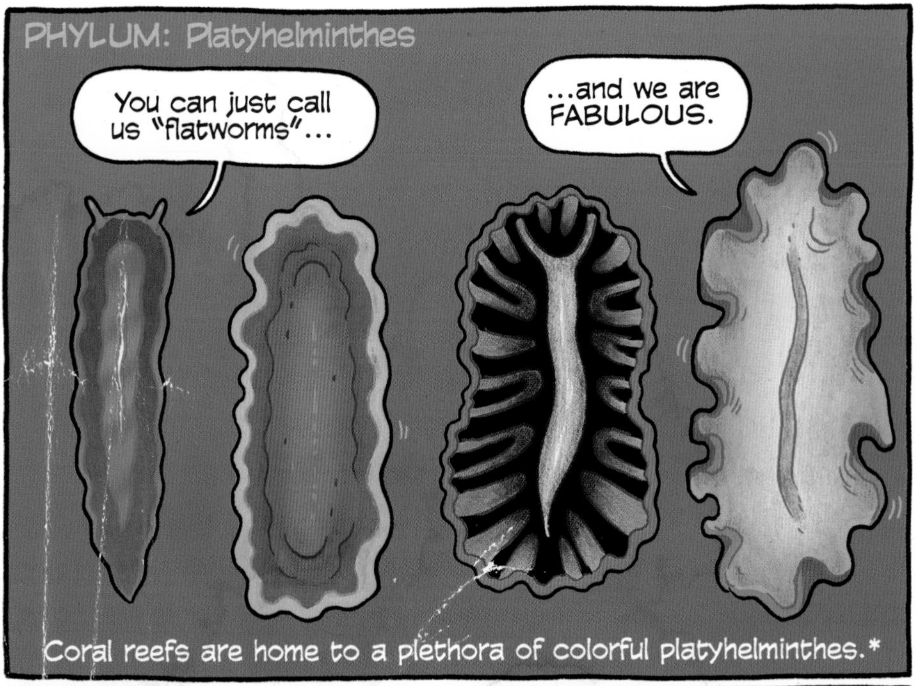
PHYLUM: Platyhelminthes
You can just call us "flatworms"...
...and we are FABULOUS.
Coral reefs are home to a plethora of colorful platyhelminthes.*

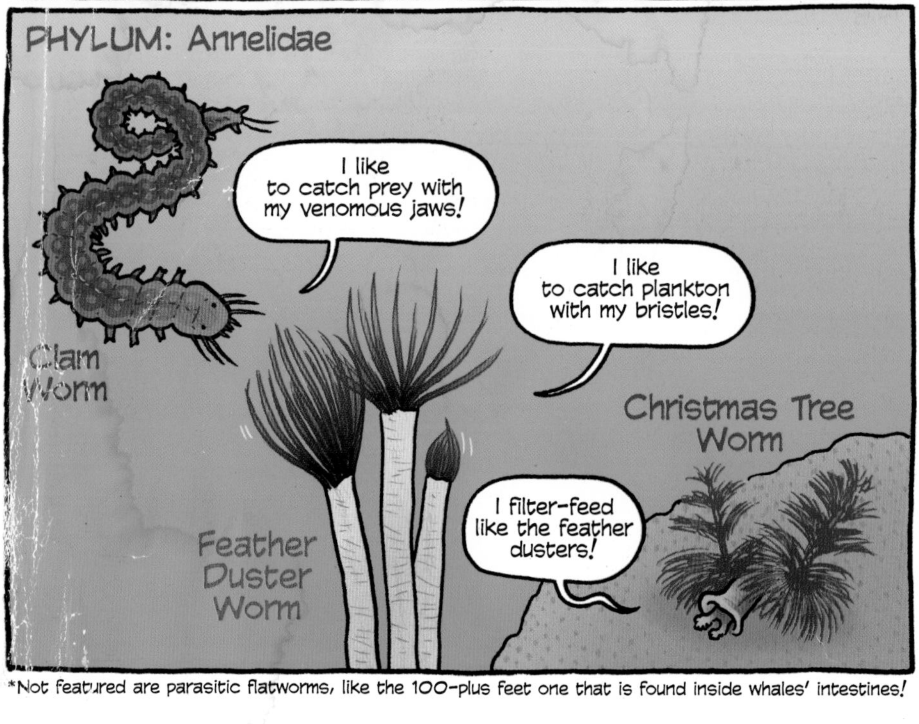
PHYLUM: Annelidae
I like to catch prey with my venomous jaws!
I like to catch plankton with my bristles!
I filter-feed like the feather dusters!
Clam Worm
Feather Duster Worm
Christmas Tree Worm

*Not featured are parasitic flatworms, like the 100-plus feet one that is found inside whales' intestines!

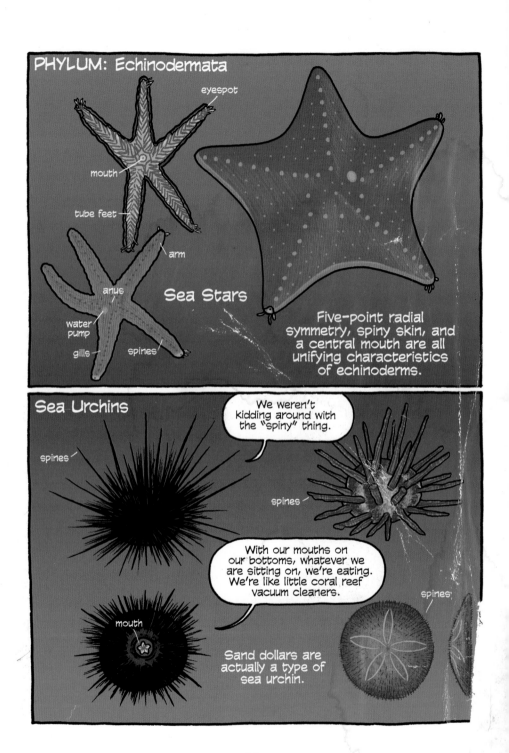

PHYLUM: Echinodermata

eyespot

mouth

tube feet

arm

Sea Stars

anus

water pump

gills   spines

Five-point radial symmetry, spiny skin, and a central mouth are all unifying characteristics of echinoderms.

Sea Urchins

spines

We weren't kidding around with the "spiny" thing.

spines

With our mouths on our bottoms, whatever we are sitting on, we're eating. We're like little coral reef vacuum cleaners.

mouth

spines

Sand dollars are actually a type of sea urchin.

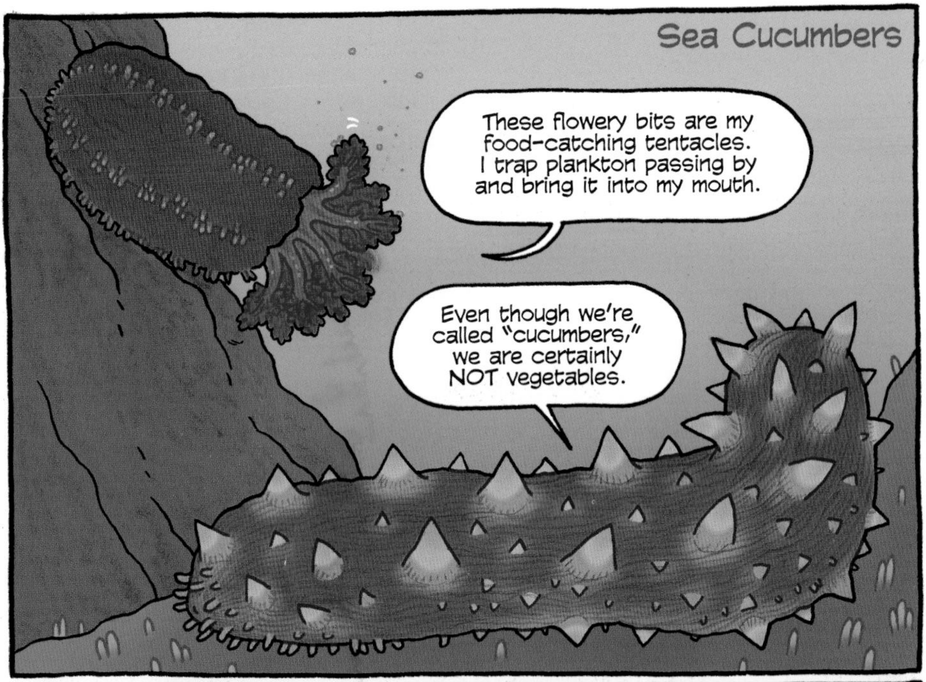
Sea Cucumbers
These flowery bits are my food-catching tentacles. I trap plankton passing by and bring it into my mouth.
Even though we're called "cucumbers," we are certainly NOT vegetables.

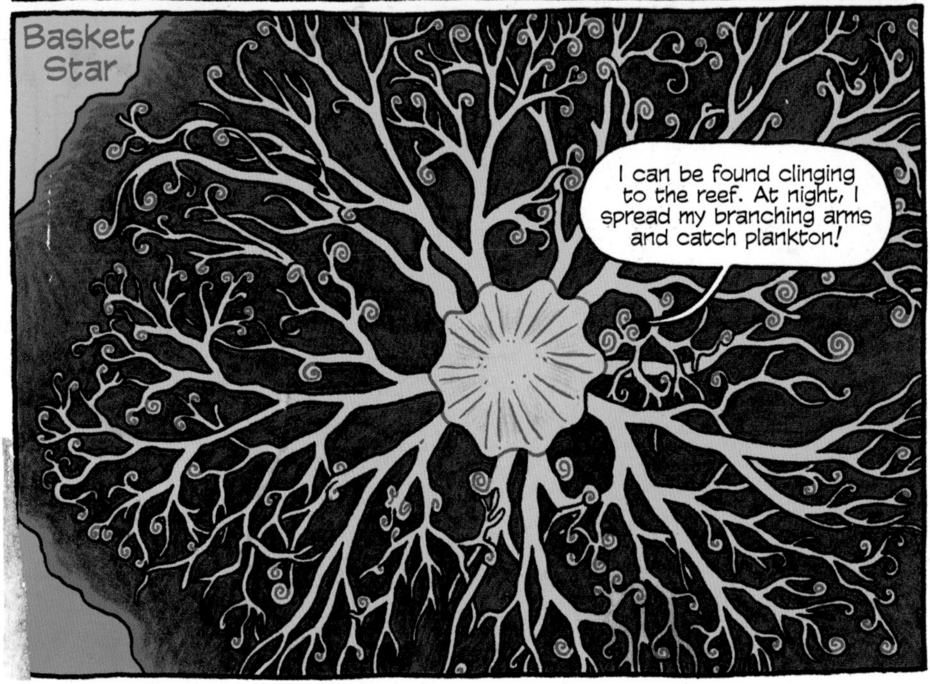
Basket Star
I can be found clinging to the reef. At night, I spread my branching arms and catch plankton!

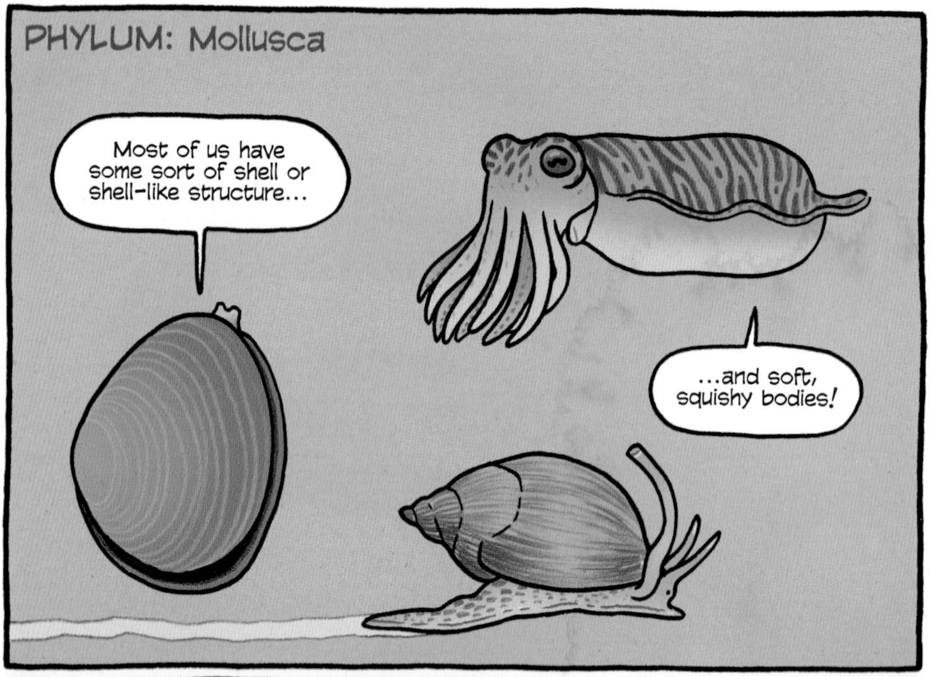
PHYLUM: Mollusca
Most of us have some sort of shell or shell-like structure...
...and soft, squishy bodies!

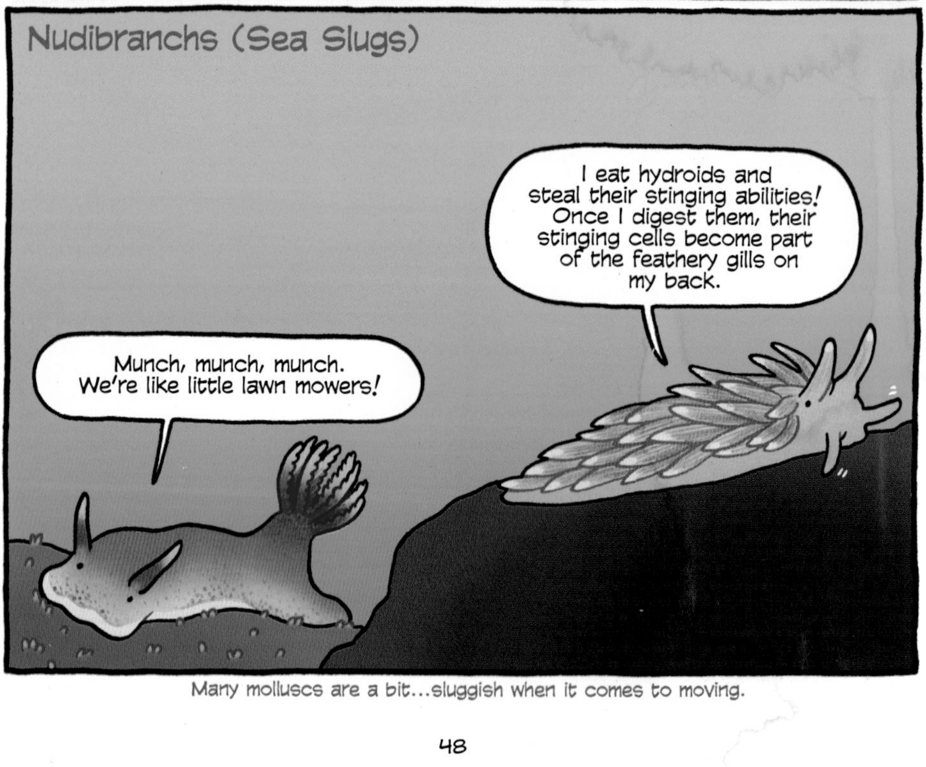
Nudibranchs (Sea Slugs)
I eat hydroids and steal their stinging abilities! Once I digest them, their stinging cells become part of the feathery gills on my back.
Munch, munch, munch. We're like little lawn mowers!

Many molluscs are a bit...sluggish when it comes to moving.

Flamingo Tongue Snail
I live on soft corals like this gorgonian and eat the fleshy part of the coral. Mmmm-mm-mmm.
My shell is actually cream-colored; it's my soft mantle (body) that gives me these fantastic markings.
om nom nom
Queen Conch
Kneel before me, loyal subjects!!
Despite my large size, I am actually a herbivore. My diet consists of algae; I am another vacuum cleaner of the reef. But a royal vacuum cleaner.
Cone Snail
I am one of the most DEADLY animals in the world; my venom is strong enough to kill even the biggest animal. But I use it to kill my prey...which happens to be small fish.
I deliver my venom via a built-in harpoon.
Hah! You're just a snail—
AHHHHHH

harpoon'd!

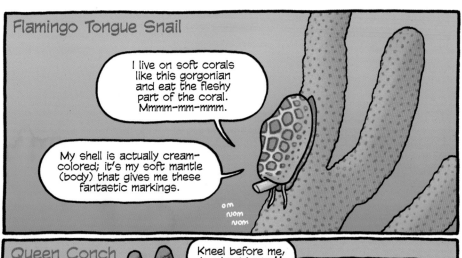

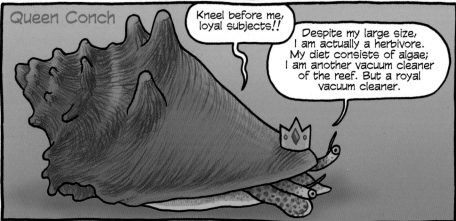

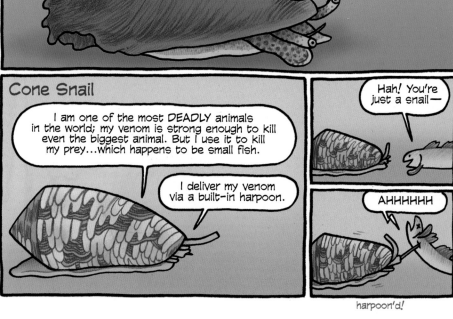

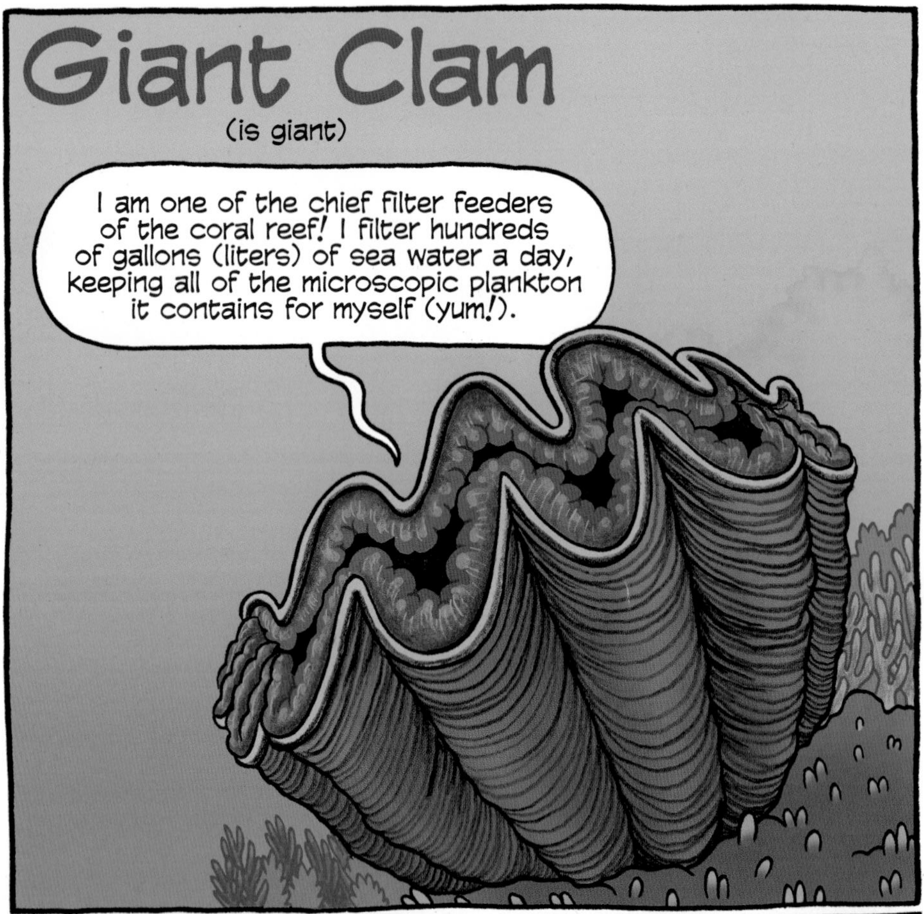
Giant Clam
(is giant)
I am one of the chief filter feeders of the coral reef! I filter hundreds of gallons (liters) of sea water a day, keeping all of the microscopic plankton it contains for myself (yum!).

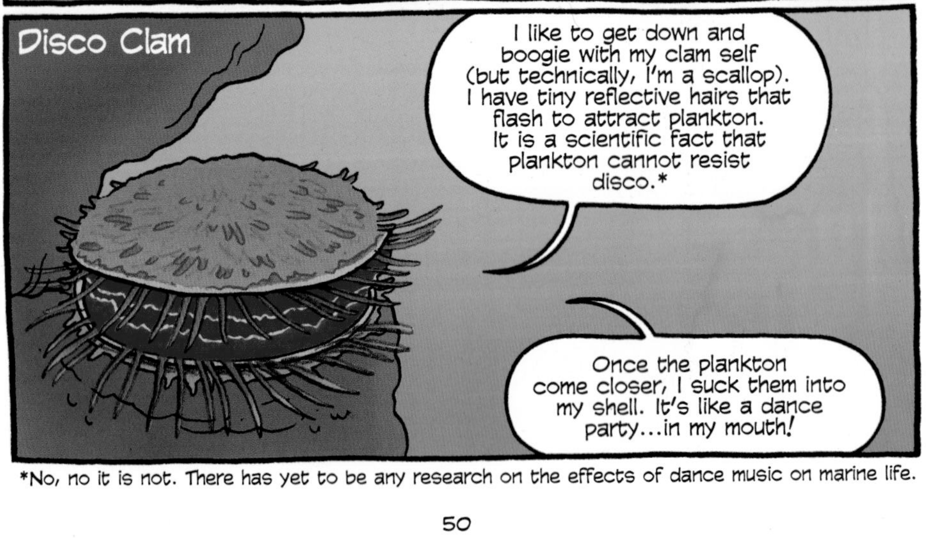
Disco Clam
I like to get down and boogie with my clam self (but technically, I'm a scallop). I have tiny reflective hairs that flash to attract plankton. It is a scientific fact that plankton cannot resist disco.*
Once the plankton come closer, I suck them into my shell. It's like a dance party...in my mouth!

*No, no it is not. There has yet to be any research on the effects of dance music on marine life.

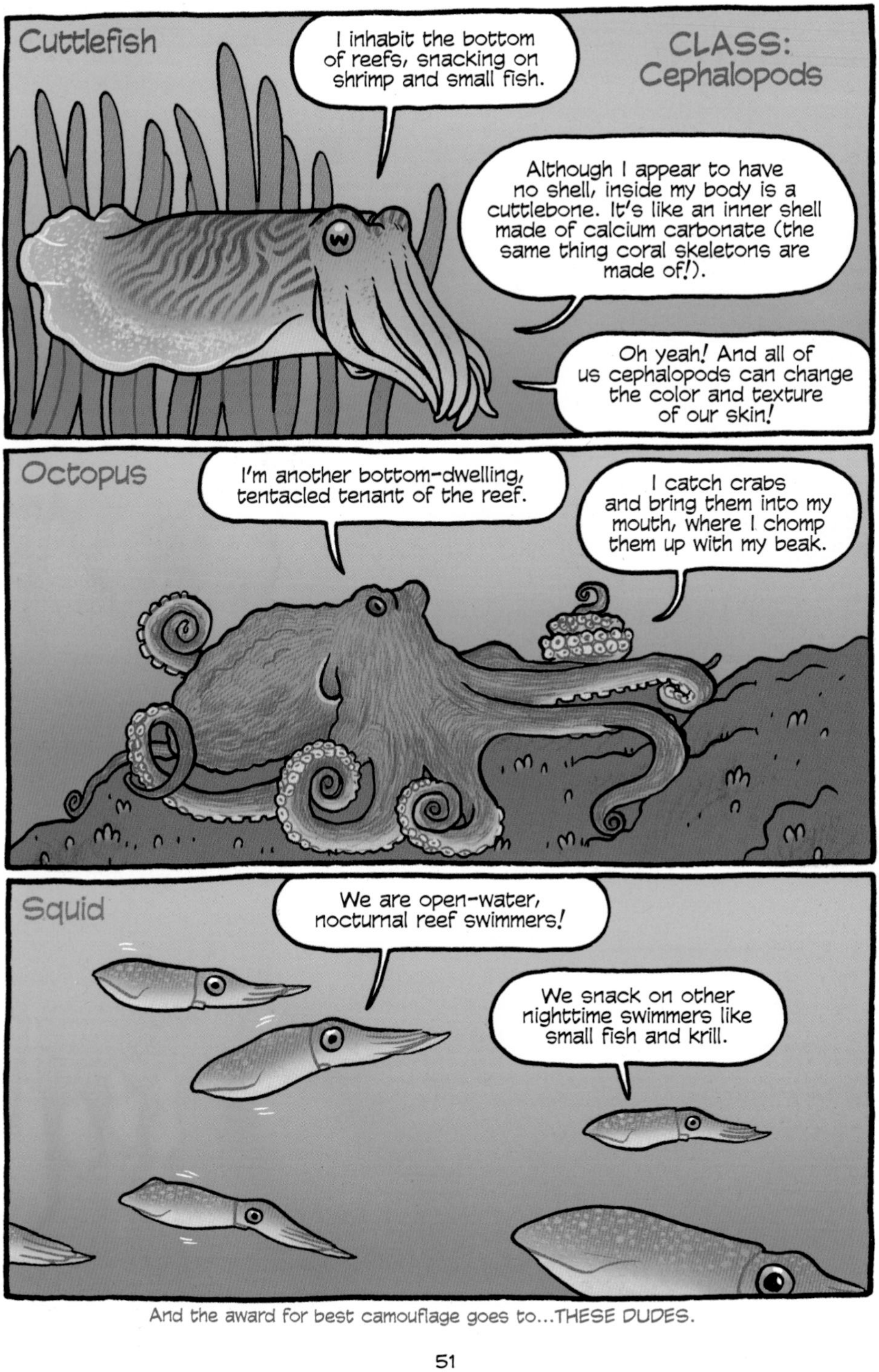
Cuttlefish
I inhabit the bottom of reefs, snacking on shrimp and small fish.
CLASS: Cephalopods
Although I appear to have no shell, inside my body is a cuttlebone. It's like an inner shell made of calcium carbonate (the same thing coral skeletons are made of!).
Oh yeah! And all of us cephalopods can change the color and texture of our skin!
Octopus
I'm another bottom-dwelling, tentacled tenant of the reef.
I catch crabs and bring them into my mouth, where I chomp them up with my beak.
Squid
We are open-water, nocturnal reef swimmers!
We snack on other nighttime swimmers like small fish and krill.

And the award for best camouflage goes to...THESE DUDES.

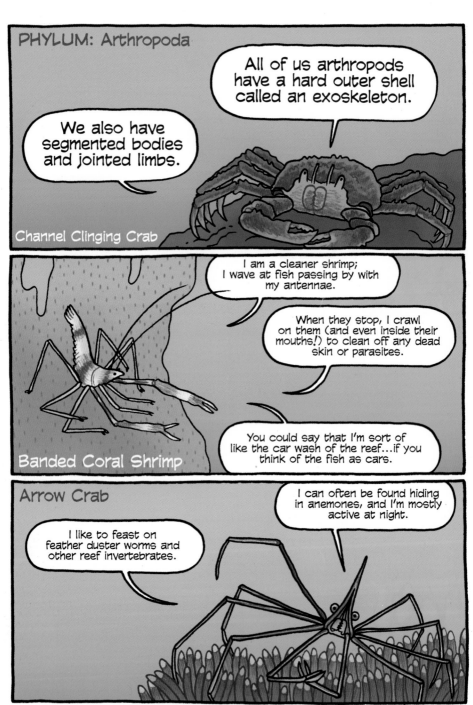

PHYLUM: Arthropoda

All of us arthropods have a hard outer shell called an exoskeleton.

We also have segmented bodies and jointed limbs.

Channel Clinging Crab

I am a cleaner shrimp; I wave at fish passing by with my antennae.

When they stop, I crawl on them (and even inside their mouths!) to clean off any dead skin or parasites.

You could say that I'm sort of like the car wash of the reef...if you think of the fish as cars.

Banded Coral Shrimp

Arrow Crab

I can often be found hiding in anemones, and I'm mostly active at night.

I like to feast on feather duster worms and other reef invertebrates.

BEEP BEEP make way for the fishmobile!

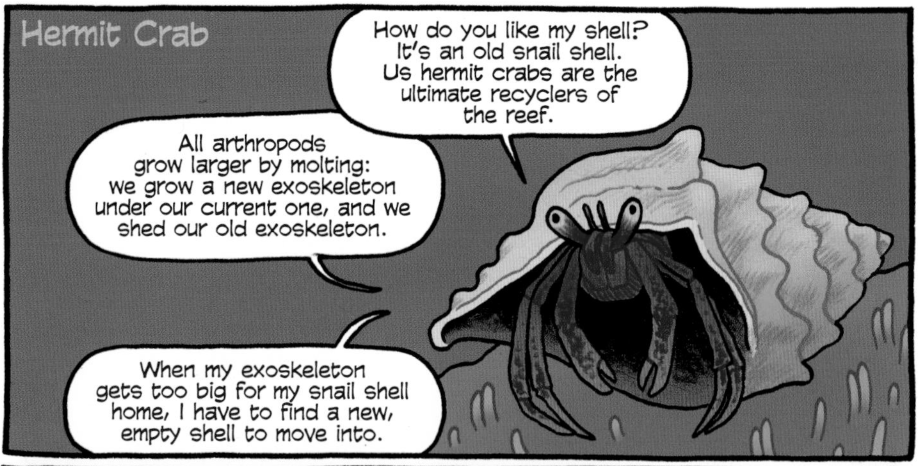
Hermit Crab
How do you like my shell? It's an old snail shell. Us hermit crabs are the ultimate recyclers of the reef.
All arthropods grow larger by molting: we grow a new exoskeleton under our current one, and we shed our old exoskeleton.
When my exoskeleton gets too big for my snail shell home, I have to find a new, empty shell to move into.

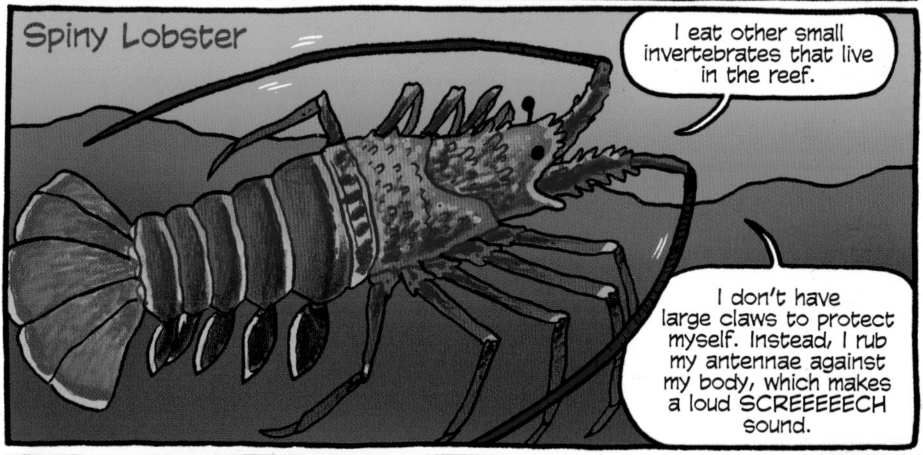
Spiny Lobster
I eat other small invertebrates that live in the reef.
I don't have large claws to protect myself. Instead, I rub my antennae against my body, which makes a loud SCREEEEECH sound.

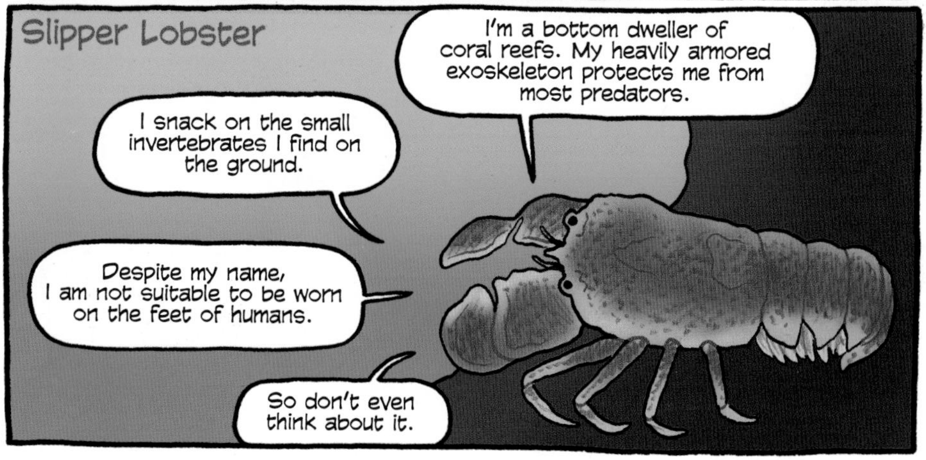
Slipper Lobster
I'm a bottom dweller of coral reefs. My heavily armored exoskeleton protects me from most predators.
I snack on the small invertebrates I find on the ground.
Despite my name, I am not suitable to be worn on the feet of humans.
So don't even think about it.

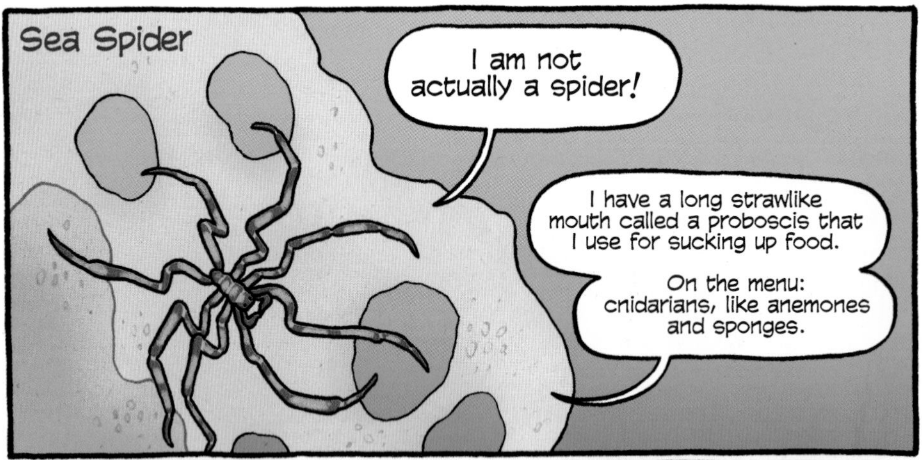
Sea Spider
I am not actually a spider!
I have a long strawlike mouth called a proboscis that I use for sucking up food.
On the menu: cnidarians, like anemones and sponges.

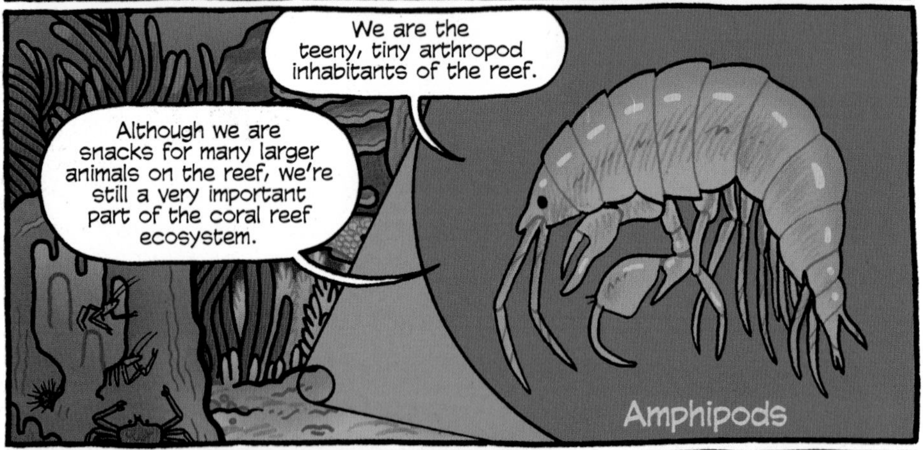
We are the teeny, tiny arthropod inhabitants of the reef.
Although we are snacks for many larger animals on the reef, we're still a very important part of the coral reef ecosystem.
Amphipods

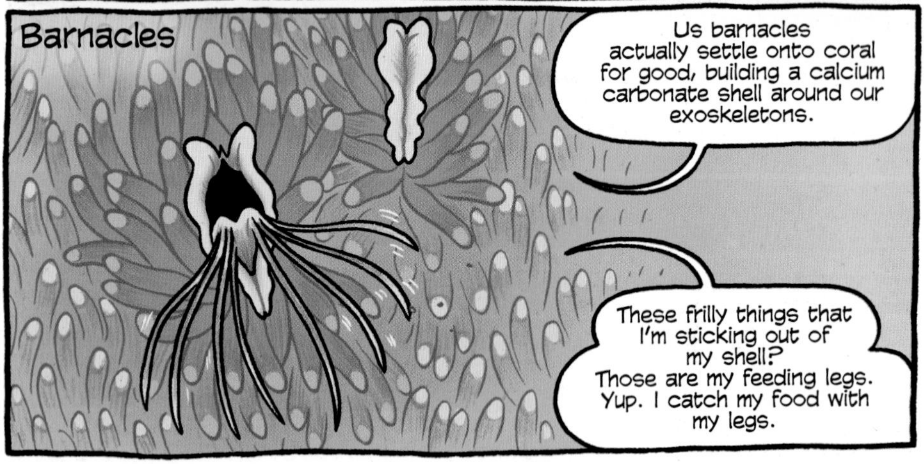
Barnacles
Us barnacles actually settle onto coral for good, building a calcium carbonate shell around our exoskeletons.
These frilly things that I'm sticking out of my shell? Those are my feeding legs. Yup. I catch my food with my legs.

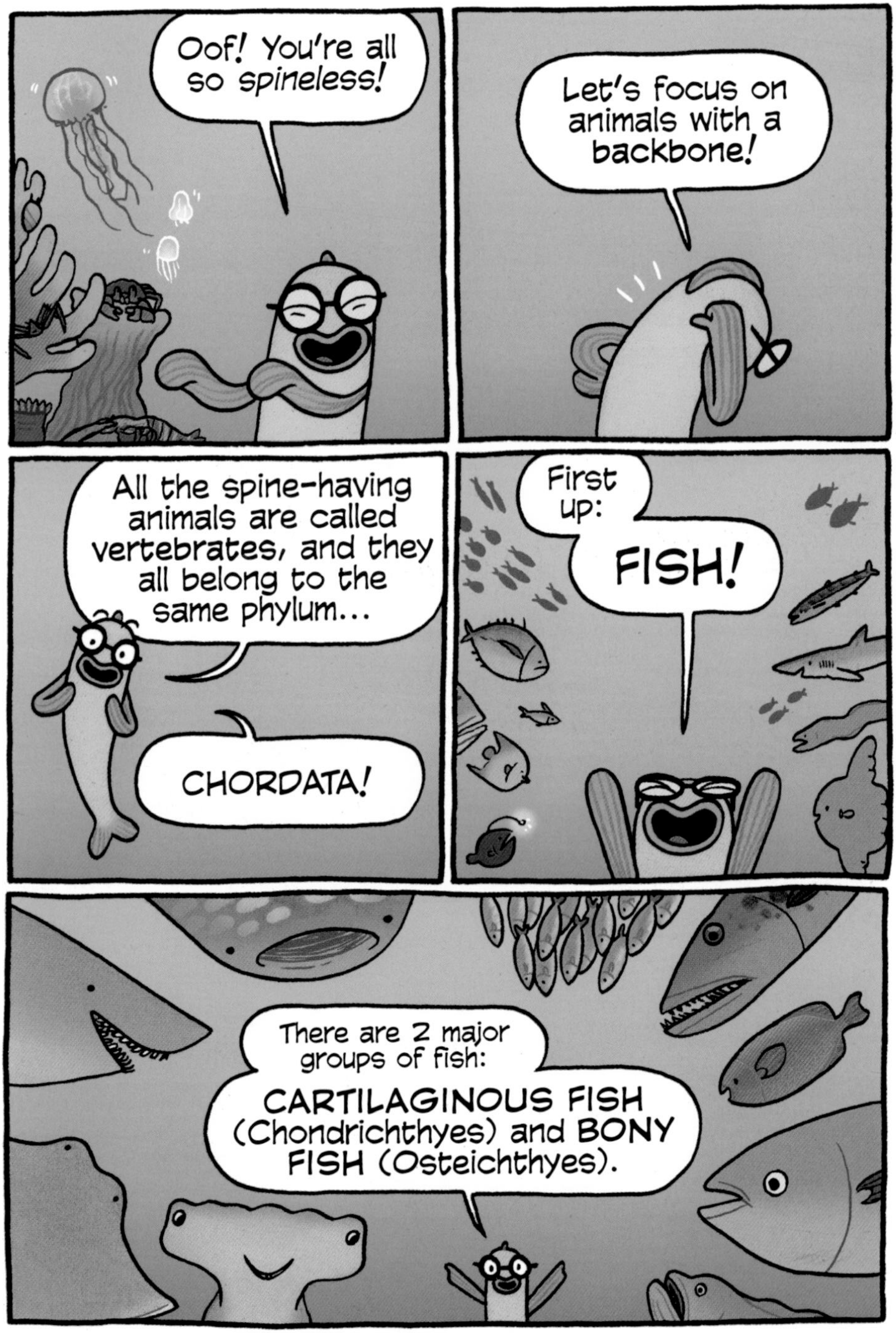
Oof! You're all so spineless!
Let's focus on animals with a backbone!
All the spine-having animals are called vertebrates, and they all belong to the same phylum...
CHORDATA!
First up:
FISH!
There are 2 major groups of fish:
CARTILAGINOUS FISH (Chondrichthyes) and BONY FISH (Osteichthyes).

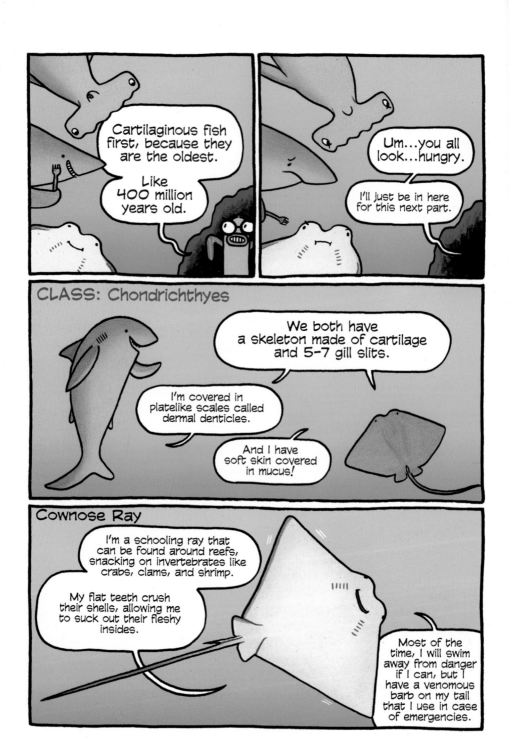

Cartilaginous fish first, because they are the oldest.

Like 400 million years old.

Um...you all look...hungry.

I'll just be in here for this next part.

CLASS: Chondrichthyes

We both have a skeleton made of cartilage and 5-7 gill slits.

I'm covered in platelike scales called dermal denticles.

And I have soft skin covered in mucus!

Cownose Ray

I'm a schooling ray that can be found around reefs, snacking on invertebrates like crabs, clams, and shrimp.

My flat teeth crush their shells, allowing me to suck out their fleshy insides.

Most of the time, I will swim away from danger if I can, but I have a venomous barb on my tail that I use in case of emergencies.

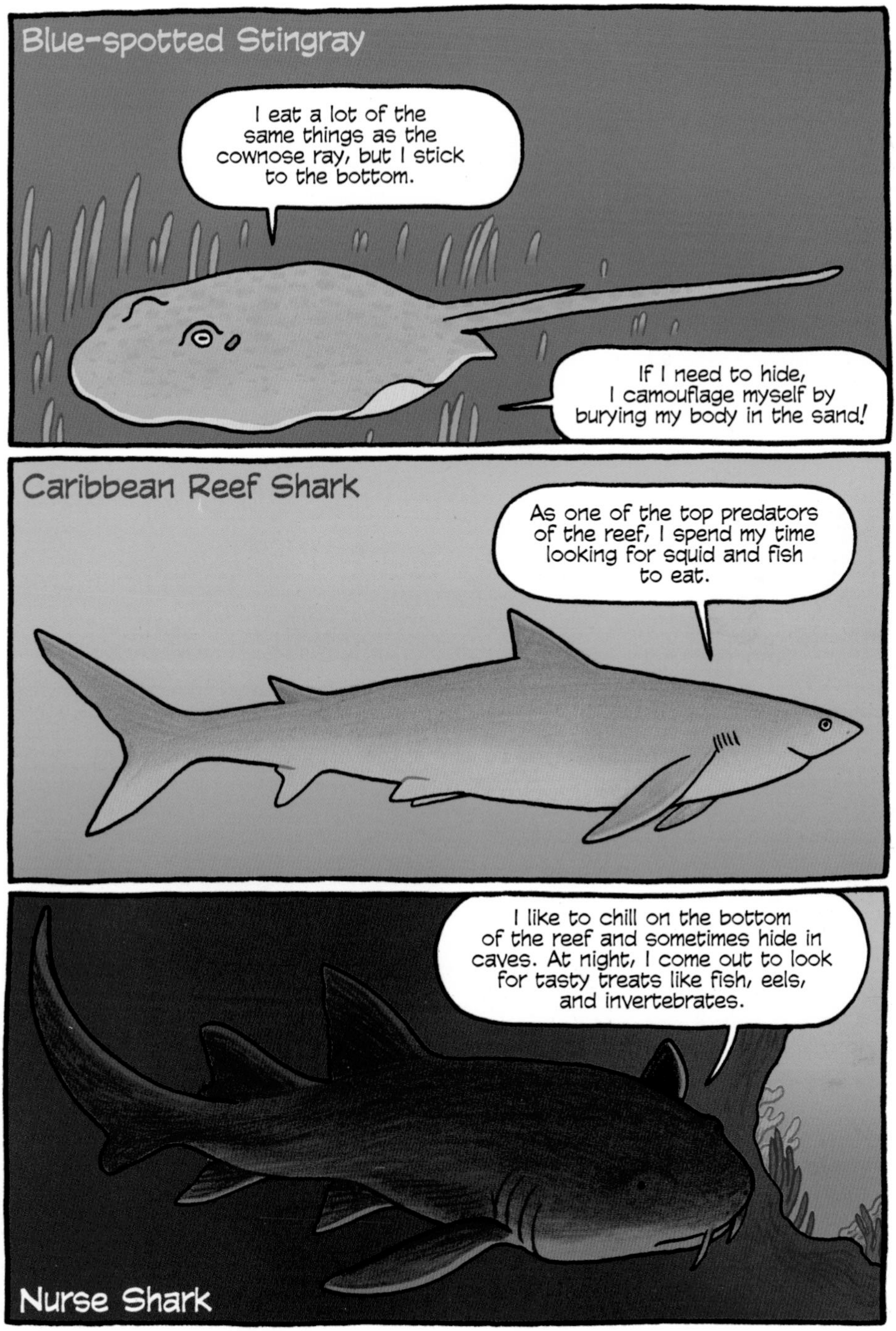
Blue-spotted Stingray
I eat a lot of the same things as the cownose ray, but I stick to the bottom.
If I need to hide, I camouflage myself by burying my body in the sand!
Caribbean Reef Shark
As one of the top predators of the reef, I spend my time looking for squid and fish to eat.
I like to chill on the bottom of the reef and sometimes hide in caves. At night, I come out to look for tasty treats like fish, eels, and invertebrates.
Nurse Shark

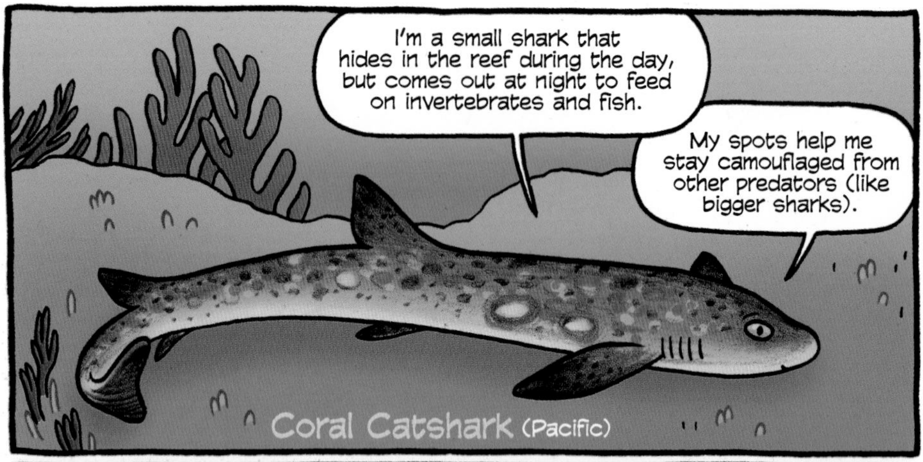
I'm a small shark that hides in the reef during the day, but comes out at night to feed on invertebrates and fish.
My spots help me stay camouflaged from other predators (like bigger sharks).
Coral Catshark (Pacific)

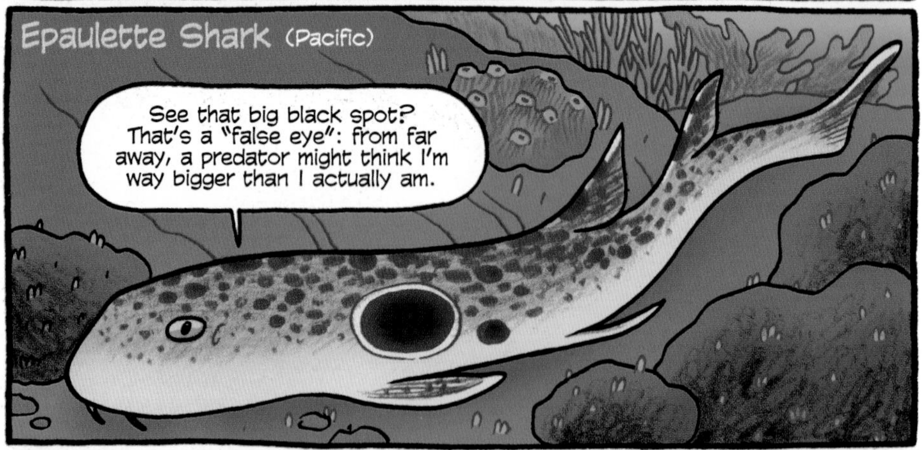
Epaulette Shark (Pacific)
See that big black spot? That's a "false eye": from far away, a predator might think I'm way bigger than I actually am.

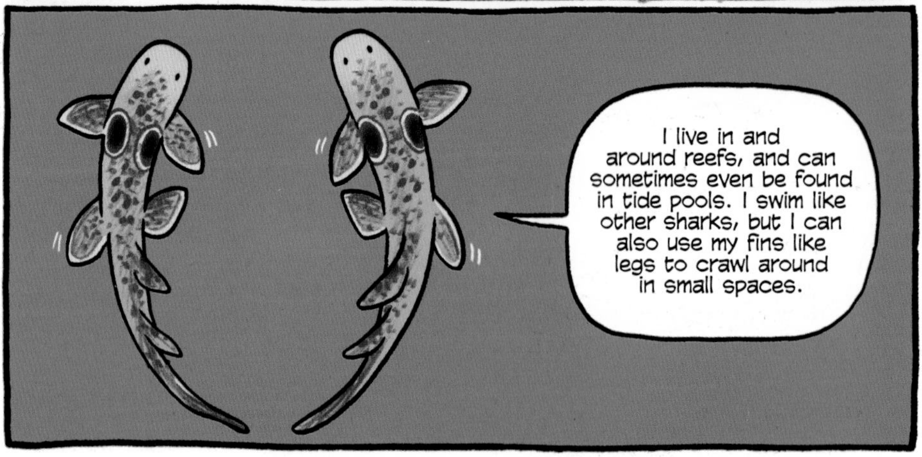
I live in and around reefs, and can sometimes even be found in tide pools. I swim like other sharks, but I can also use my fins like legs to crawl around in small spaces.

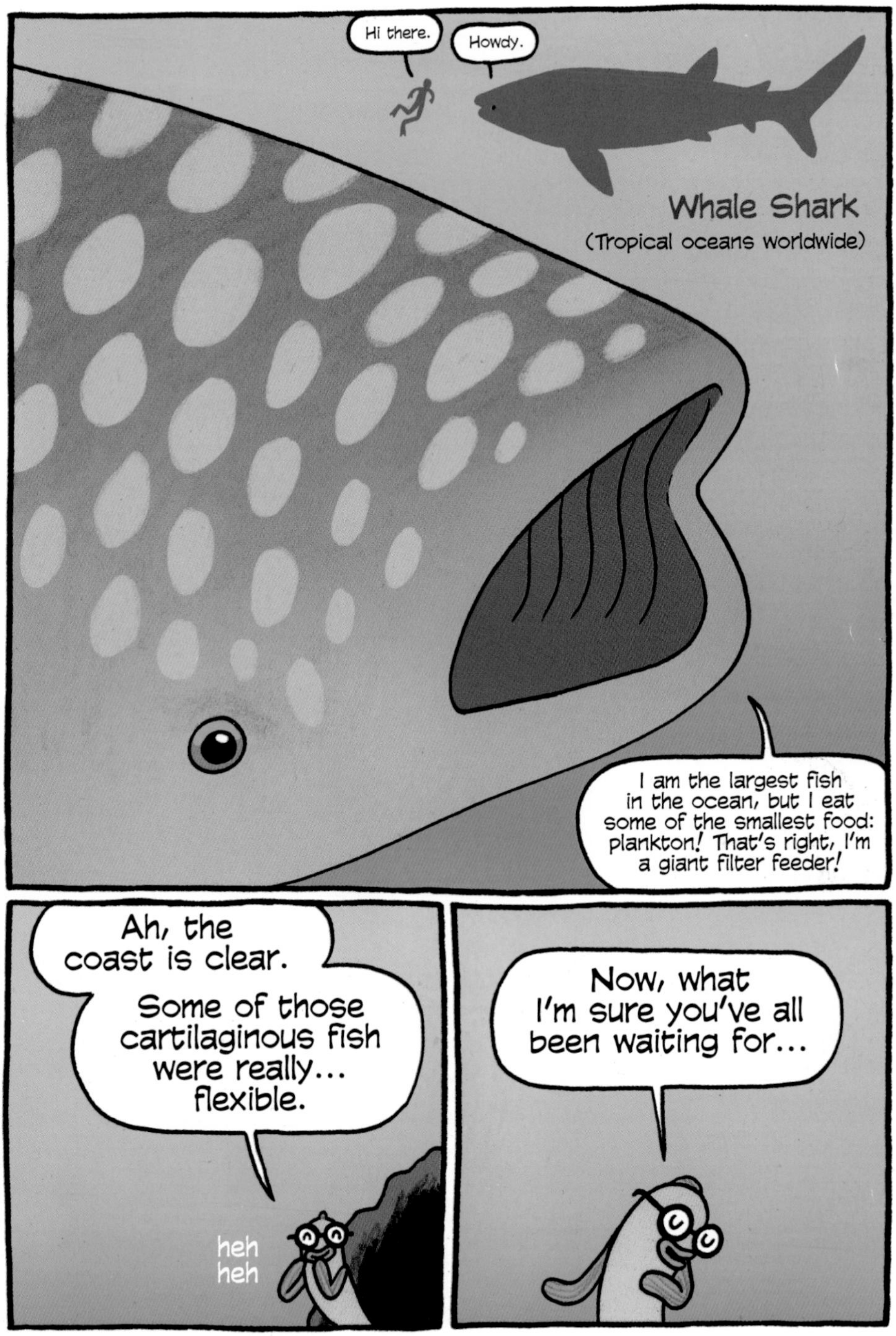
Hi there.
Howdy.
Whale Shark
(Tropical oceans worldwide)
I am the largest fish in the ocean, but I eat some of the smallest food: plankton! That's right, I'm a giant filter feeder!
Ah, the coast is clear.
Some of those cartilaginous fish were really... flexible.
heh heh
Now, what I'm sure you've all been waiting for...

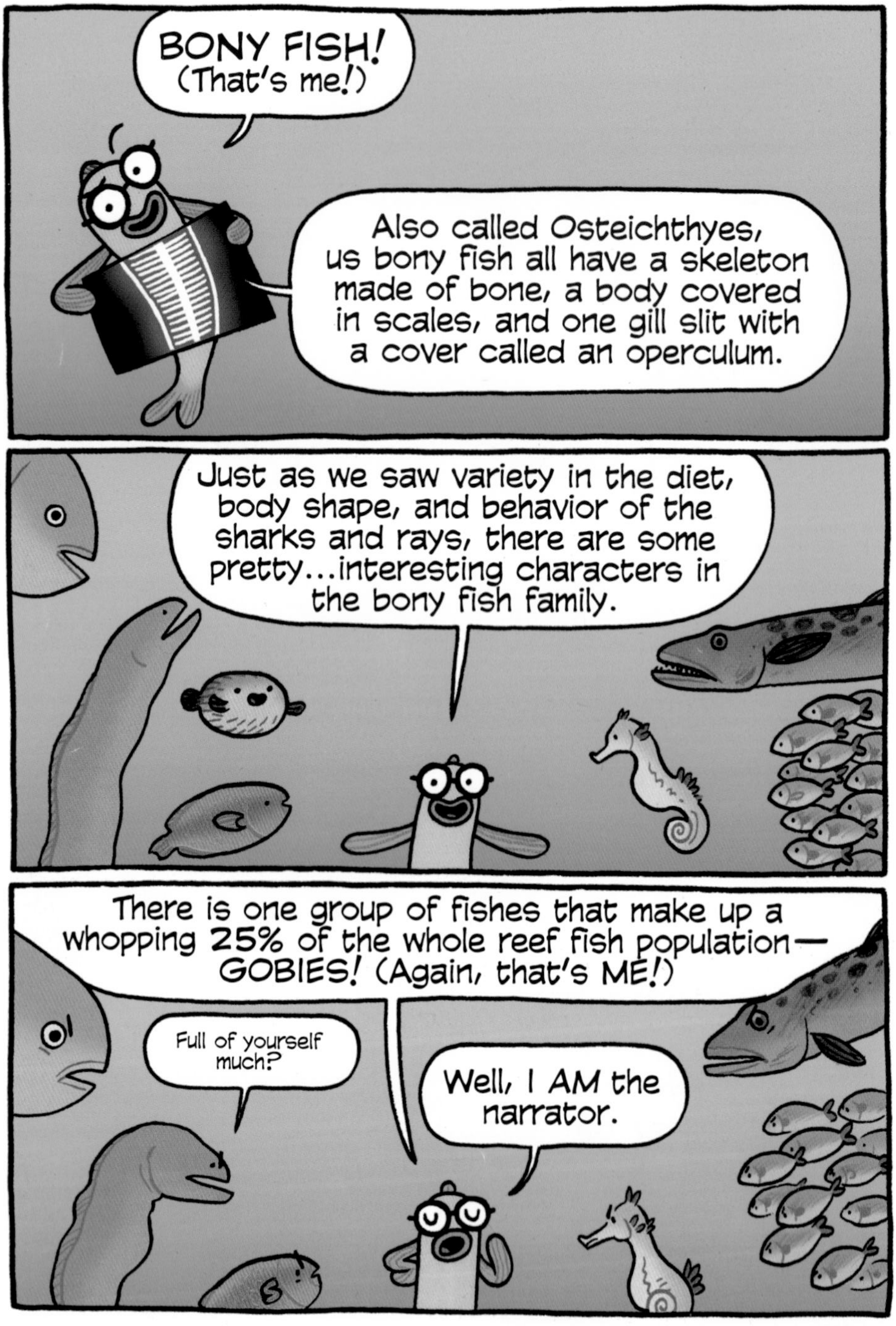
BONY FISH! (That's me!)
Also called Osteichthyes, us bony fish all have a skeleton made of bone, a body covered in scales, and one gill slit with a cover called an operculum.
Just as we saw variety in the diet, body shape, and behavior of the sharks and rays, there are some pretty...interesting characters in the bony fish family.
There is one group of fishes that make up a whopping 25% of the whole reef fish population— GOBIES! (Again, that's ME!)
Full of yourself much?
Well, I AM the narrator.

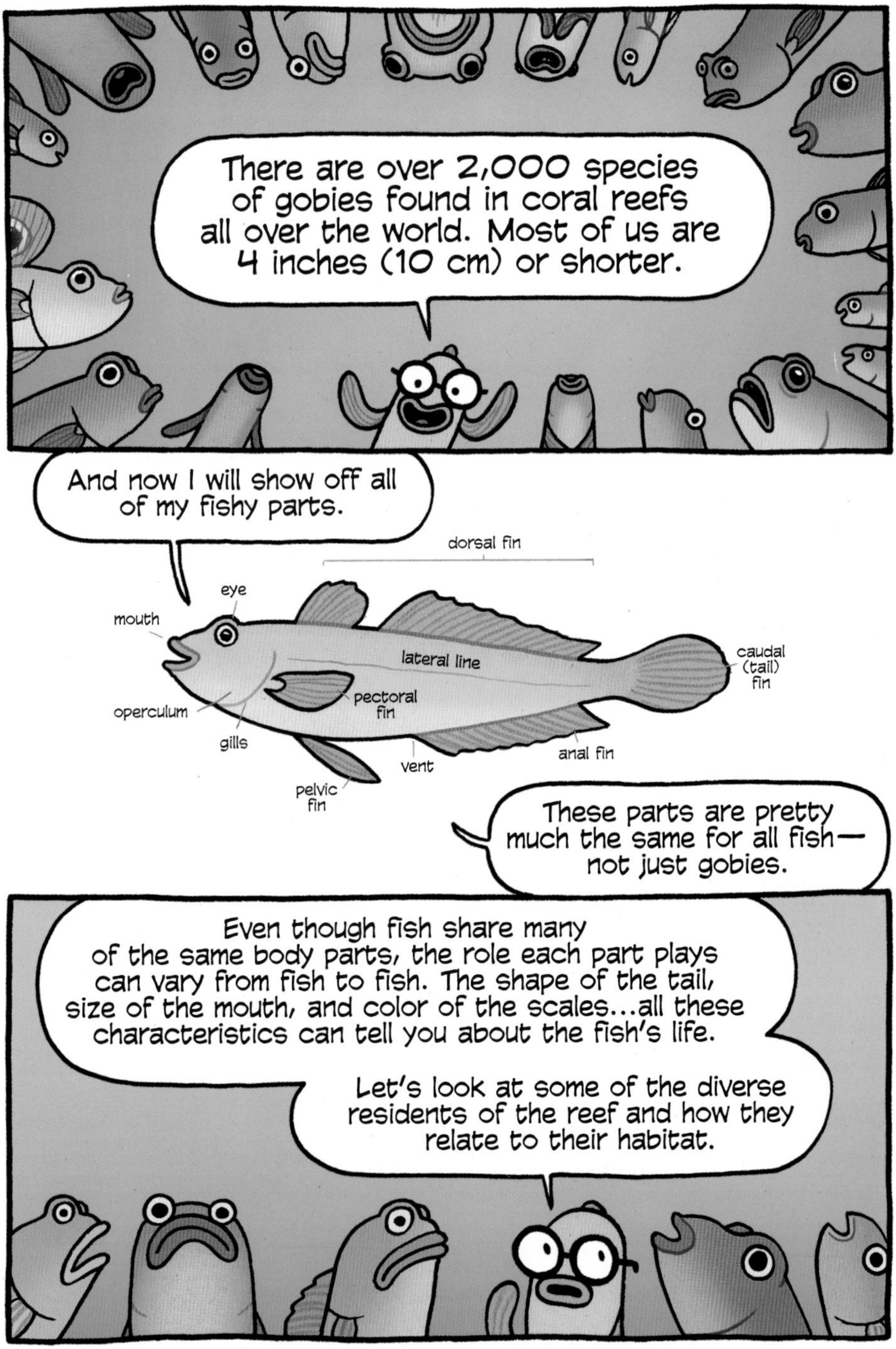
There are over 2,000 species of gobies found in coral reefs all over the world. Most of us are 4 inches (10 cm) or shorter.
And now I will show off all of my fishy parts.
dorsal fin
eye
mouth
lateral line
caudal (tail) fin
pectoral fin
operculum
gills
vent
anal fin
pelvic fin
These parts are pretty much the same for all fish—not just gobies.
Even though fish share many of the same body parts, the role each part plays can vary from fish to fish. The shape of the tail, size of the mouth, and color of the scales...all these characteristics can tell you about the fish's life.
Let's look at some of the diverse residents of the reef and how they relate to their habitat.

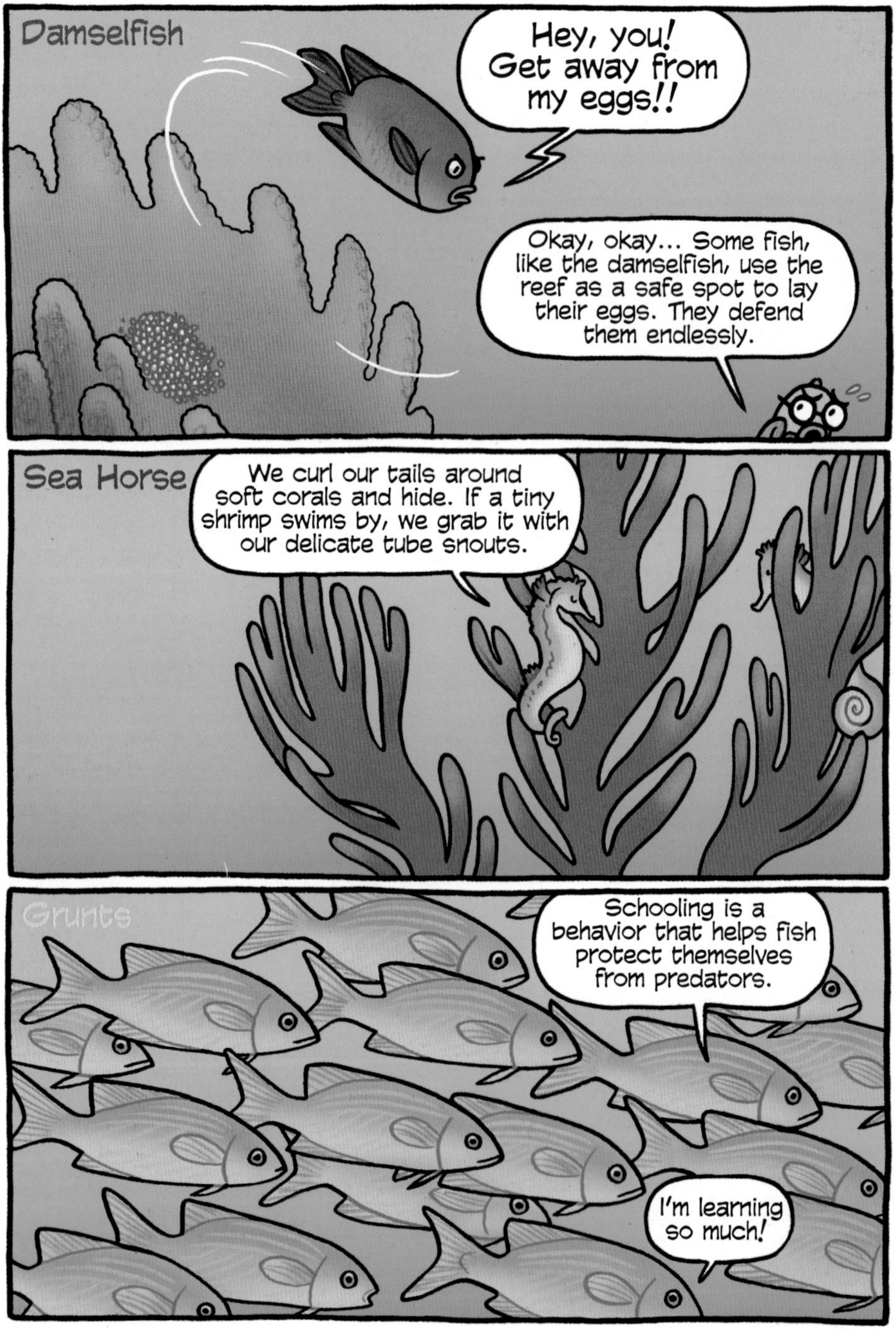
Damselfish
Hey, you! Get away from my eggs!!
Okay, okay... Some fish, like the damselfish, use the reef as a safe spot to lay their eggs. They defend them endlessly.
Sea Horse
We curl our tails around soft corals and hide. If a tiny shrimp swims by, we grab it with our delicate tube snouts.
Grunts
Schooling is a behavior that helps fish protect themselves from predators.
I'm learning so much!

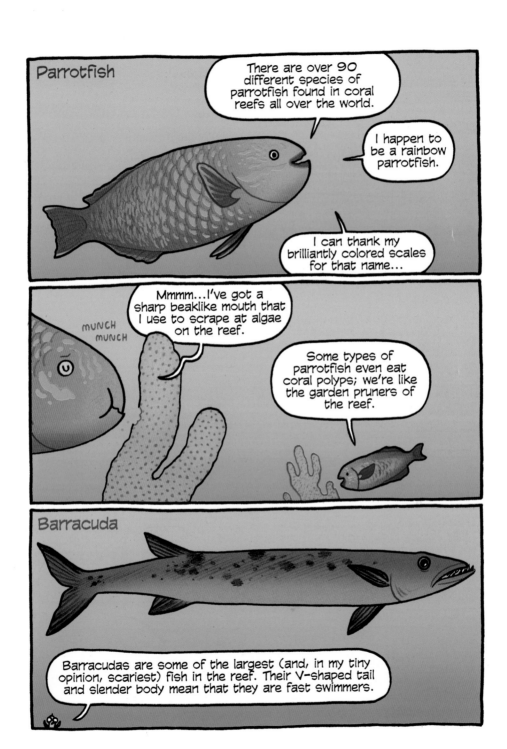

Parrotfish

There are over 90 different species of parrotfish found in coral reefs all over the world.

I happen to be a rainbow parrotfish.

I can thank my brilliantly colored scales for that name...

MUNCH MUNCH

Mmmm...I've got a sharp beaklike mouth that I use to scrape at algae on the reef.

Some types of parrotfish even eat coral polyps; we're like the garden pruners of the reef.

Barracuda

Barracudas are some of the largest (and, in my tiny opinion, scariest) fish in the reef. Their V-shaped tail and slender body mean that they are fast swimmers.

Moray Eel

Psst.

Over here.

In the cave.

I'm an apex predator, which means I'm at the top of the food chain. I'm what you would call an ambush feeder. I hide in caves all day, and when an unsuspecting fish swims by...

CHOMP!

...I grab them with my strong jaws. I even have ANOTHER set of jaws in my throat that helps pull my catch in further.

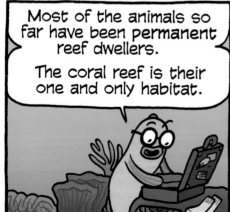

Most of the animals so far have been permanent reef dwellers.

The coral reef is their one and only habitat.

Many migratory animals visit the reef throughout the year and depend on it for food and/or shelter.

It's impolite to talk with your mouth full, Mr. Moray.

ORDER: Reptilia

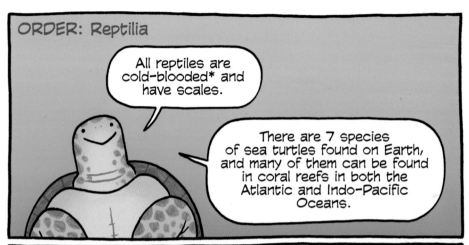

All reptiles are cold-blooded* and have scales.

There are 7 species of sea turtles found on Earth, and many of them can be found in coral reefs in both the Atlantic and Indo-Pacific Oceans.

Sea turtles spend their lives swimming all over the ocean (and world!), but the coral reef is just as important to them as the open ocean.

Reefs provide two valuable resources: a place to rest...

...and a place to eat.

*With one exception: the leatherback sea turtle can regulate its body temperature!

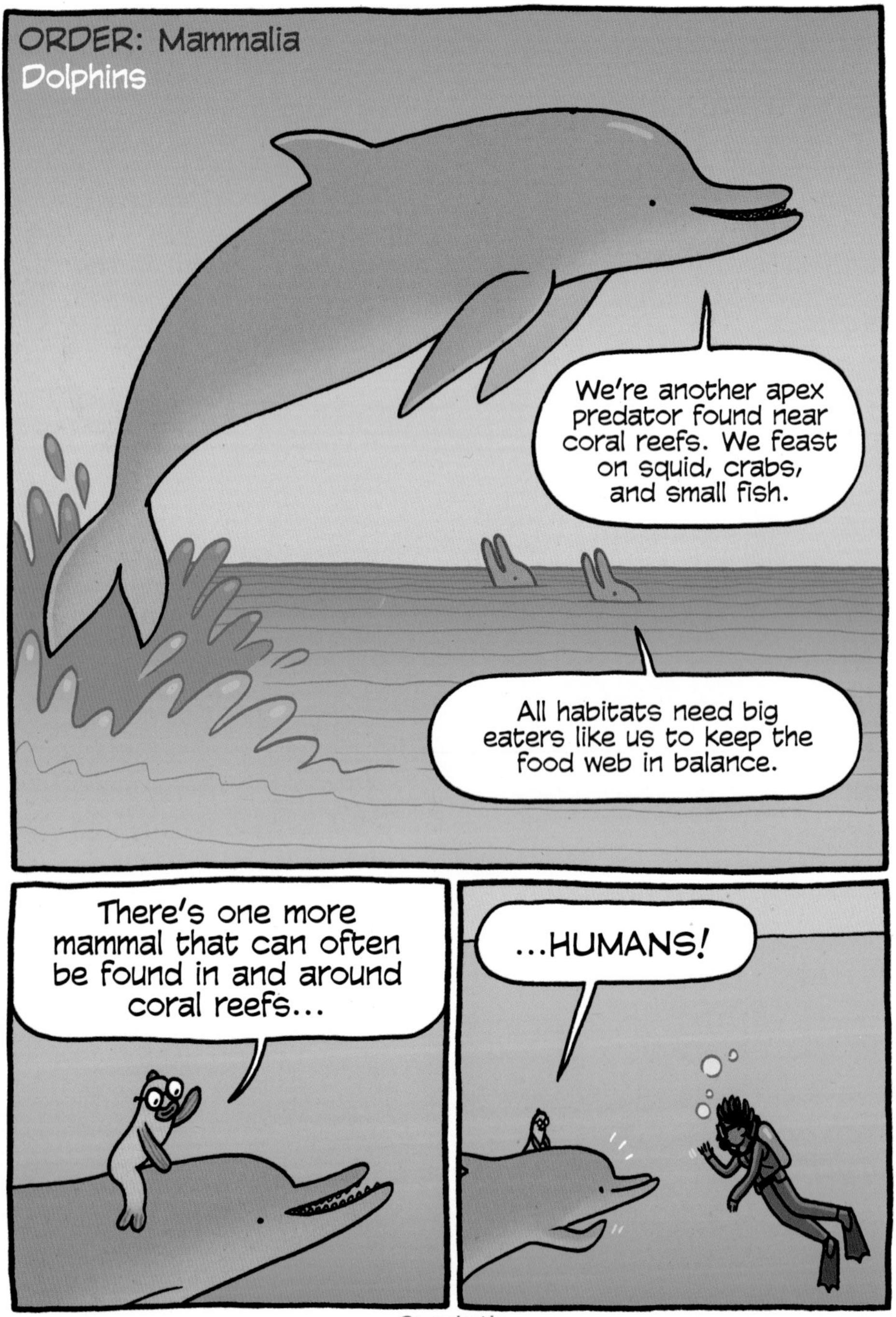
ORDER: Mammalia
Dolphins
We're another apex predator found near coral reefs. We feast on squid, crabs, and small fish.
All habitats need big eaters like us to keep the food web in balance.
There's one more mammal that can often be found in and around coral reefs...
...HUMANS!

So majestic.

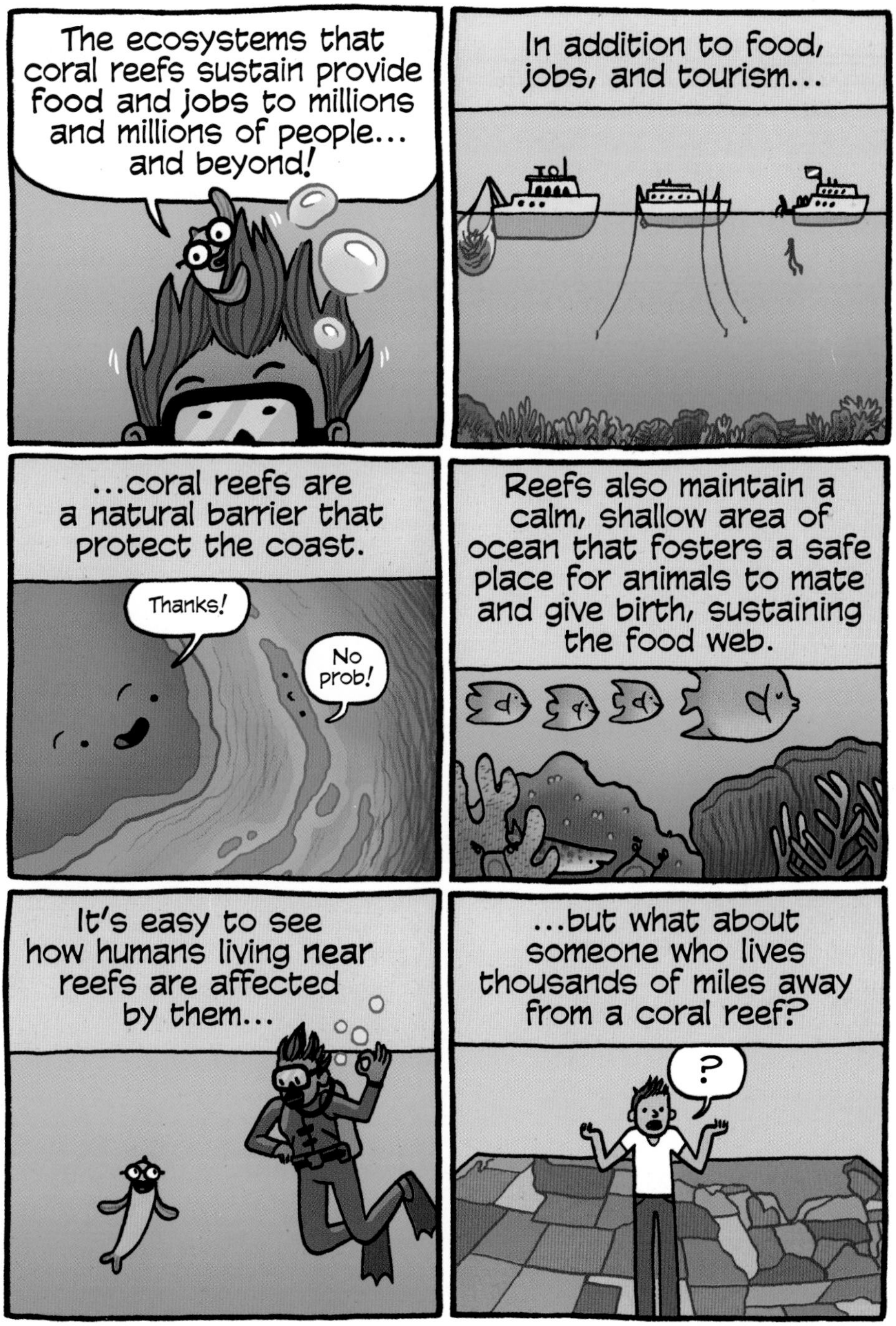
The ecosystems that coral reefs sustain provide food and jobs to millions and millions of people... and beyond!
In addition to food, jobs, and tourism...
...coral reefs are a natural barrier that protect the coast.
Thanks!
No prob!
Reefs also maintain a calm, shallow area of ocean that fosters a safe place for animals to mate and give birth, sustaining the food web.
It's easy to see how humans living near reefs are affected by them...
...but what about someone who lives thousands of miles away from a coral reef?
?

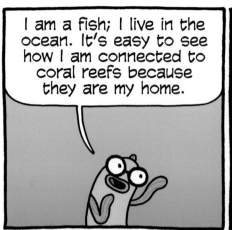

I am a fish; I live in the ocean. It's easy to see how I am connected to coral reefs because they are my home.

But what about the places where there are no reefs? The other 99.9% of the planet?

CHAPTER FOUR:
HOW ARE CORAL REEFS CONNECTED TO THE REST OF THE PLANET?

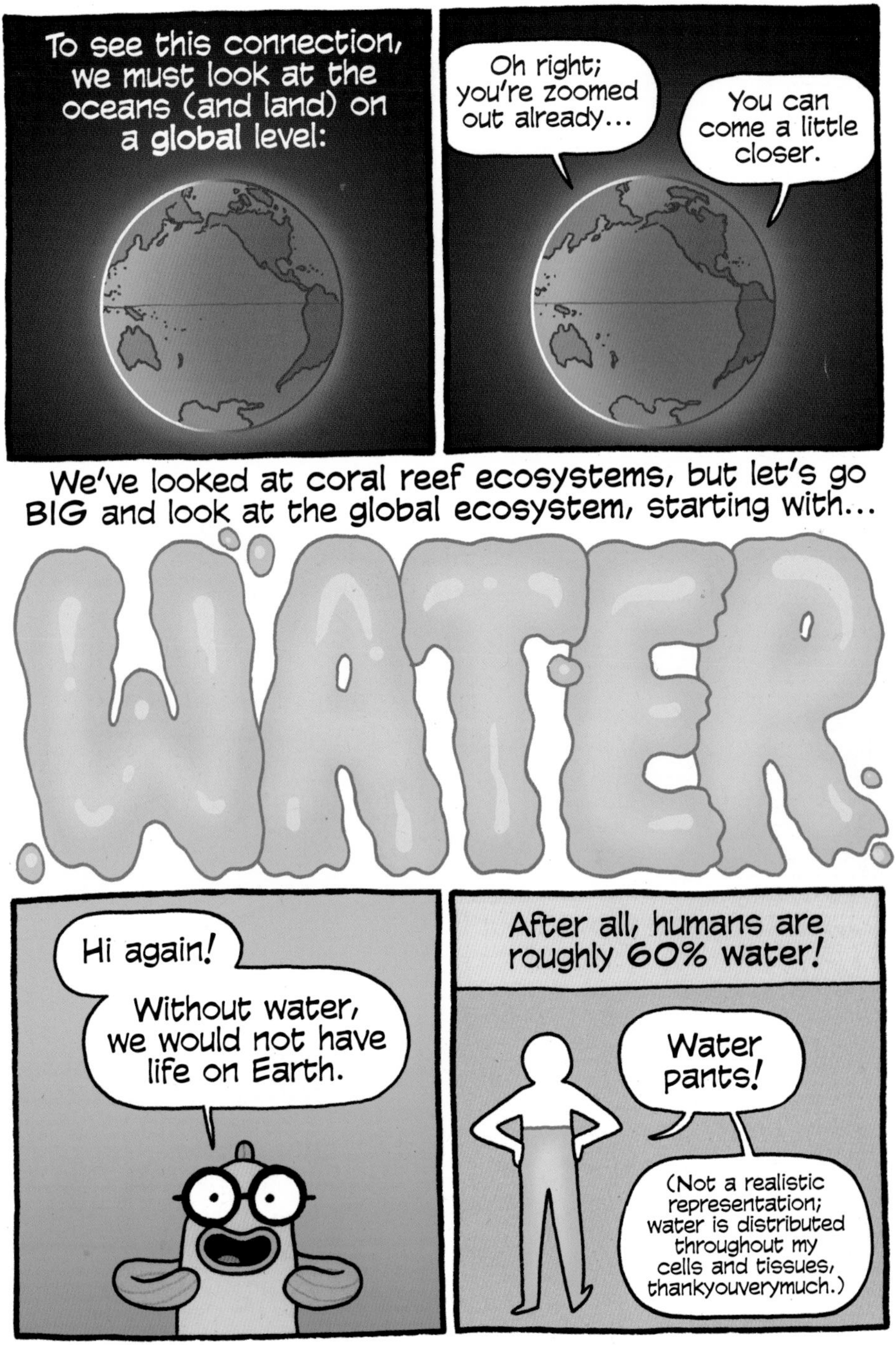
To see this connection, we must look at the oceans (and land) on a **global** level:
Oh right; you're zoomed out already...
You can come a little closer.
We've looked at coral reef ecosystems, but let's go BIG and look at the global ecosystem, starting with...
WATER
Hi again!
Without water, we would not have life on Earth.
After all, humans are roughly 60% water!
Water pants!
(Not a realistic representation; water is distributed throughout my cells and tissues, thankyouverymuch.)

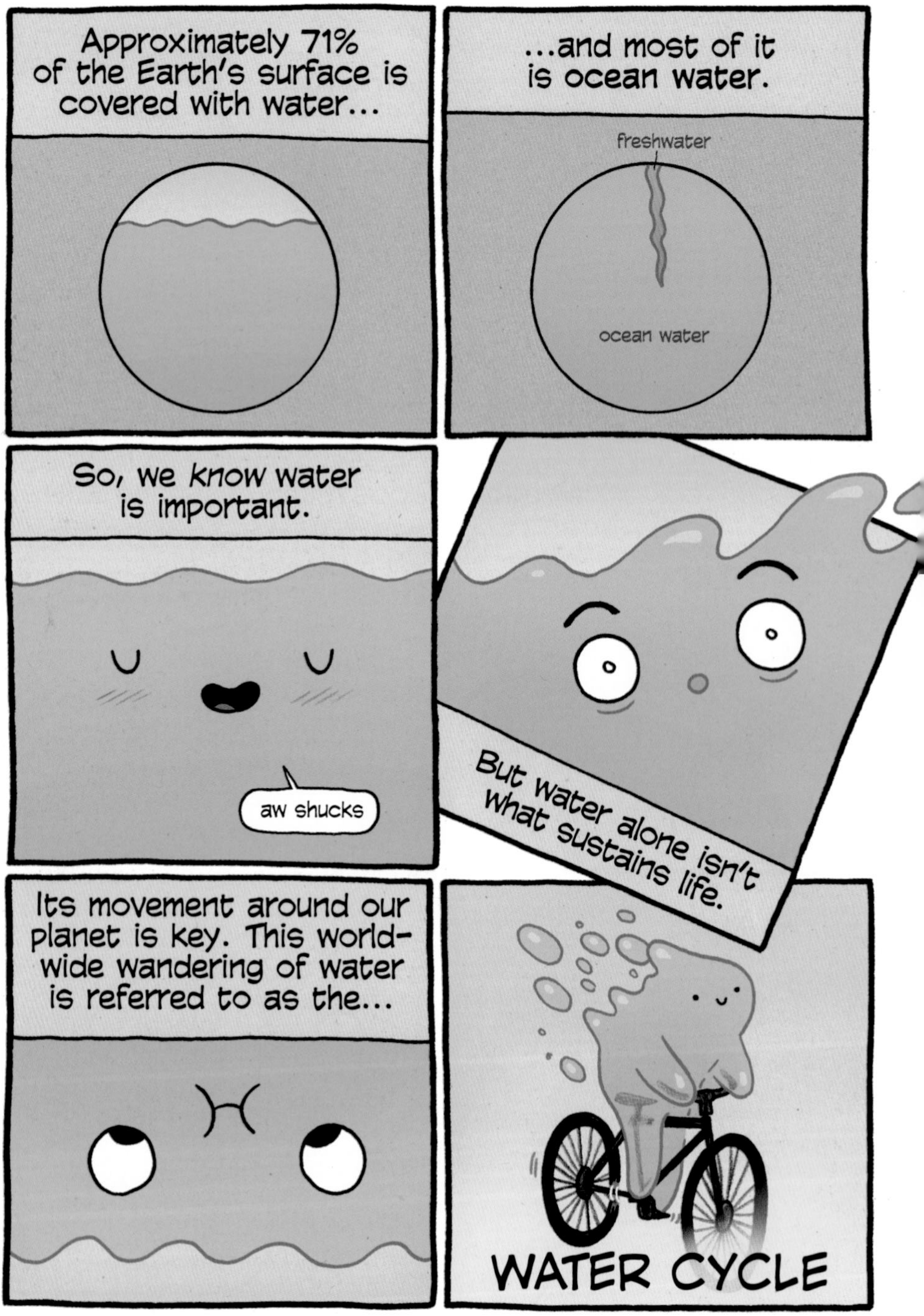

Approximately 71% of the Earth's surface is covered with water...
...and most of it is ocean water.
freshwater
ocean water
So, we *know* water is important.
aw shucks
But water alone isn't what sustains life.
Its movement around our planet is key. This world-wide wandering of water is referred to as the...
WATER CYCLE

Um, not THAT kind of cycle.

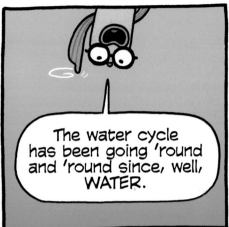

The water cycle has been going 'round and 'round since, well, WATER.

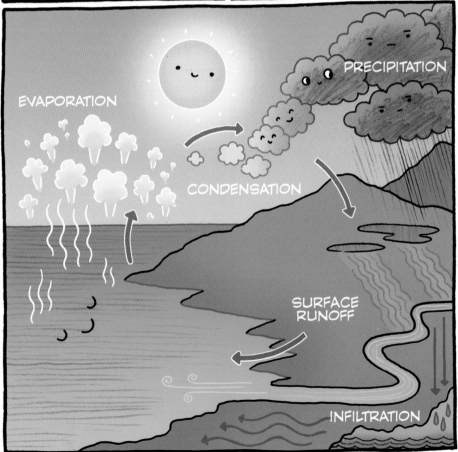

EVAPORATION

PRECIPITATION

CONDENSATION

SURFACE RUNOFF

INFILTRATION

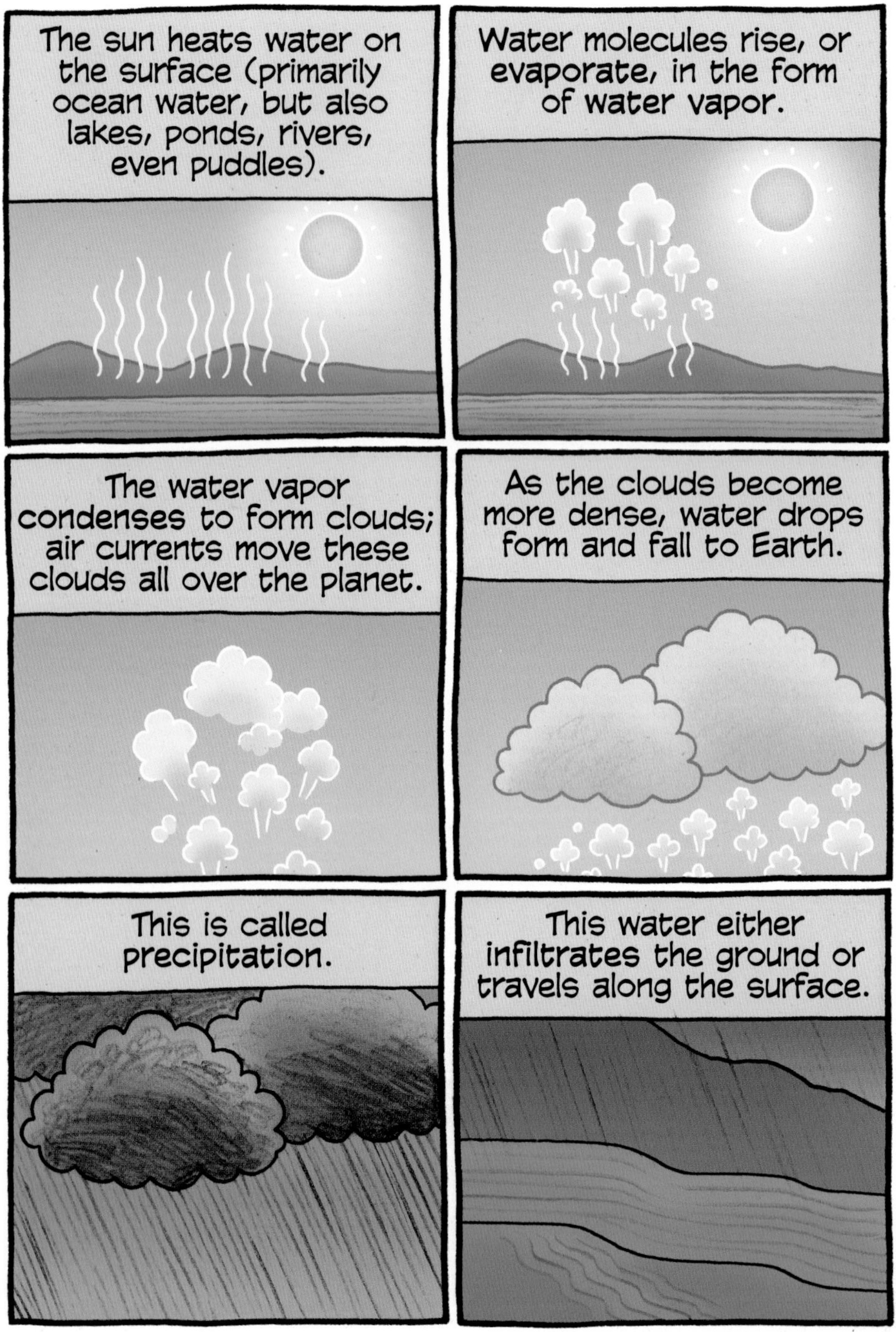
The sun heats water on the surface (primarily ocean water, but also lakes, ponds, rivers, even puddles).
Water molecules rise, or evaporate, in the form of water vapor.
The water vapor condenses to form clouds; air currents move these clouds all over the planet.
As the clouds become more dense, water drops form and fall to Earth.
This is called precipitation.
This water either infiltrates the ground or travels along the surface.

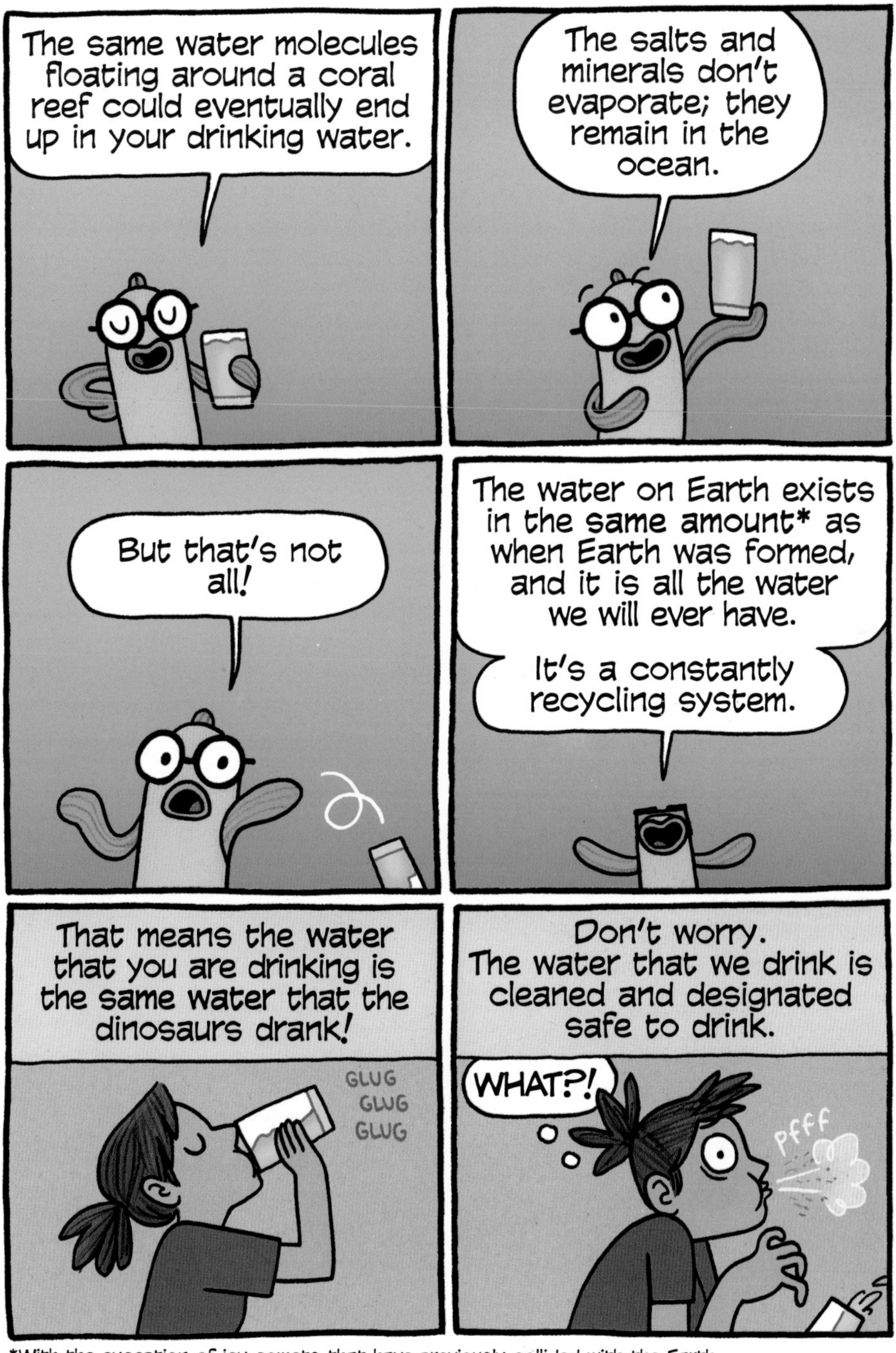
The same water molecules floating around a coral reef could eventually end up in your drinking water.
The salts and minerals don't evaporate; they remain in the ocean.
But that's not all!
The water on Earth exists in the same amount* as when Earth was formed, and it is all the water we will ever have.
It's a constantly recycling system.
That means the water that you are drinking is the same water that the dinosaurs drank!
GLUG
GLUG
GLUG
Don't worry. The water that we drink is cleaned and designated safe to drink.
WHAT?!
pfff

*With the exception of icy comets that have previously collided with the Earth.

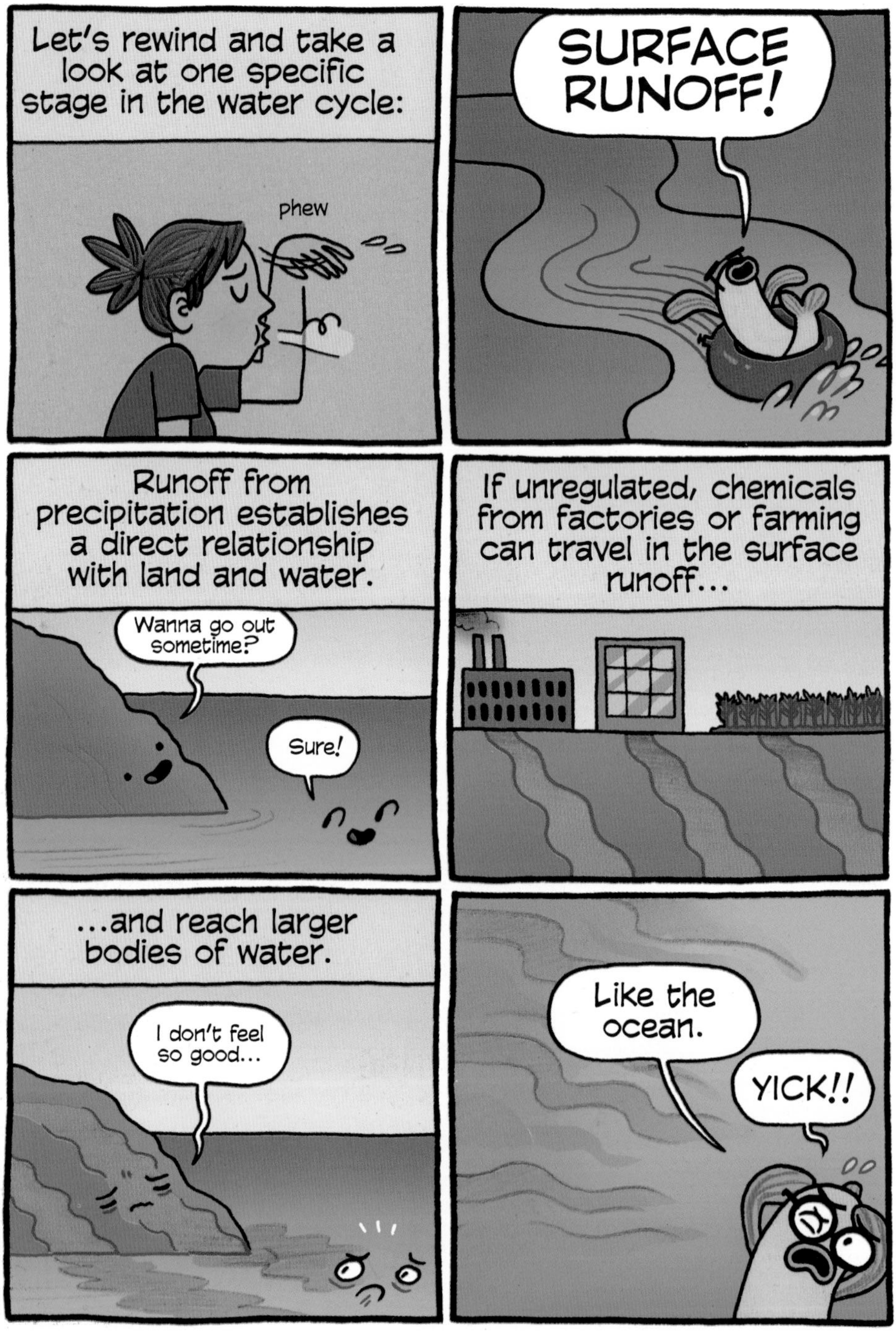
Let's rewind and take a look at one specific stage in the water cycle:
phew
SURFACE RUNOFF!
Runoff from precipitation establishes a direct relationship with land and water.
Wanna go out sometime?
Sure!
If unregulated, chemicals from factories or farming can travel in the surface runoff...
...and reach larger bodies of water.
I don't feel so good...
Like the ocean.
YICK!!

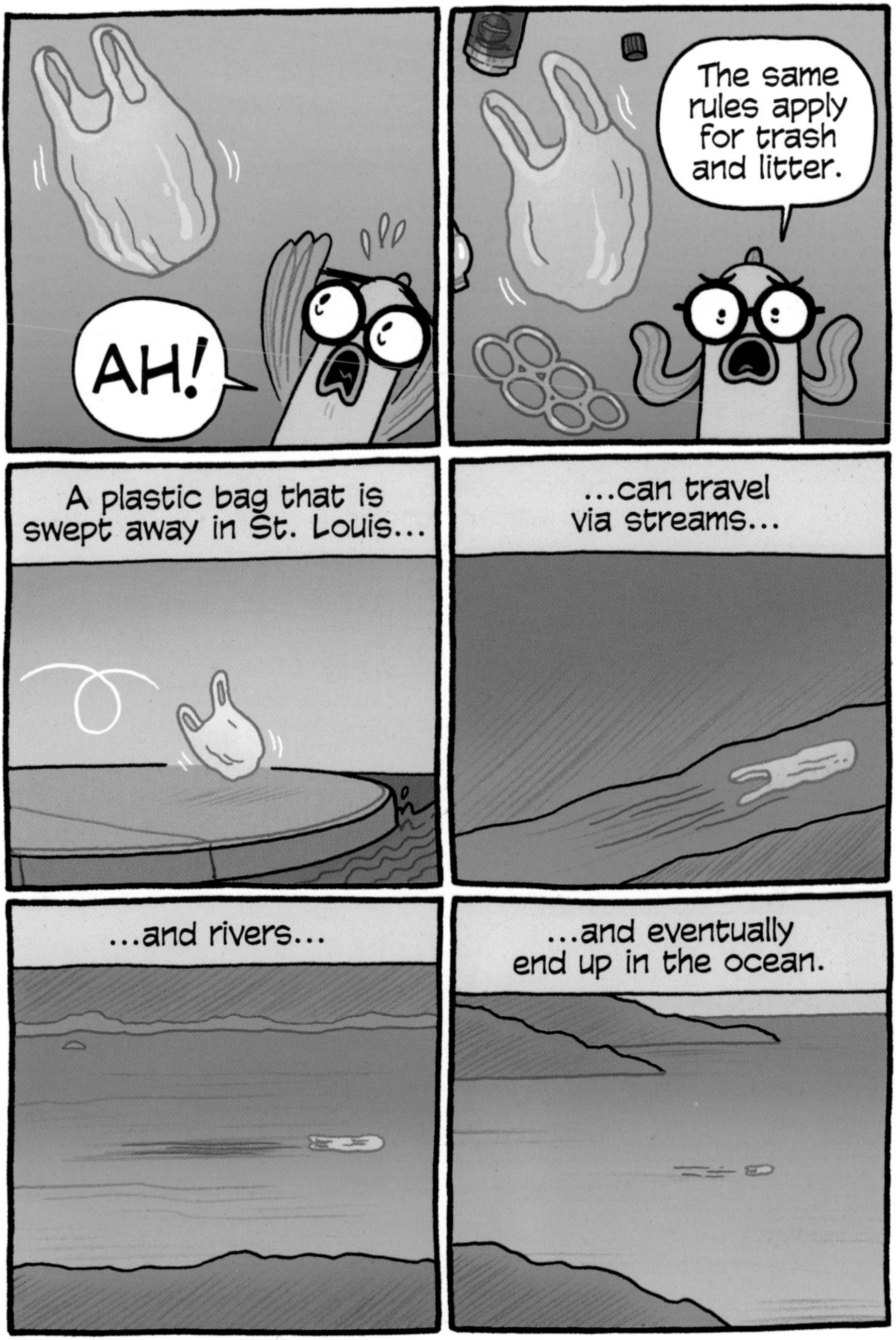
AH!
The same rules apply for trash and litter.
A plastic bag that is swept away in St. Louis...
...can travel via streams...
...and rivers...
...and eventually end up in the ocean.

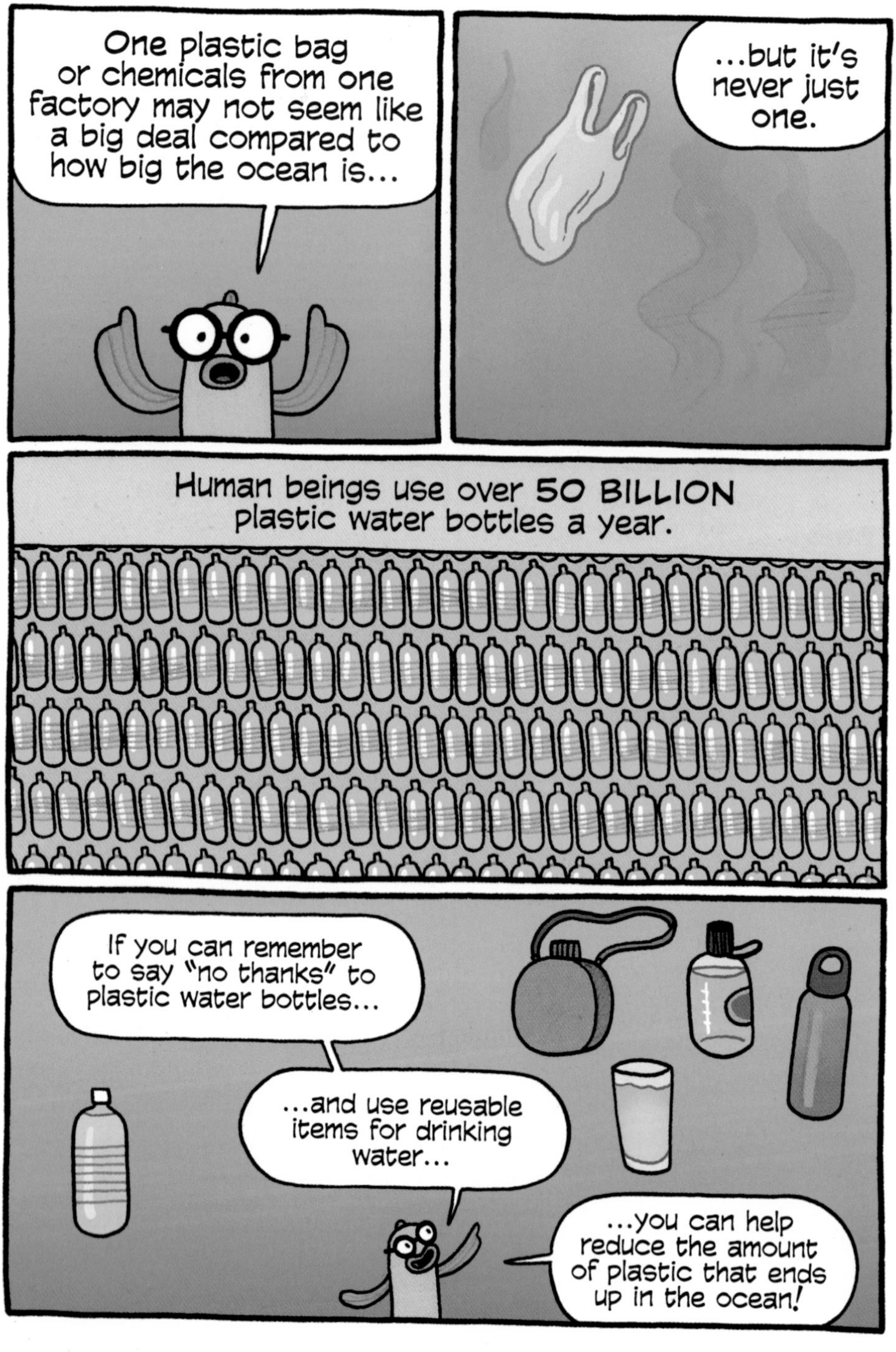
One plastic bag or chemicals from one factory may not seem like a big deal compared to how big the ocean is...
...but it's never just one.
Human beings use over 50 BILLION plastic water bottles a year.
If you can remember to say "no thanks" to plastic water bottles...
...and use reusable items for drinking water...
...you can help reduce the amount of plastic that ends up in the ocean!

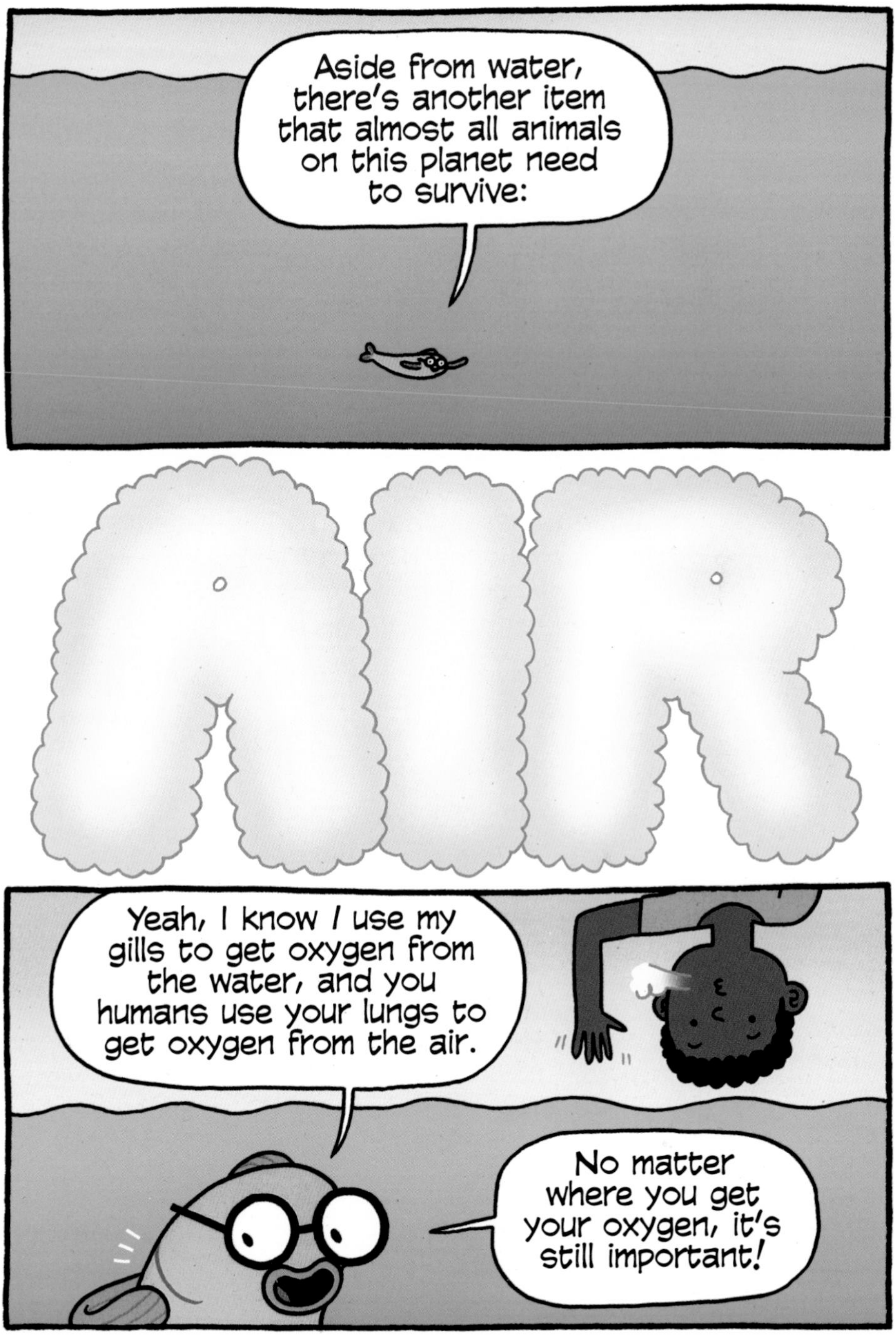
Aside from water, there's another item that almost all animals on this planet need to survive:
AIR
Yeah, I know I use my gills to get oxygen from the water, and you humans use your lungs to get oxygen from the air.
No matter where you get your oxygen, it's still important!

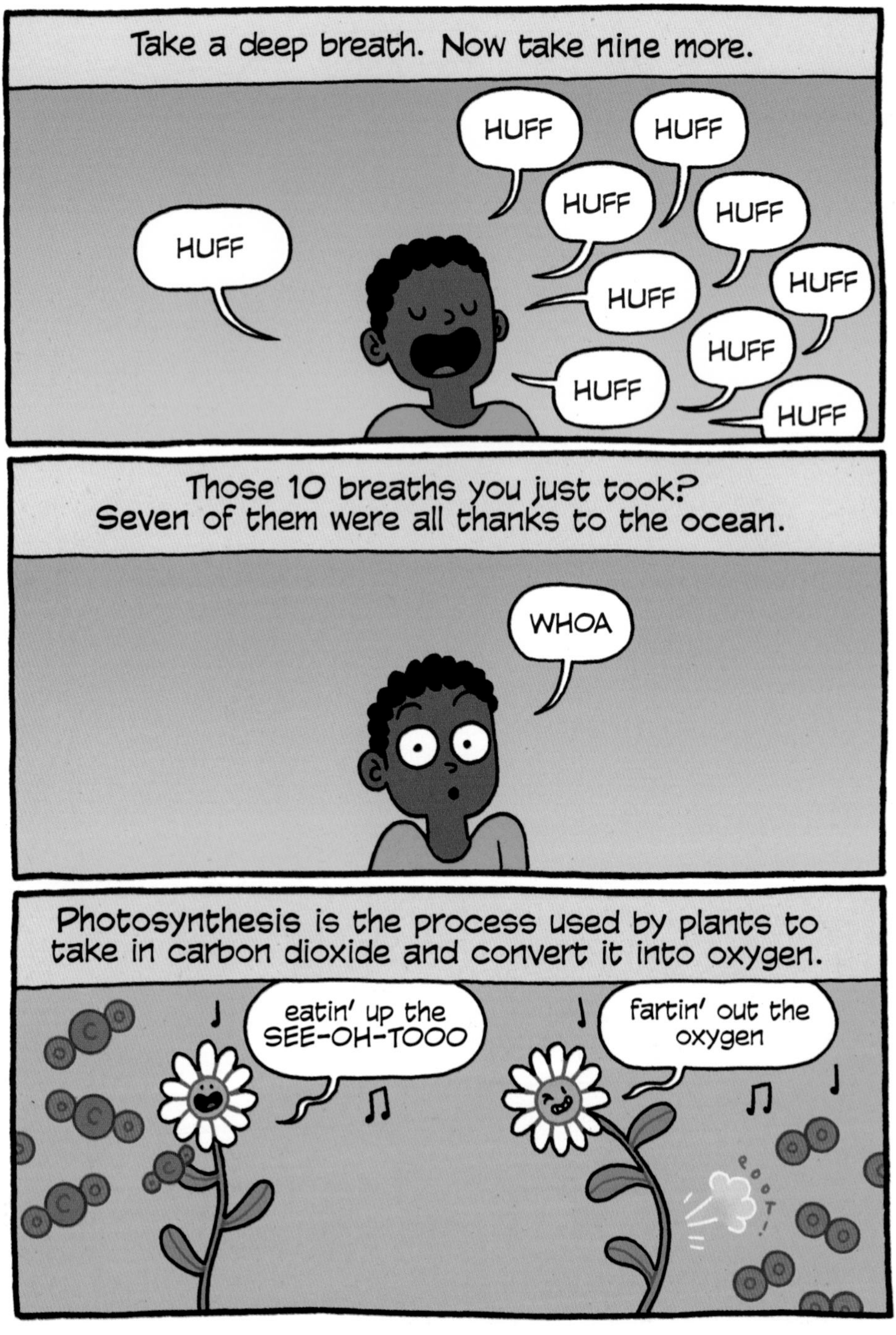
Take a deep breath. Now take nine more.
HUFF
HUFF
HUFF
HUFF
HUFF
HUFF
HUFF
HUFF
HUFF
HUFF
Those 10 breaths you just took?
Seven of them were all thanks to the ocean.
WHOA
Photosynthesis is the process used by plants to take in carbon dioxide and convert it into oxygen.
eatin' up the SEE-OH-TOOO
fartin' out the oxygen
POOT!

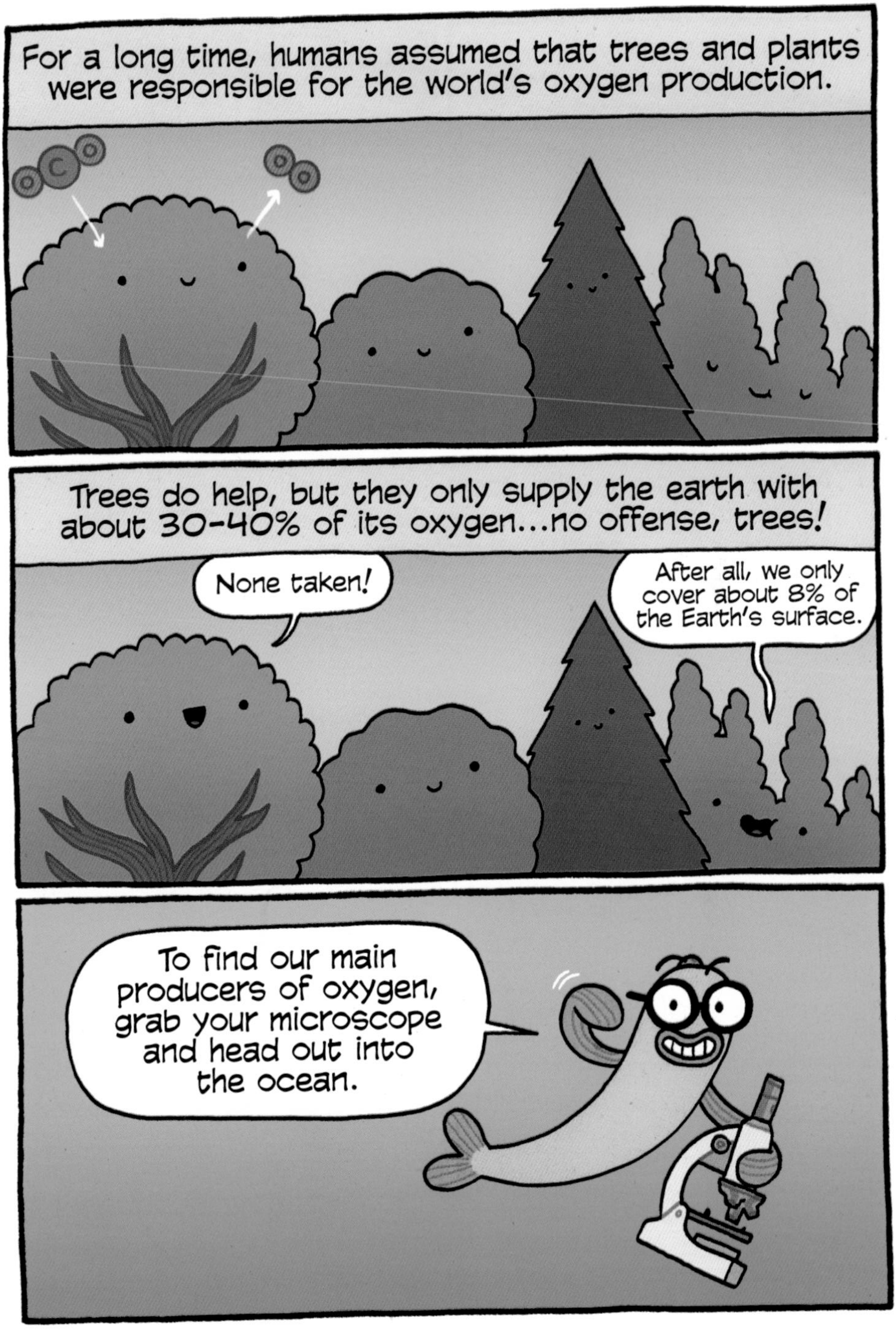
For a long time, humans assumed that trees and plants were responsible for the world's oxygen production.
Trees do help, but they only supply the earth with about 30-40% of its oxygen...no offense, trees!
None taken!
After all, we only cover about 8% of the Earth's surface.
To find our main producers of oxygen, grab your microscope and head out into the ocean.

Just because you are tiny doesn't mean that you are not important...
...isn't that right, little dudes?
POOT
POOT!
POOT!
POOT!
POOT
POOT!
Algae and phytoplankton (an umbrella term for all plantlike plankton) contribute the other 60-70% of the world's oxygen.
The ocean has played a major role in the global climate for BILLIONS of years, starting with cyanobacteria.
When I was your age, I had to float around the ocean all by myself!
Ugh... THIS story again?

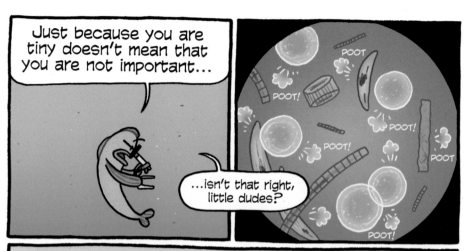

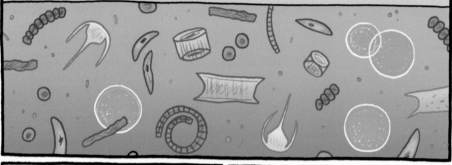

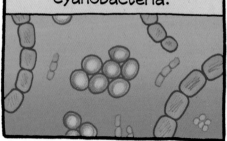

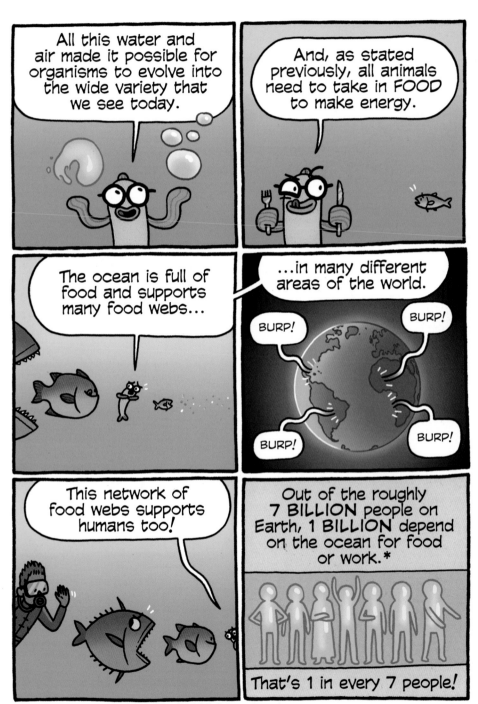

All this water and air made it possible for organisms to evolve into the wide variety that we see today.

And, as stated previously, all animals need to take in FOOD to make energy.

The ocean is full of food and supports many food webs...

...in many different areas of the world.

BURP!

BURP!

BURP!

BURP!

This network of food webs supports humans too!

Out of the roughly 7 BILLION people on Earth, 1 BILLION depend on the ocean for food or work.*

That's 1 in every 7 people!

*This is the number of people that DIRECTLY depend on the ocean.

Even if YOU don't eat seafood or work on a boat...

...you still depend on the ocean for air.

I'm a vegetarian.

phew!

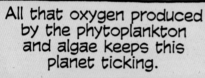

All that oxygen produced by the phytoplankton and algae keeps this planet ticking.

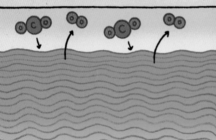

This balance is key to the health of the whole planet.

No matter how far you live from the ocean (and coral reefs), your basic needs are supported by the sea.

Let's take a look at some of the challenges that our planet faces, and how to keep it healthy...

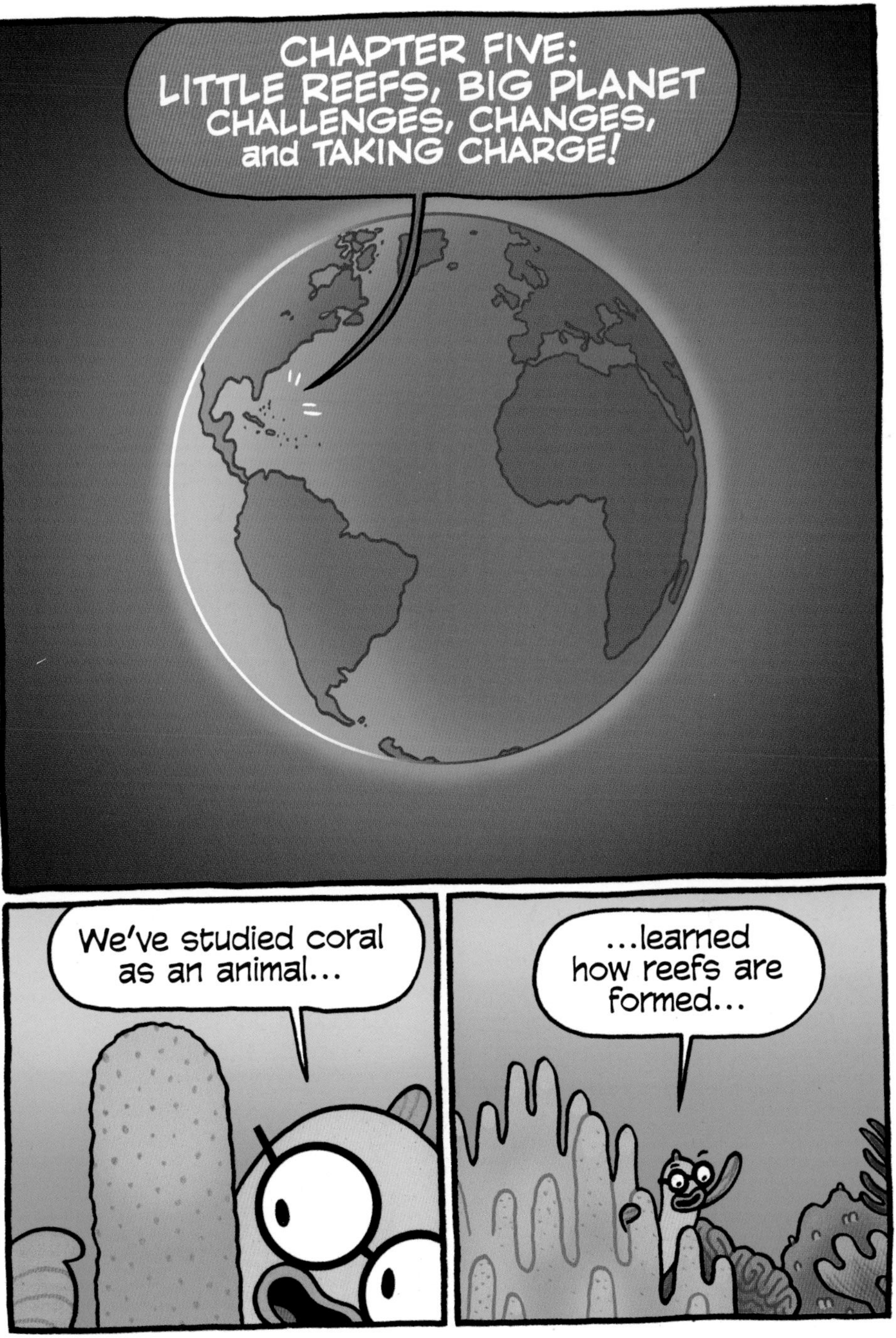
CHAPTER FIVE:
LITTLE REEFS, BIG PLANET
CHALLENGES, CHANGES,
and TAKING CHARGE!
We've studied coral as an animal...
...learned how reefs are formed...

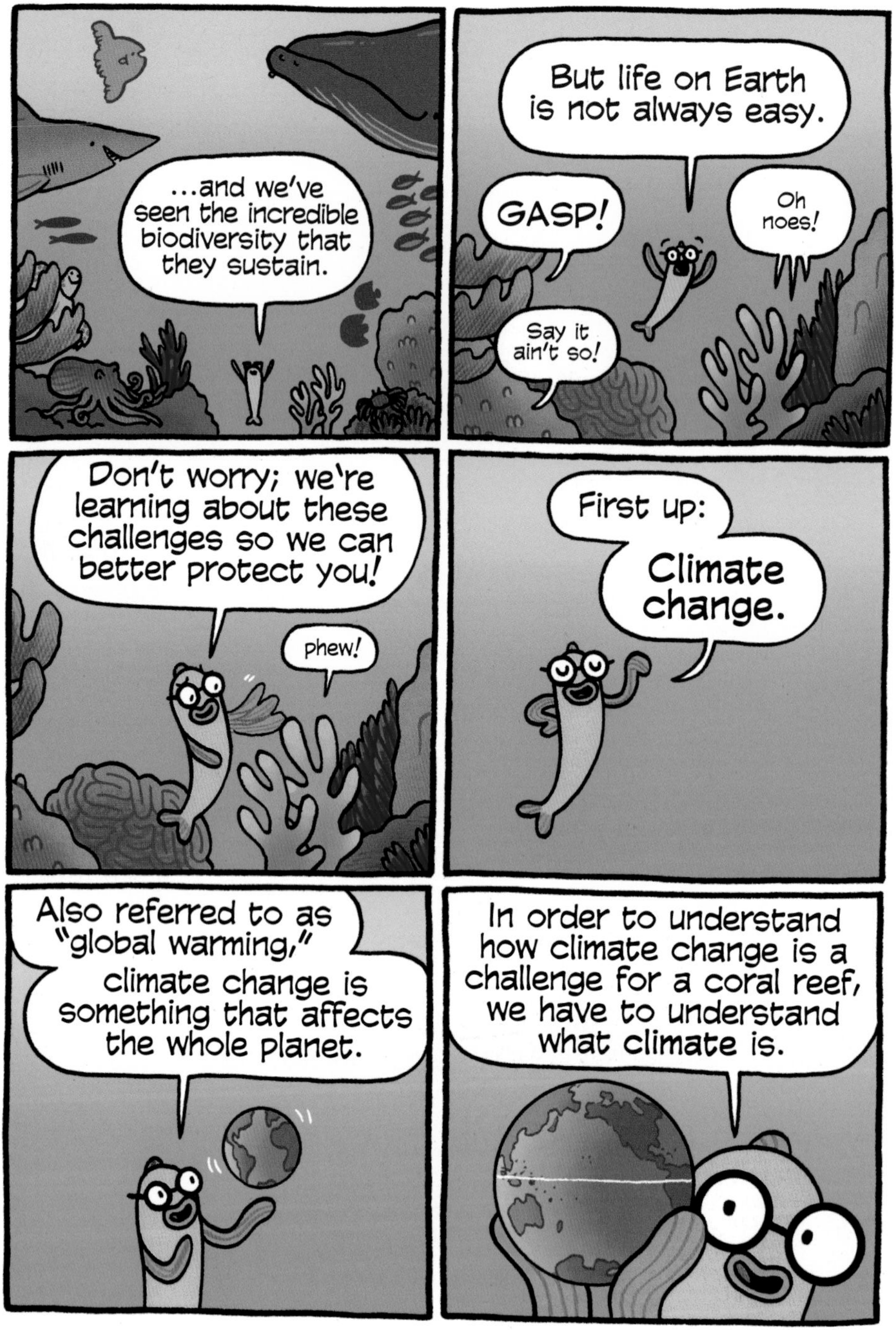
...and we've seen the incredible biodiversity that they sustain.
But life on Earth is not always easy.
GASP!
Oh noes!
Say it ain't so!
Don't worry; we're learning about these challenges so we can better protect you!
phew!
First up:
Climate change.
Also referred to as "global warming,"
climate change is something that affects the whole planet.
In order to understand how climate change is a challenge for a coral reef, we have to understand what climate is.

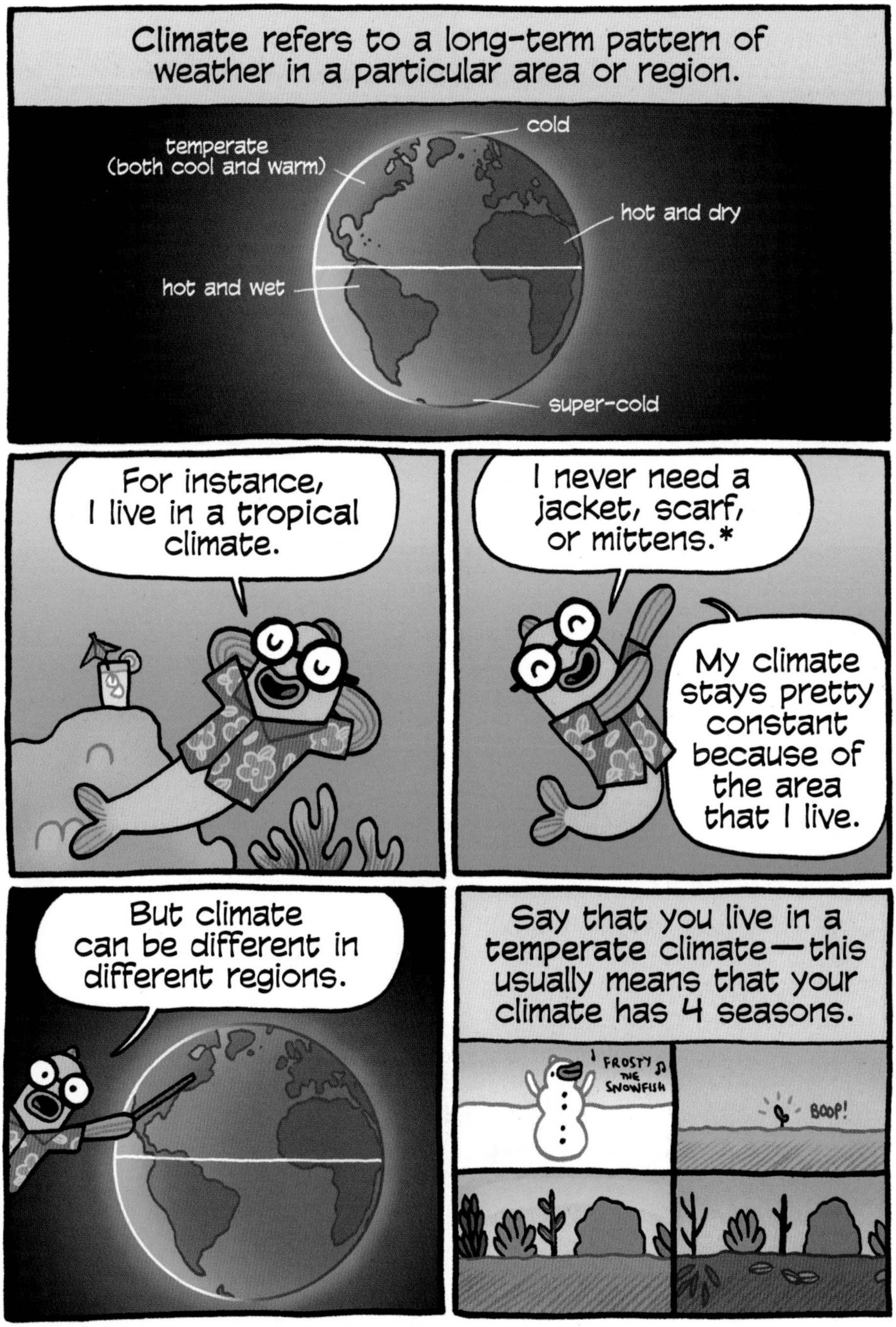
Climate refers to a long-term pattern of weather in a particular area or region.
cold
temperate (both cool and warm)
hot and dry
hot and wet
super-cold
For instance, I live in a tropical climate.
I never need a jacket, scarf, or mittens.*
My climate stays pretty constant because of the area that I live.
But climate can be different in different regions.
Say that you live in a temperate climate—this usually means that your climate has 4 seasons.
FROSTY THE SNOWFISH
BOOP!

*Or, like, any clothes at all. Because fish don't wear clothes.

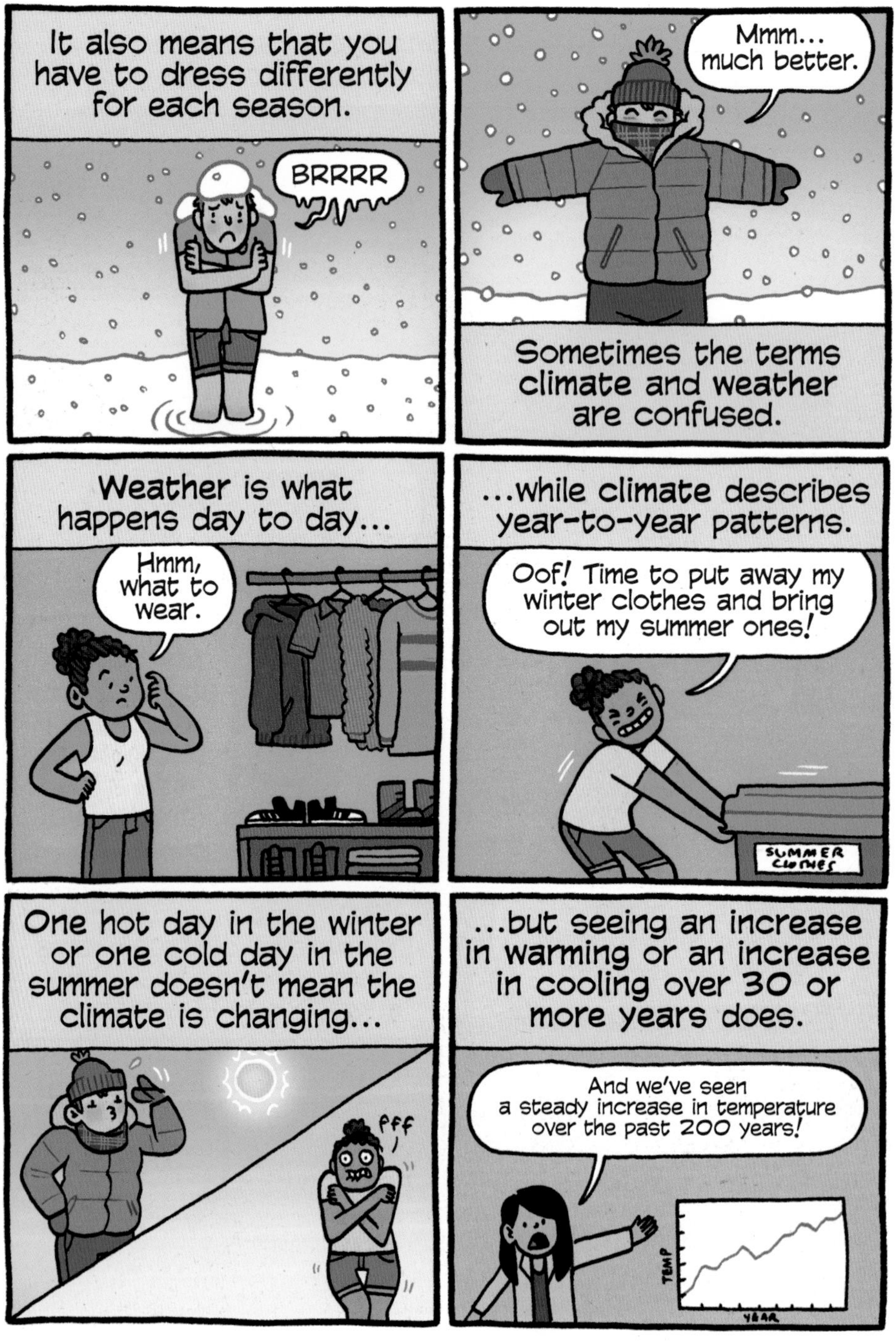
It also means that you have to dress differently for each season.
BRRRR
Mmm... much better.
Sometimes the terms climate and weather are confused.
Weather is what happens day to day...
Hmm, what to wear.
...while climate describes year-to-year patterns.
Oof! Time to put away my winter clothes and bring out my summer ones!
SUMMER CLOTHES
One hot day in the winter or one cold day in the summer doesn't mean the climate is changing...
PFF
...but seeing an increase in warming or an increase in cooling over 30 or more years does.
And we've seen a steady increase in temperature over the past 200 years!
TEMP
YEAR

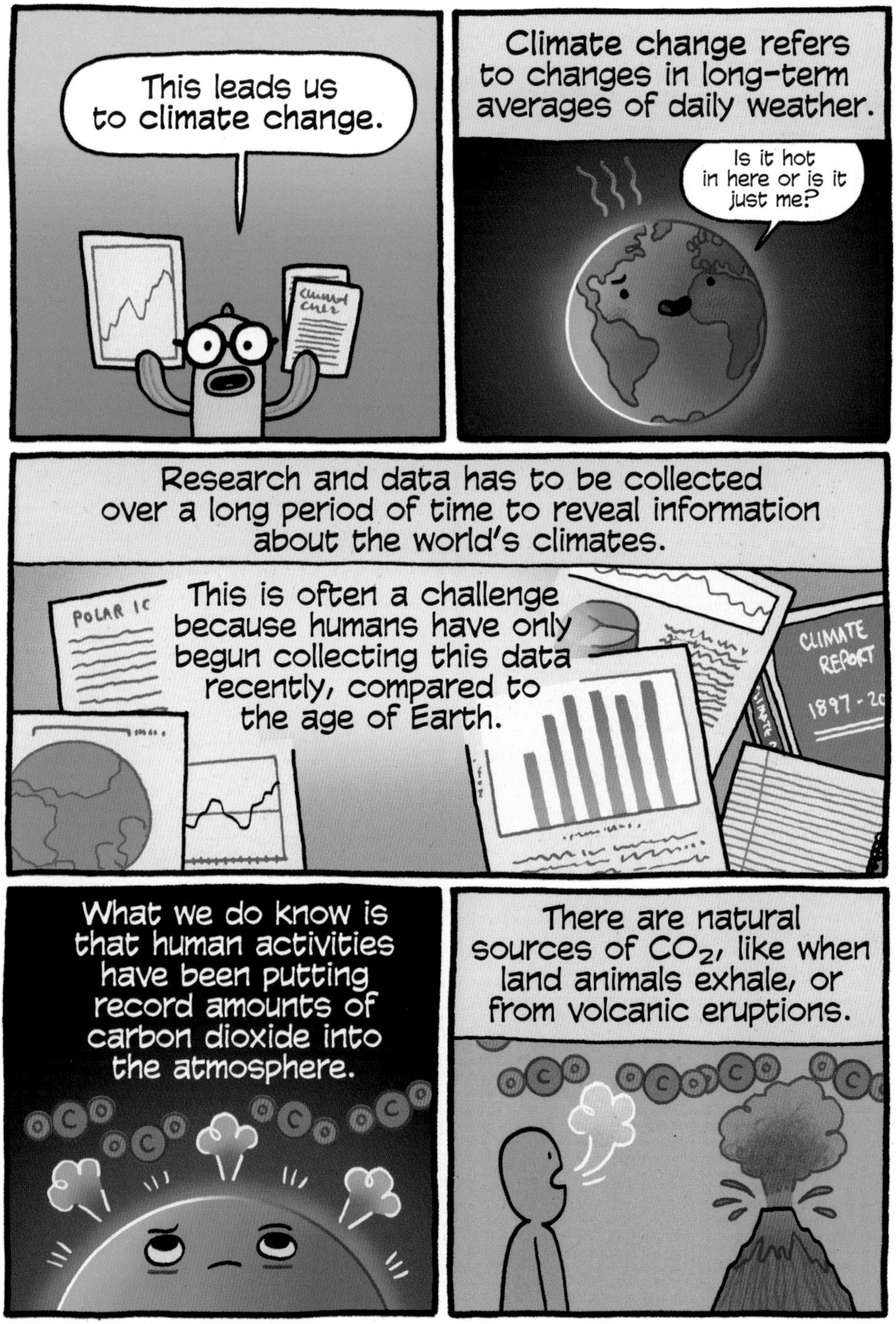
This leads us to climate change.
Climate change refers to changes in long-term averages of daily weather.
Is it hot in here or is it just me?
Research and data has to be collected over a long period of time to reveal information about the world's climates.
This is often a challenge because humans have only begun collecting this data recently, compared to the age of Earth.
POLAR IC
CLIMATE REPORT
What we do know is that human activities have been putting record amounts of carbon dioxide into the atmosphere.
There are natural sources of CO_2, like when land animals exhale, or from volcanic eruptions.

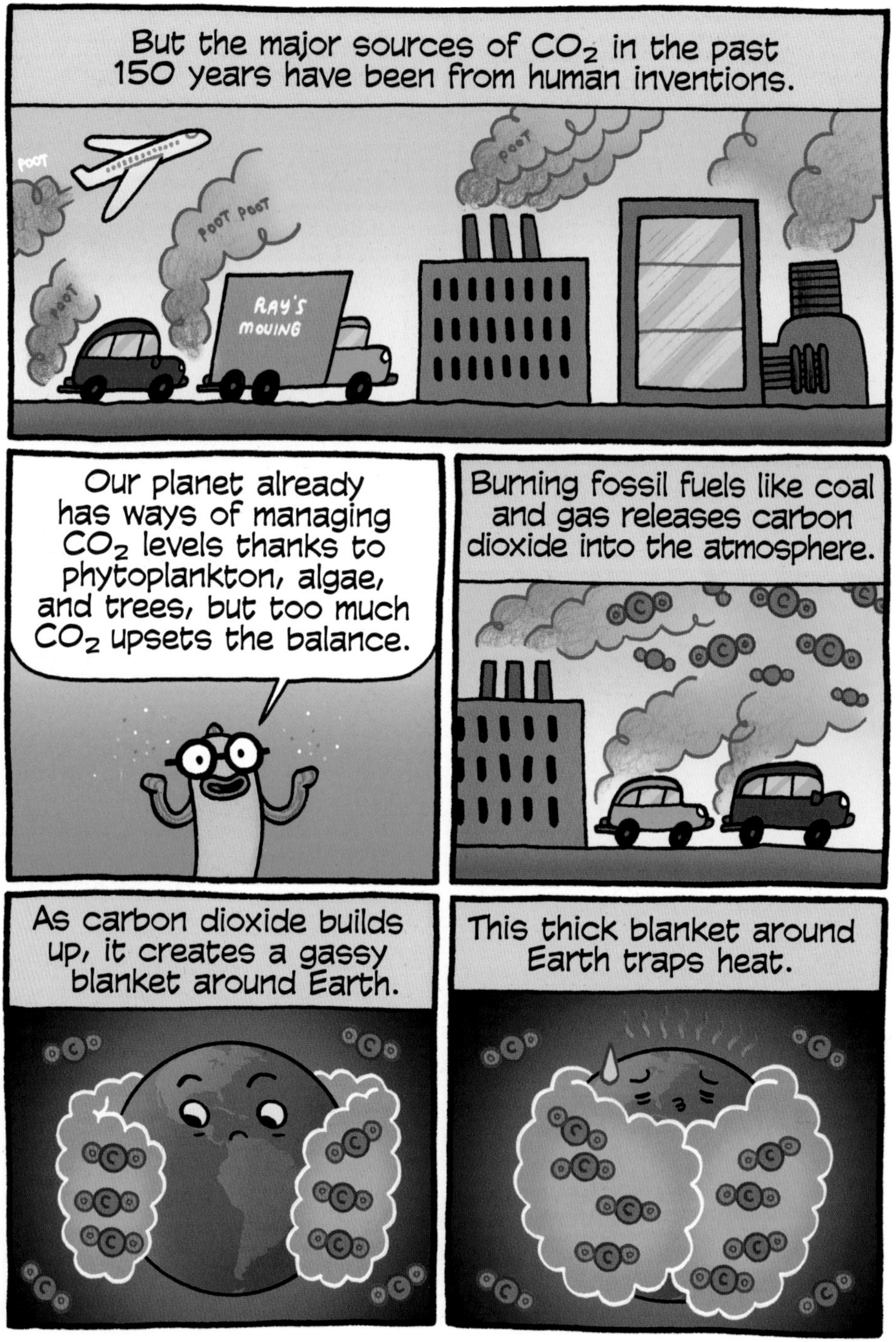
But the major sources of CO_2 in the past 150 years have been from human inventions.
POOT
POOT POOT
POOT
POOT
RAY'S MOVING
Our planet already has ways of managing CO_2 levels thanks to phytoplankton, algae, and trees, but too much CO_2 upsets the balance.
Burning fossil fuels like coal and gas releases carbon dioxide into the atmosphere.
As carbon dioxide builds up, it creates a gassy blanket around Earth.
This thick blanket around Earth traps heat.

And all that trapped heat warms up the oceans.

This causes the global temperature to rise, having a negative impact on ecosystems that are accustomed to very slow environmental changes.

Melting polar ice, droughts, and sea level rise are just a few of the dangers from climate change.

Well, this can't be good.

Yeah, definitely NOT GOOD.

We've been looking at how climate change affects the whole planet...

Let's shift our focus to how it affects coral reefs.

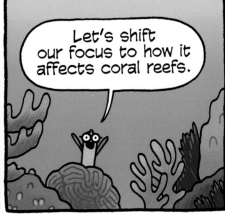

CORAL BLEACHING

Remember that symbiotic relationship the corals had with the tiny algae, zooxanthellae?

And that some coral reefs have taken more that 30 million years to form?

Because of these preexisting conditions, a temperature change as little as 1 degree can upset the balance that has been long-established by the reef.

The zooxanthellae can only thrive in a specific temperature range. If it gets too hot, too fast, they become stressed and leave.

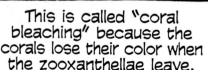

This is called "coral bleaching" because the corals lose their color when the zooxanthellae leave.

If the temperature resumes to previous levels within a short amount of time, the zooxanthellae may return.

If not, the corals can live for a while, but they will not be healthy; they may eventually die.

Changes in light and access to nutrients can also cause coral bleaching, but temperature is the most likely candidate.

OCEAN ACIDIFICATION

This is a danger for not just corals, but ANY animal in the ocean that has a shell.

When CO_2 levels increase, the ocean compensates by absorbing more CO_2 to maintain balance.

Too much CO_2 and it actually alters the chemistry of the ocean.

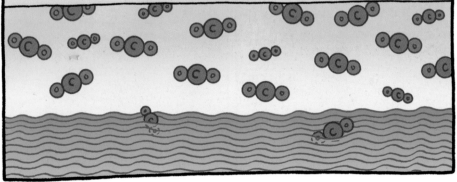

We've got to get MOLECULAR to see this happen.

Ocean water is mostly water molecules (about 97%)...

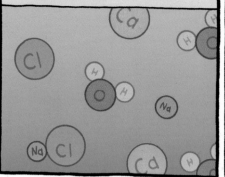

...with salts and minerals making up the rest.

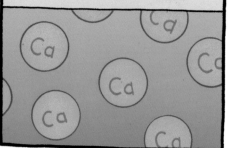

Other elements found in ocean water (like calcium) help animals to form their shells.

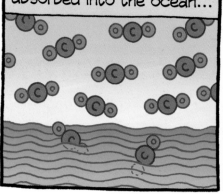

When more CO_2 is absorbed into the ocean...

...it bonds with water molecules and carbonate ions to form bicarbonate.

Which leaves less carbonate for calcium to bond with.

Less calcium carbonate in the ocean is bad news for animals that need it to form their shells.

Without calcium carbonate...

...their shells become thin and weak.

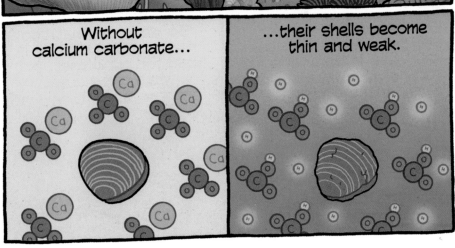

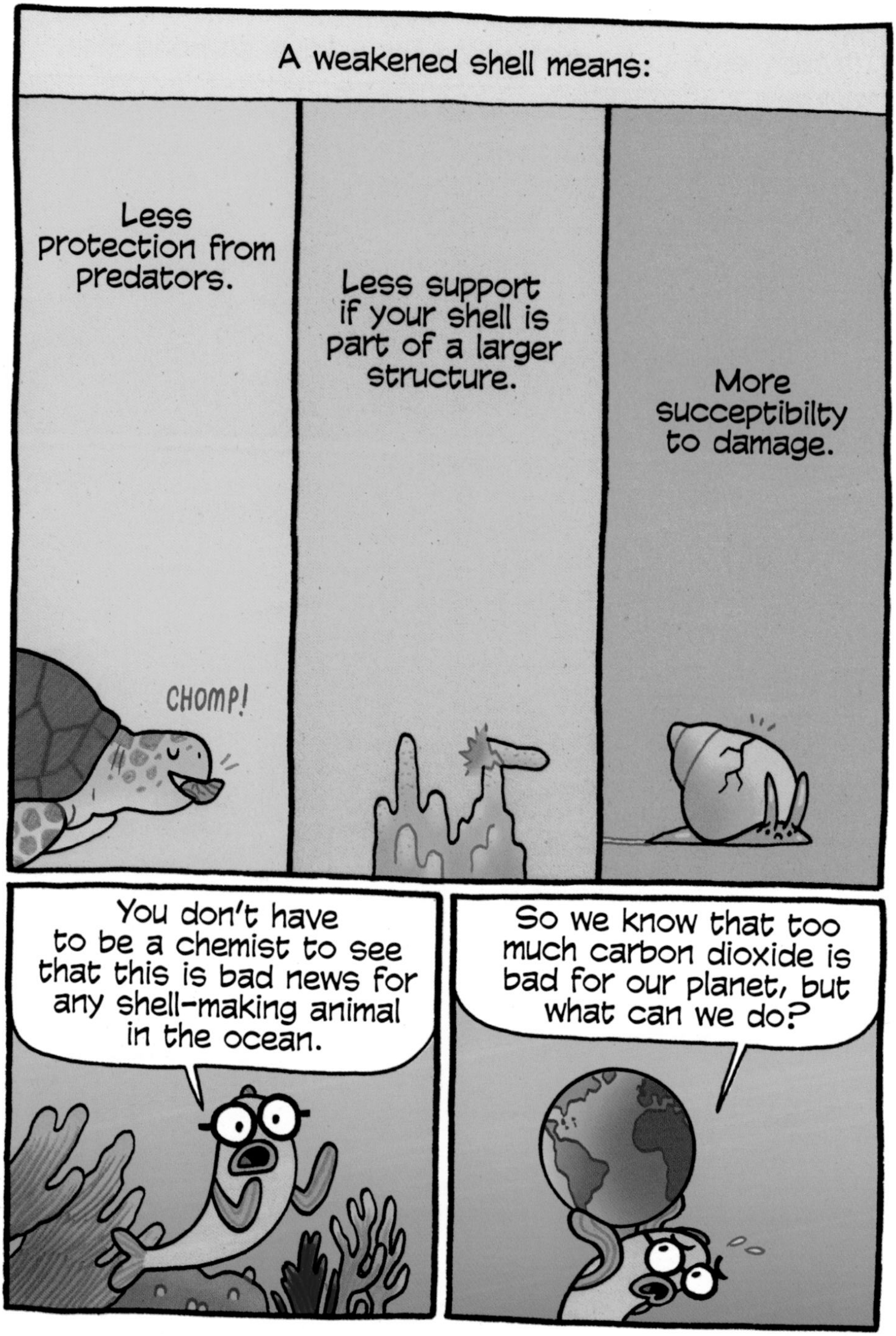
A weakened shell means:
Less protection from predators.
CHOMP!
Less support if your shell is part of a larger structure.
More succeptibilty to damage.
You don't have to be a chemist to see that this is bad news for any shell-making animal in the ocean.
So we know that too much carbon dioxide is bad for our planet, but what can we do?

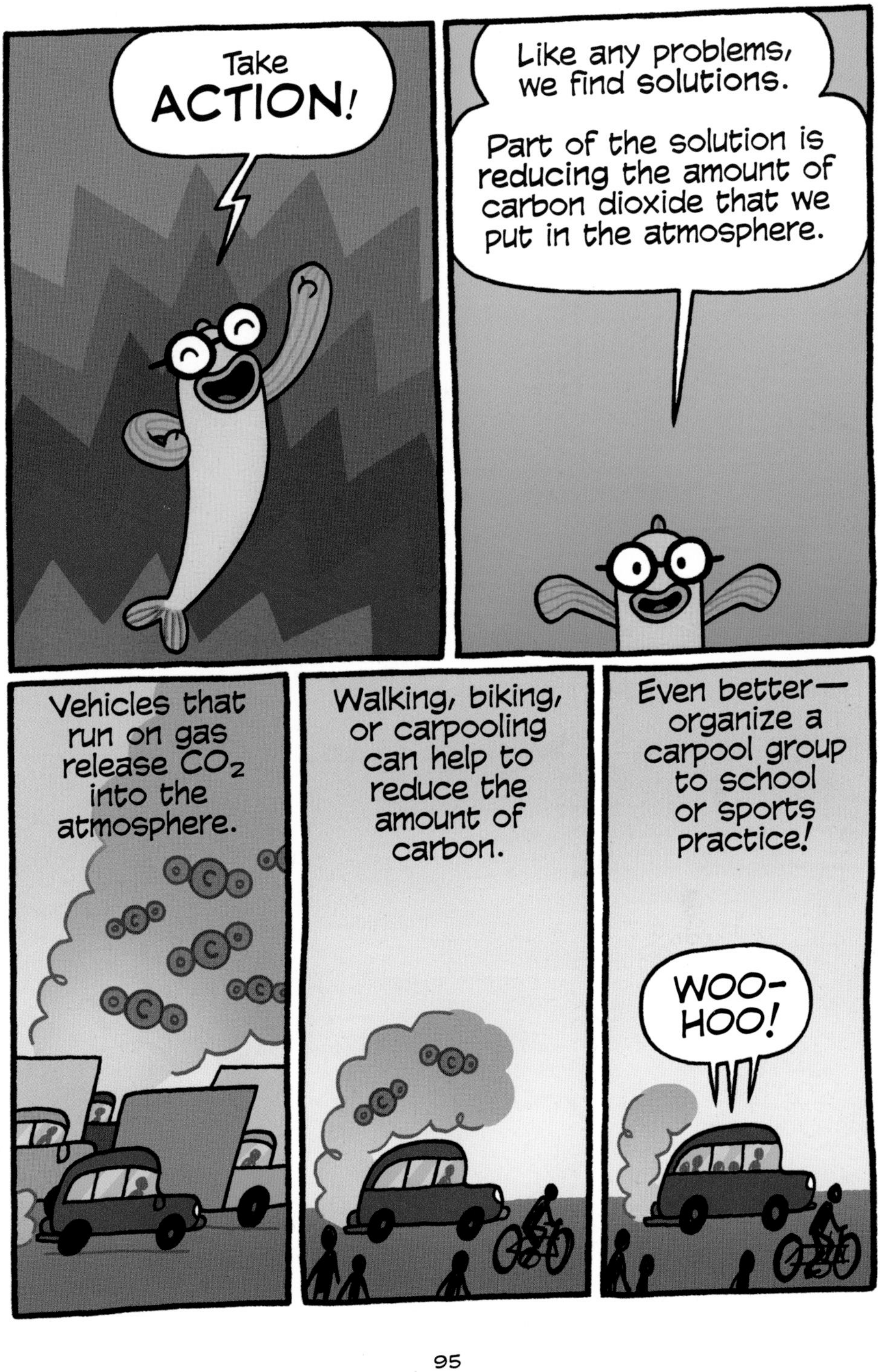
Take ACTION!
Like any problems, we find solutions.
Part of the solution is reducing the amount of carbon dioxide that we put in the atmosphere.
Vehicles that run on gas release CO_2 into the atmosphere.
Walking, biking, or carpooling can help to reduce the amount of carbon.
Even better— organize a carpool group to school or sports practice!
WOO-HOO!

Plastics are made from oil; more oil means more CO_2 in the atmosphere.

Use a reusable water bottle, lunch box, or snack bag to reduce the amount of plastic in your life.

Even better— get your school or house to be "zero waste" by starting a recycling and composting plan!

COMPOST (ORGANIC WASTE)

Get outside! Having fun outdoors helps us appreciate our awesome planet!

Plant a tree, participate in a trail or beach cleanup...

...or organize your own event for your friends and family!

WOO-HOO!

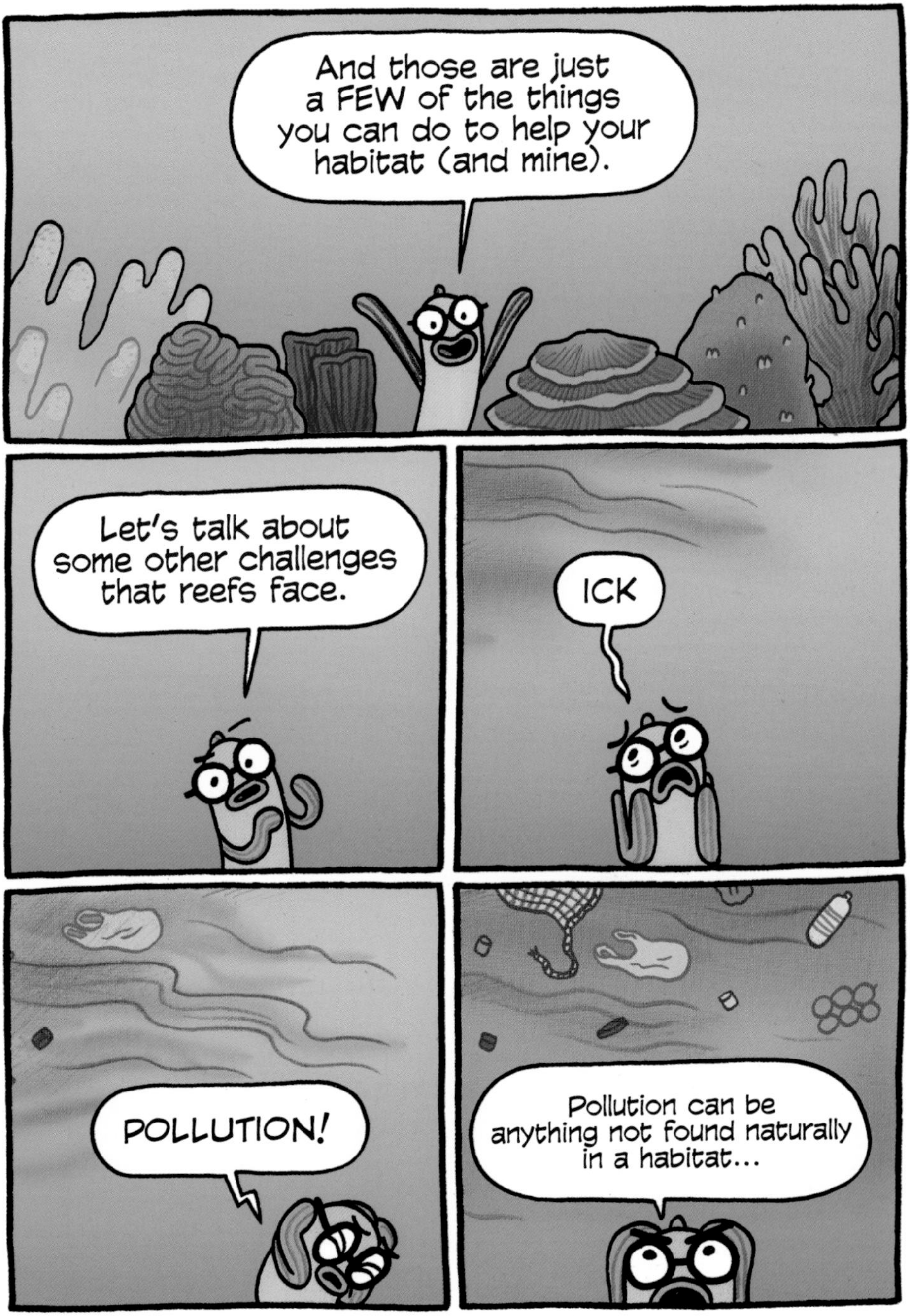

And those are just a FEW of the things you can do to help your habitat (and mine).
Let's talk about some other challenges that reefs face.
ICK
POLLUTION!
Pollution can be anything not found naturally in a habitat...

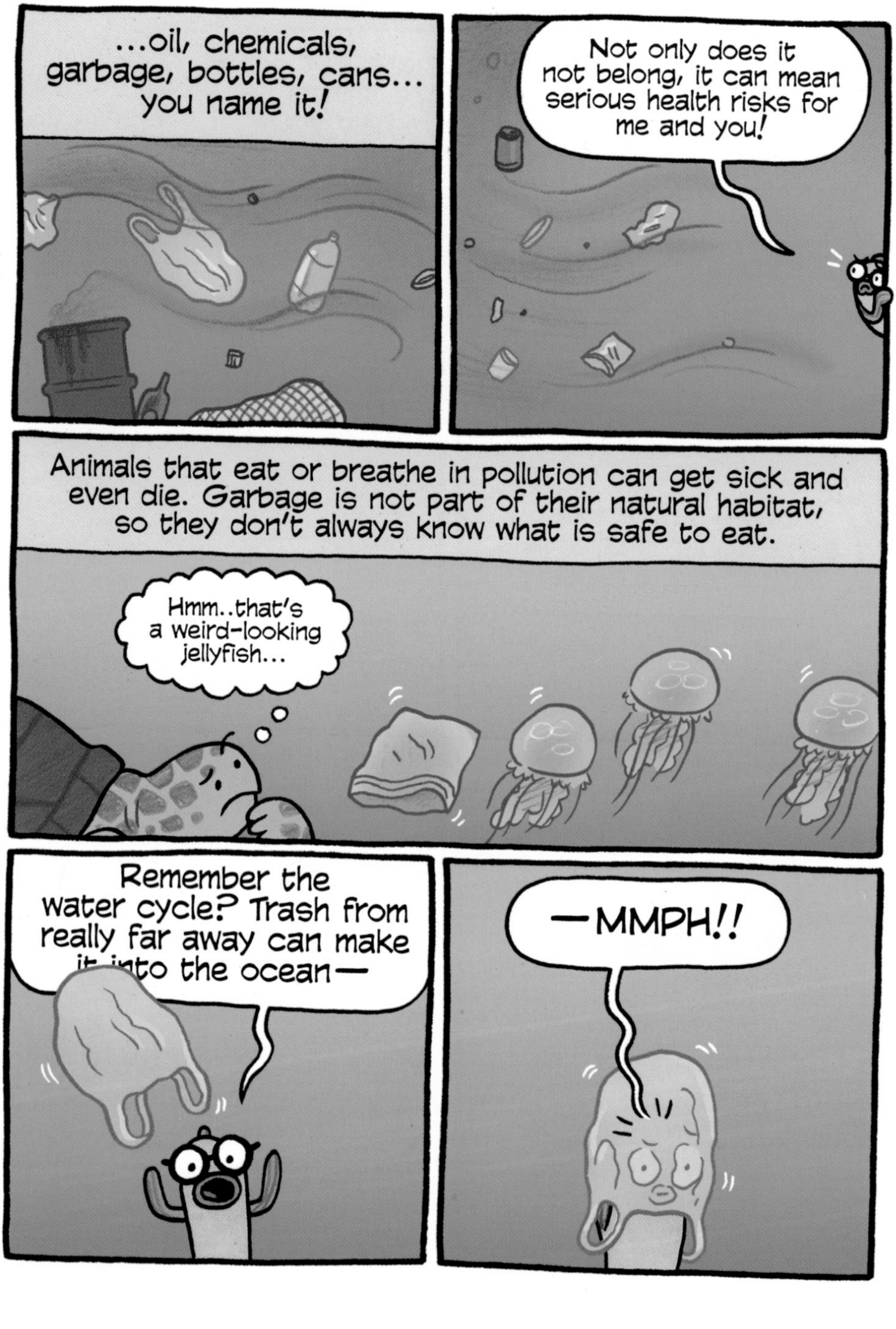
...oil, chemicals, garbage, bottles, cans... you name it!
Not only does it not belong, it can mean serious health risks for me and you!
Animals that eat or breathe in pollution can get sick and even die. Garbage is not part of their natural habitat, so they don't always know what is safe to eat.
Hmm..that's a weird-looking jellyfish...
Remember the water cycle? Trash from really far away can make
into the ocean—
—MMPH!!

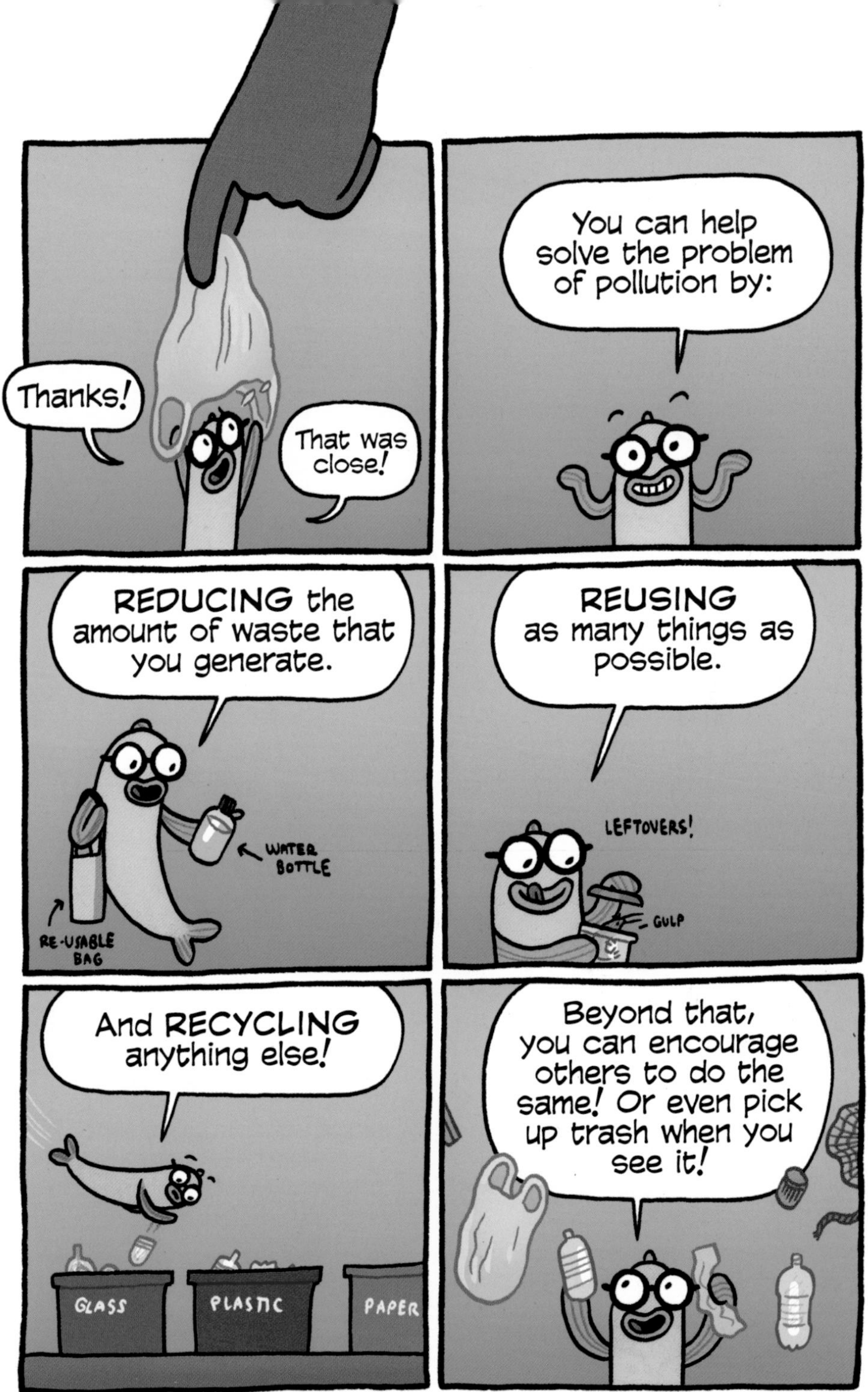
Thanks!
That was close!
You can help solve the problem of pollution by:
REDUCING the amount of waste that you generate.
WATER BOTTLE
RE-USABLE BAG
REUSING as many things as possible.
LEFTOVERS!
GULP
And RECYCLING anything else!
GLASS
PLASTIC
PAPER
Beyond that, you can encourage others to do the same! Or even pick up trash when you see it!

The notion of a fish needing a water bottle is pretty funny.

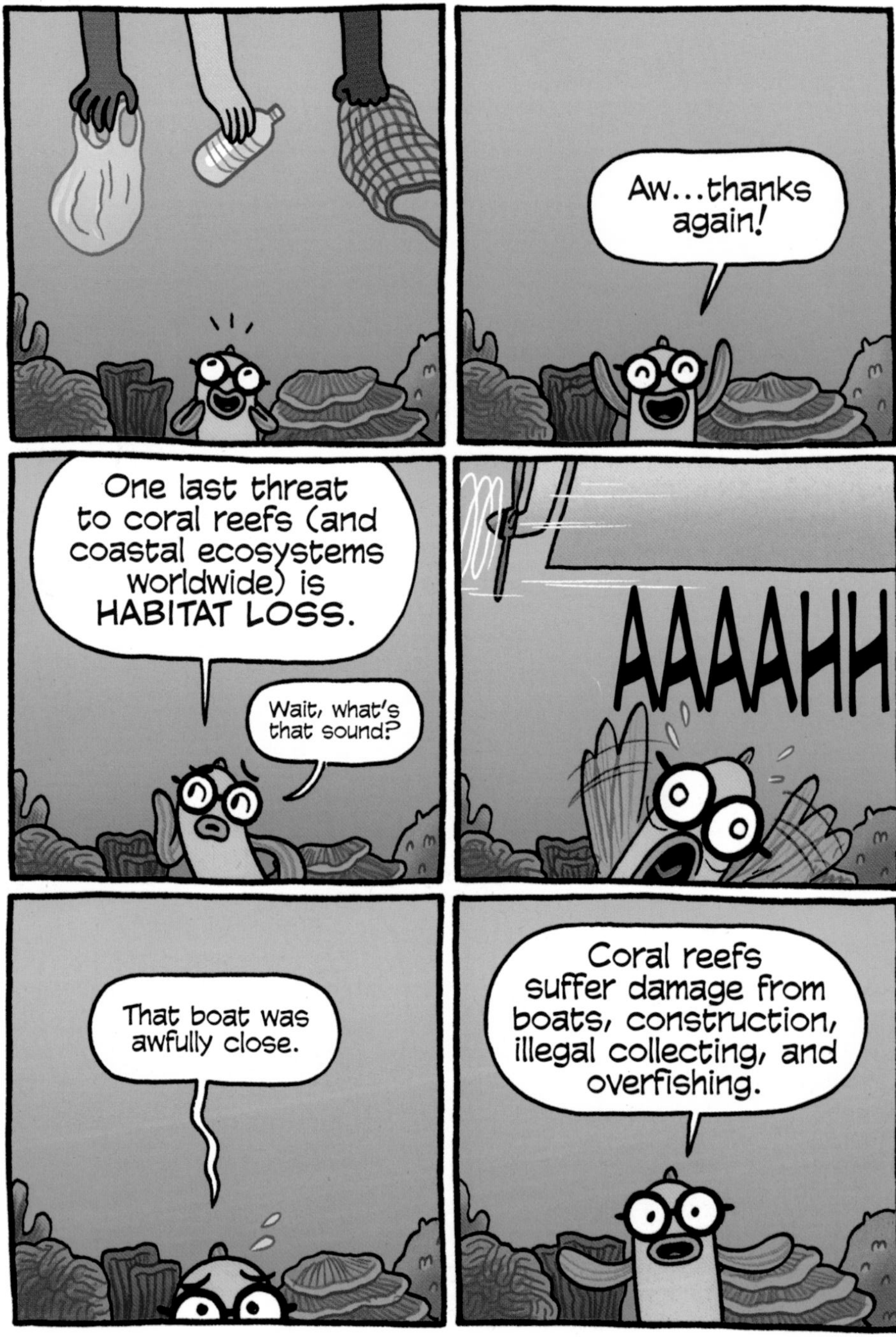
Aw...thanks again!
One last threat to coral reefs (and coastal ecosystems worldwide) is HABITAT LOSS.
Wait, what's that sound?
AAAAHH
That boat was awfully close.
Coral reefs suffer damage from boats, construction, illegal collecting, and overfishing.

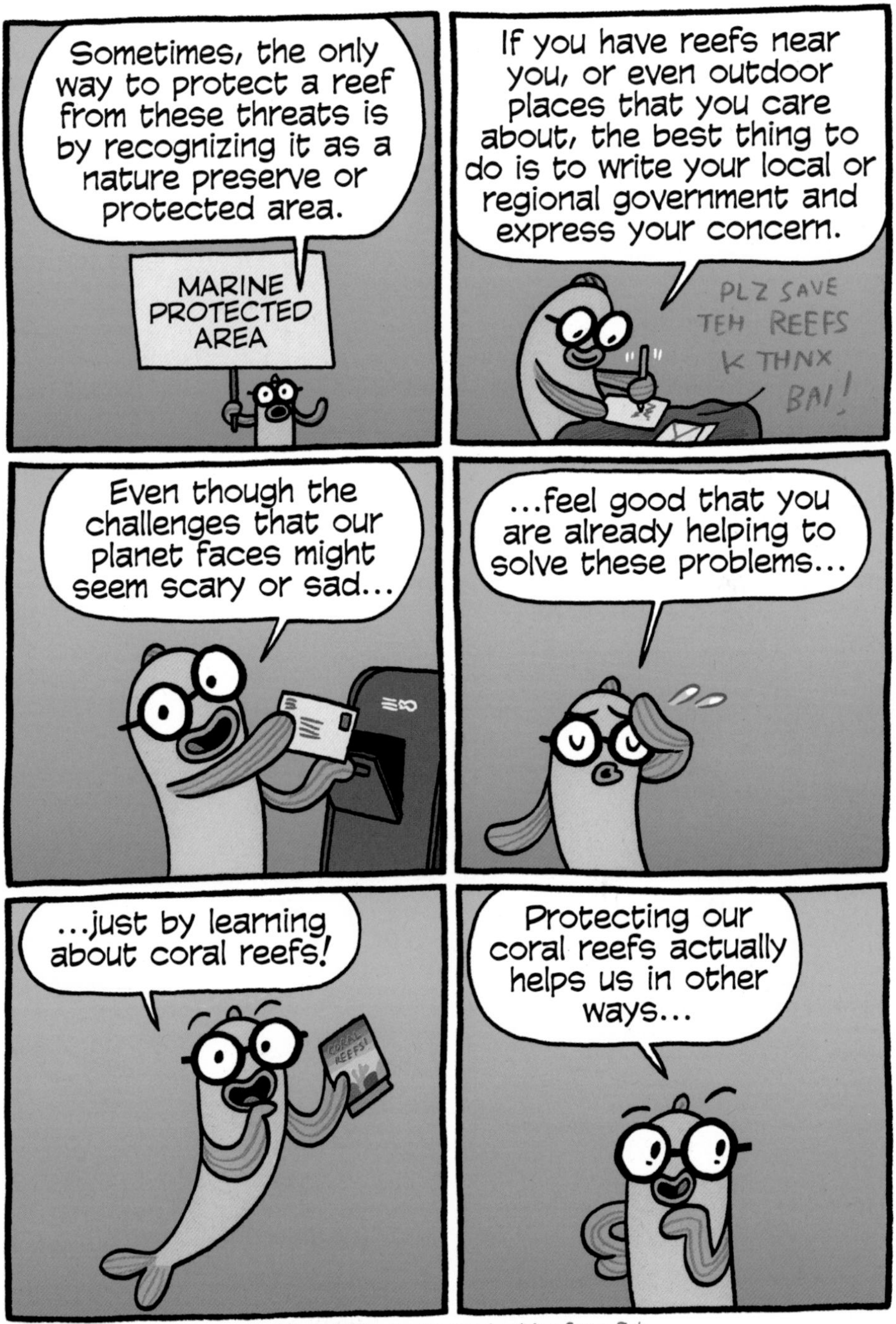
Sometimes, the only way to protect a reef from these threats is by recognizing it as a nature preserve or protected area.
MARINE PROTECTED AREA
If you have reefs near you, or even outdoor places that you care about, the best thing to do is to write your local or regional government and express your concern.
PLZ SAVE TEH REEFS K THNX BAI!
Even though the challenges that our planet faces might seem scary or sad...
...feel good that you are already helping to solve these problems...
...just by learning about coral reefs!
CORAL REEFS!
Protecting our coral reefs actually helps us in other ways...

That's actually pretty good writing for a fish.

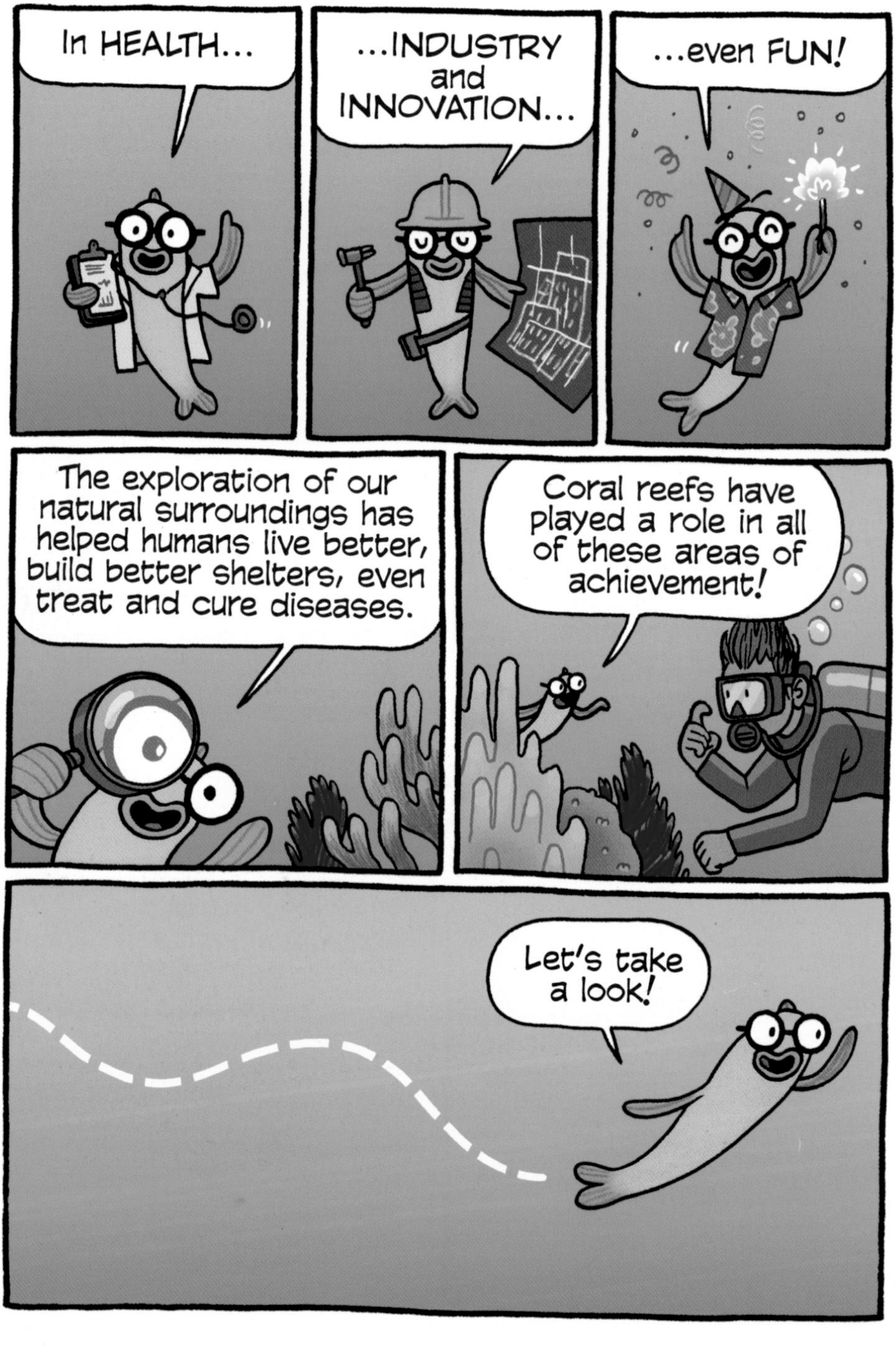

In HEALTH...
...INDUSTRY and INNOVATION...
...even FUN!
The exploration of our natural surroundings has helped humans live better, build better shelters, even treat and cure diseases.
Coral reefs have played a role in all of these areas of achievement!
Let's take a look!

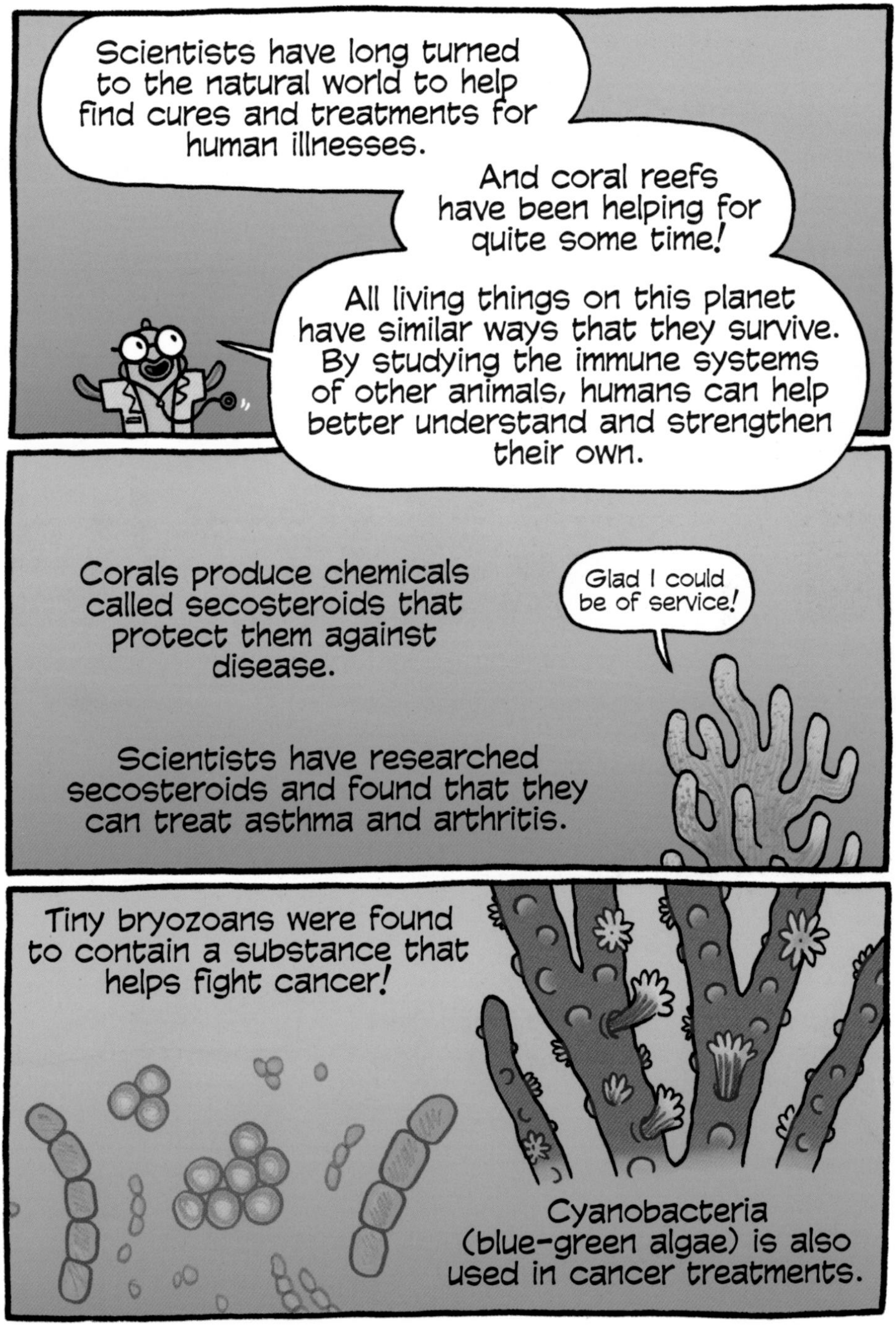
Scientists have long turned to the natural world to help find cures and treatments for human illnesses.
And coral reefs have been helping for quite some time!
All living things on this planet have similar ways that they survive. By studying the immune systems of other animals, humans can help better understand and strengthen their own.
Corals produce chemicals called secosteroids that protect them against disease.
Glad I could be of service!
Scientists have researched secosteroids and found that they can treat asthma and arthritis.
Tiny bryozoans were found to contain a substance that helps fight cancer!
Cyanobacteria (blue-green algae) is also used in cancer treatments.

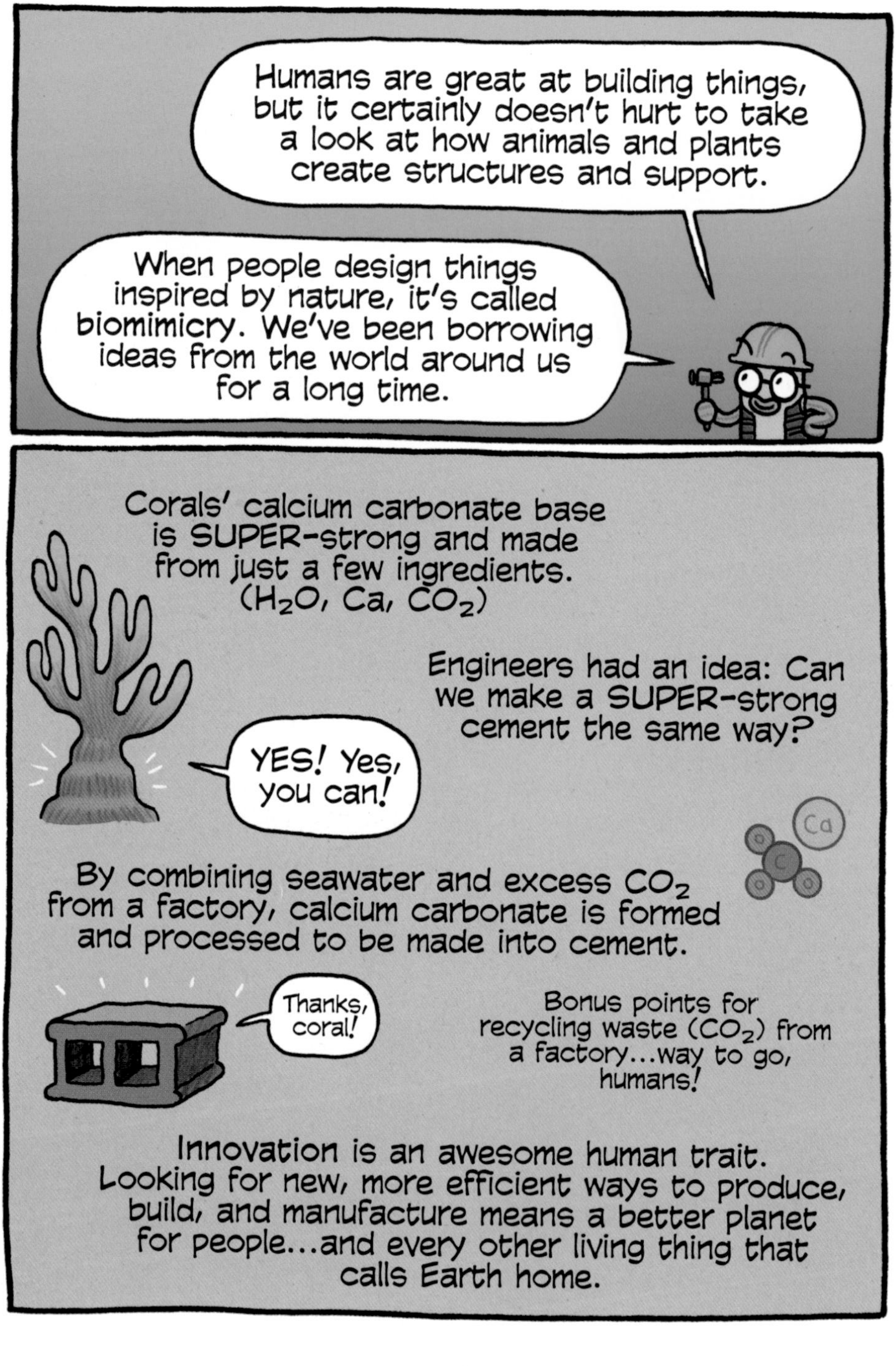

Humans are great at building things, but it certainly doesn't hurt to take a look at how animals and plants create structures and support.
When people design things inspired by nature, it's called biomimicry. We've been borrowing ideas from the world around us for a long time.
Corals' calcium carbonate base is SUPER-strong and made from just a few ingredients. (H_2O, Ca, CO_2)
Engineers had an idea: Can we make a SUPER-strong cement the same way?
YES! Yes, you can!
Ca
By combining seawater and excess CO_2 from a factory, calcium carbonate is formed and processed to be made into cement.
Thanks, coral!
Bonus points for recycling waste (CO_2) from a factory...way to go, humans!
Innovation is an awesome human trait. Looking for new, more efficient ways to produce, build, and manufacture means a better planet for people...and every other living thing that calls Earth home.

Coral reefs are home to over 25% of all the animals found in the ocean. And many of these reef inhabitants have inspired human inventions.

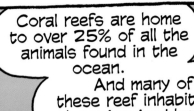

BEEP BEEP

The body shape of a trunkfish helped humans to design a more aerodynamic, fuel-efficient car.

Sharks' skin is covered in tiny, scale-like plates called dermal denticles. They provide the shark with protection and also make it more hydrodynamic in the water.

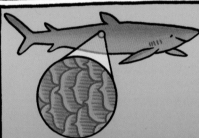

Bathing suits worn by Olympic swimmers use a similar design. The same shark technology may someday cover the bottom of boats to make them faster and more efficient.

An underwater robot inspired by the shape and movement of a cuttlefish could help humans to explore parts of the ocean that are difficult to access.

BEEP BOOP

These are all examples of biomimicry!

Also, robots are just plain cool.

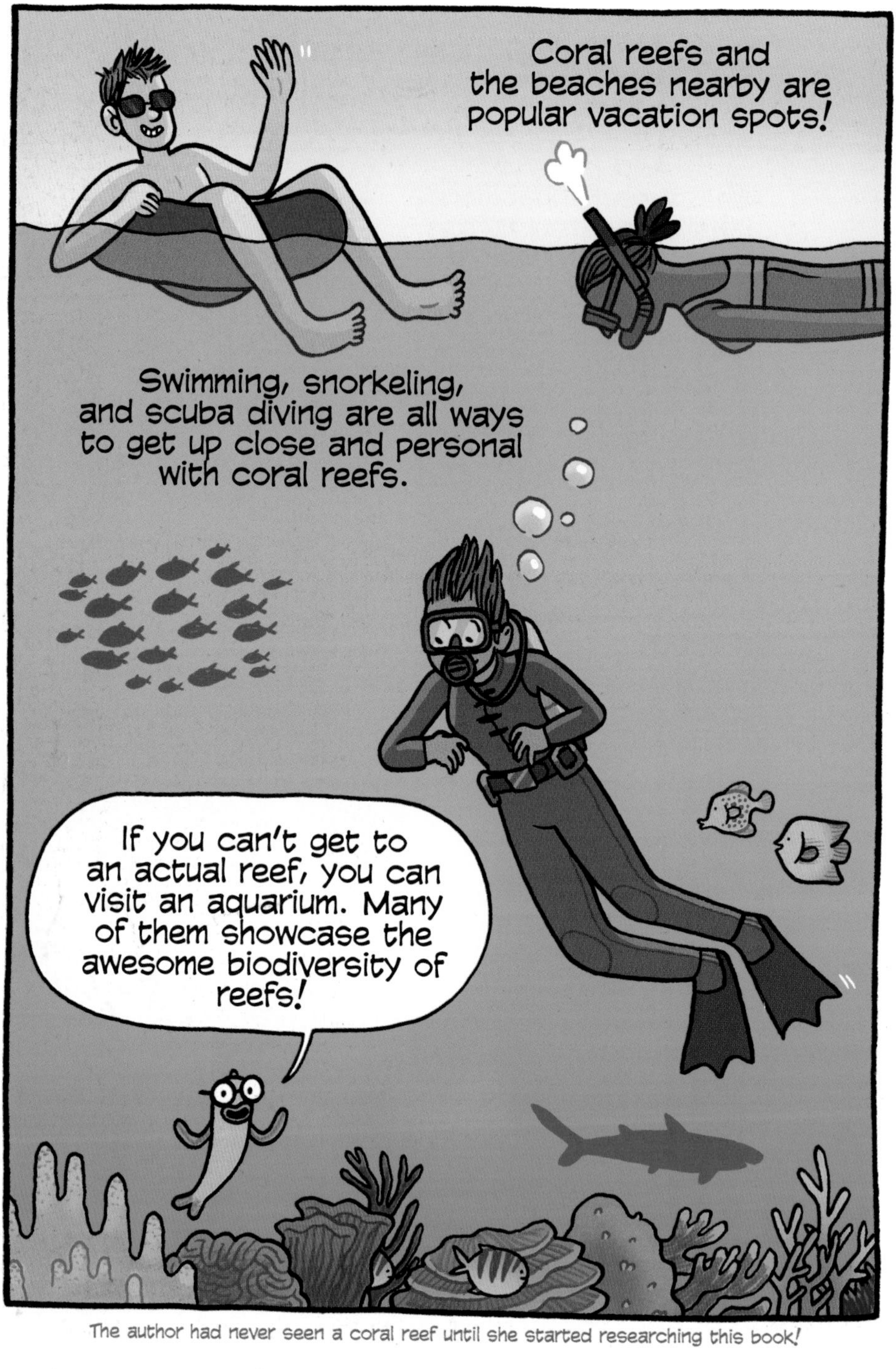
Coral reefs and the beaches nearby are popular vacation spots!
Swimming, snorkeling, and scuba diving are all ways to get up close and personal with coral reefs.
If you can't get to an actual reef, you can visit an aquarium. Many of them showcase the awesome biodiversity of reefs!

The author had never seen a coral reef until she started researching this book!

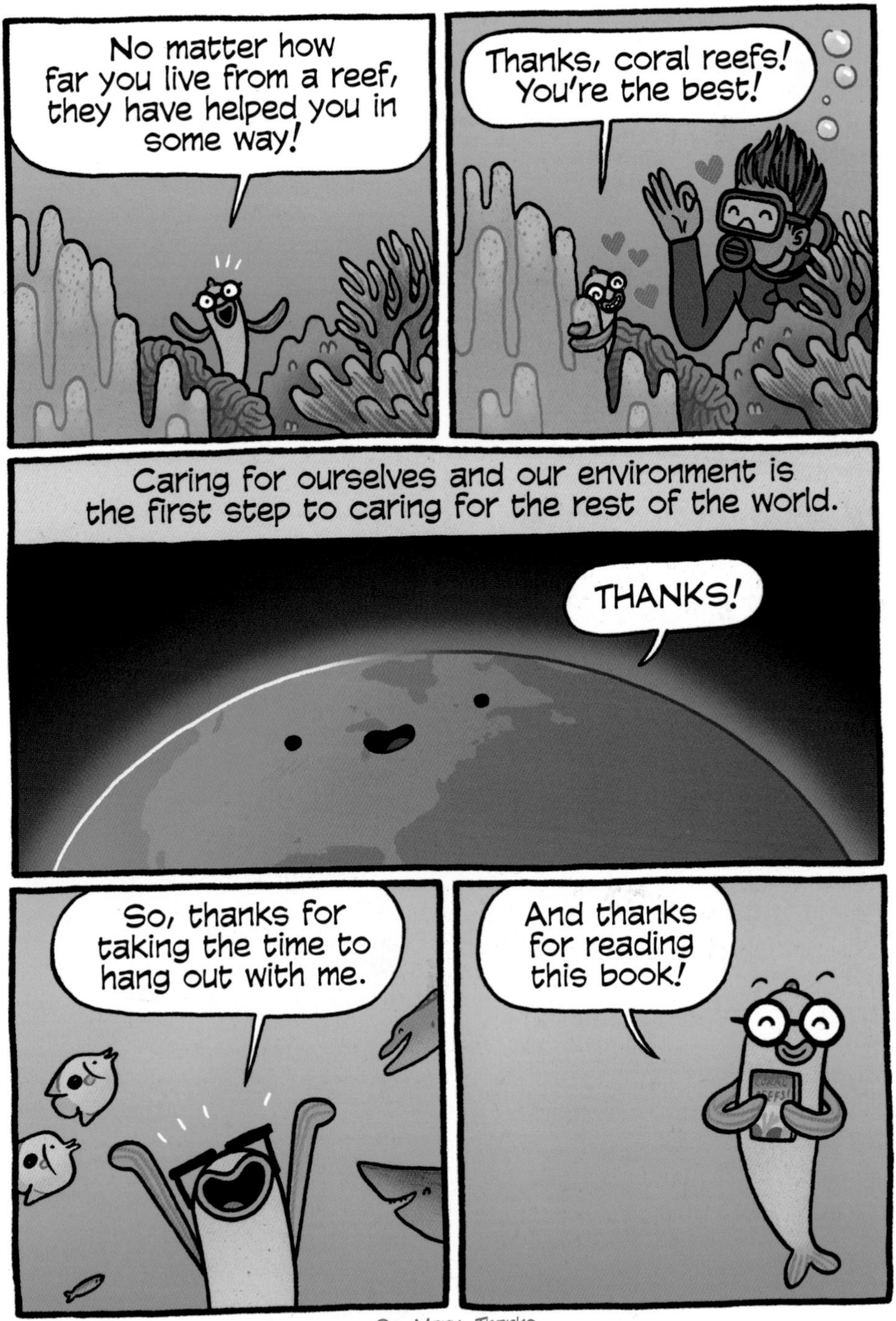
No matter how far you live from a reef, they have helped you in some way!
Thanks, coral reefs! You're the best!
Caring for ourselves and our environment is the first step to caring for the rest of the world.
THANKS!
So, thanks for taking the time to hang out with me.
And thanks for reading this book!

So. Many. Thanks.

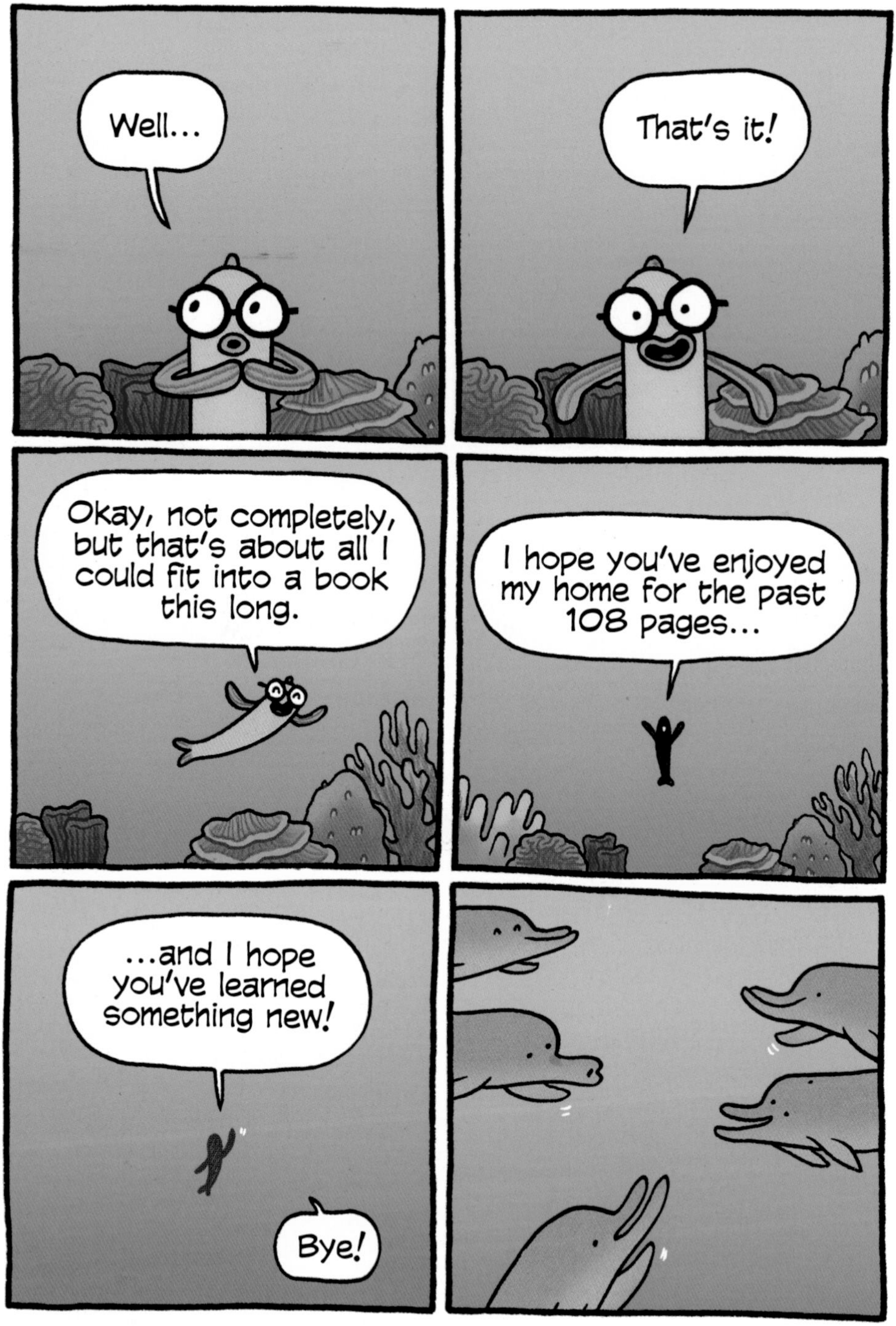
Well...
That's it!
Okay, not completely, but that's about all I could fit into a book this long.
I hope you've enjoyed my home for the past 108 pages...
...and I hope you've learned something new!
Bye!

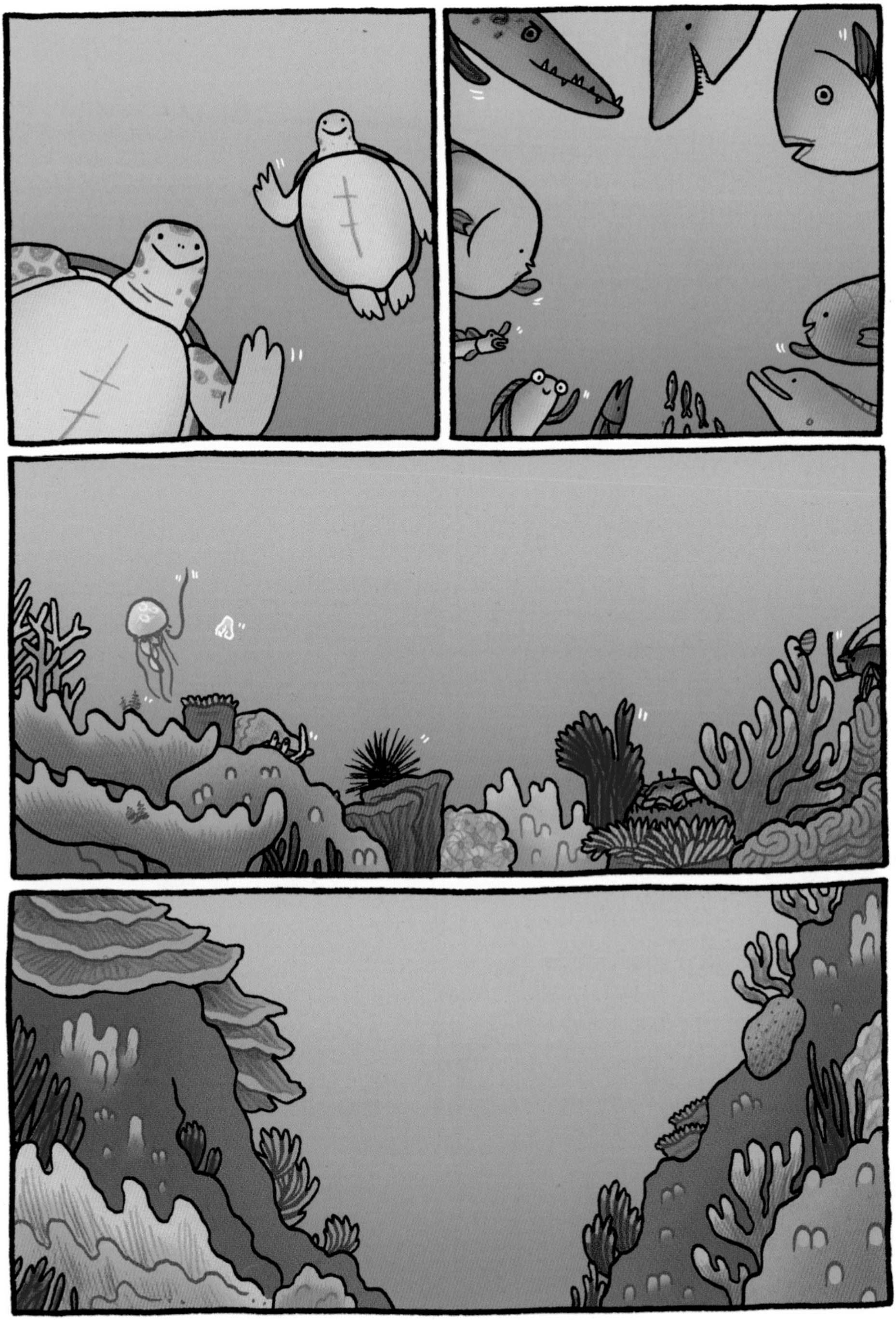

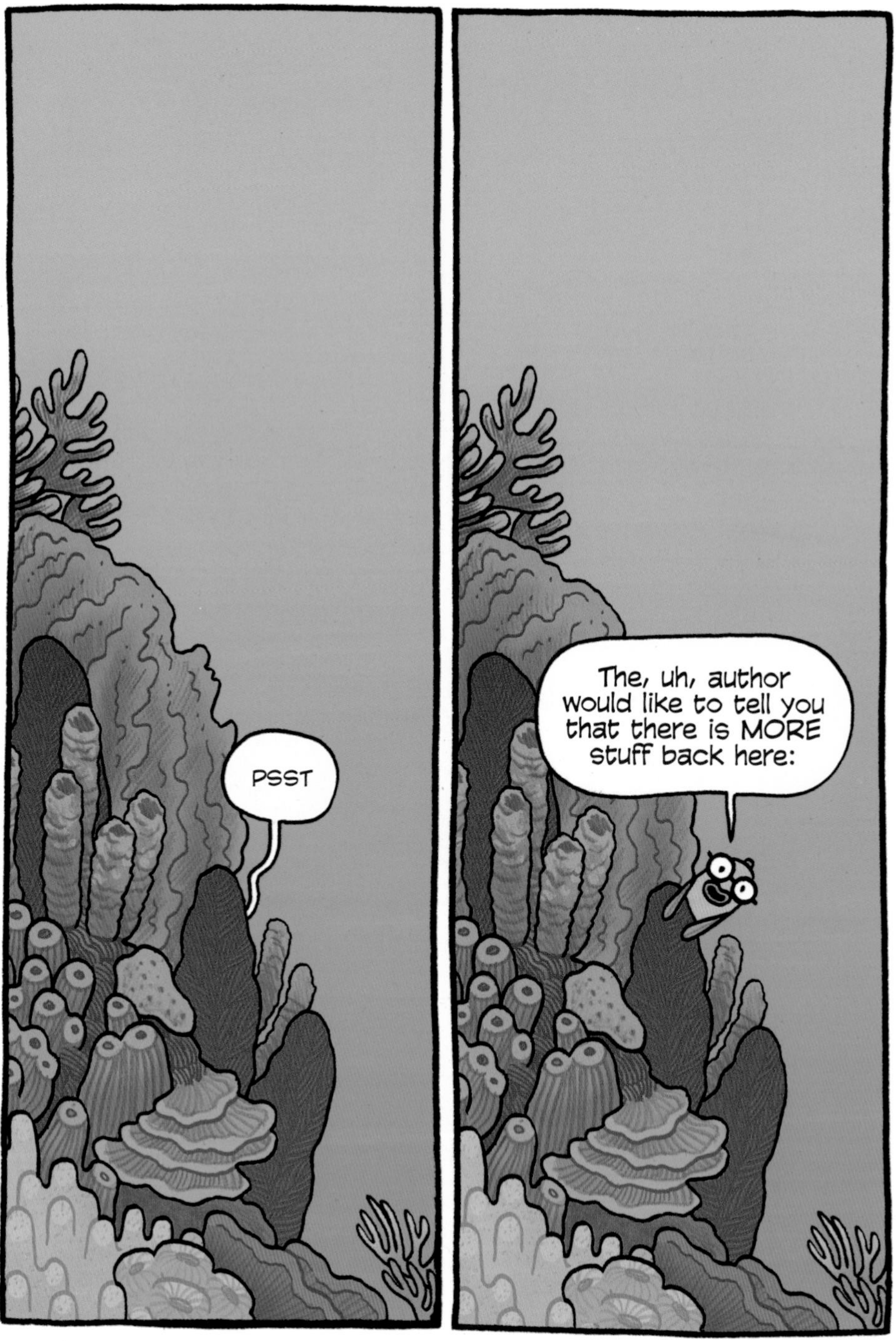
PSST
The, uh, author would like to tell you that there is MORE stuff back here:

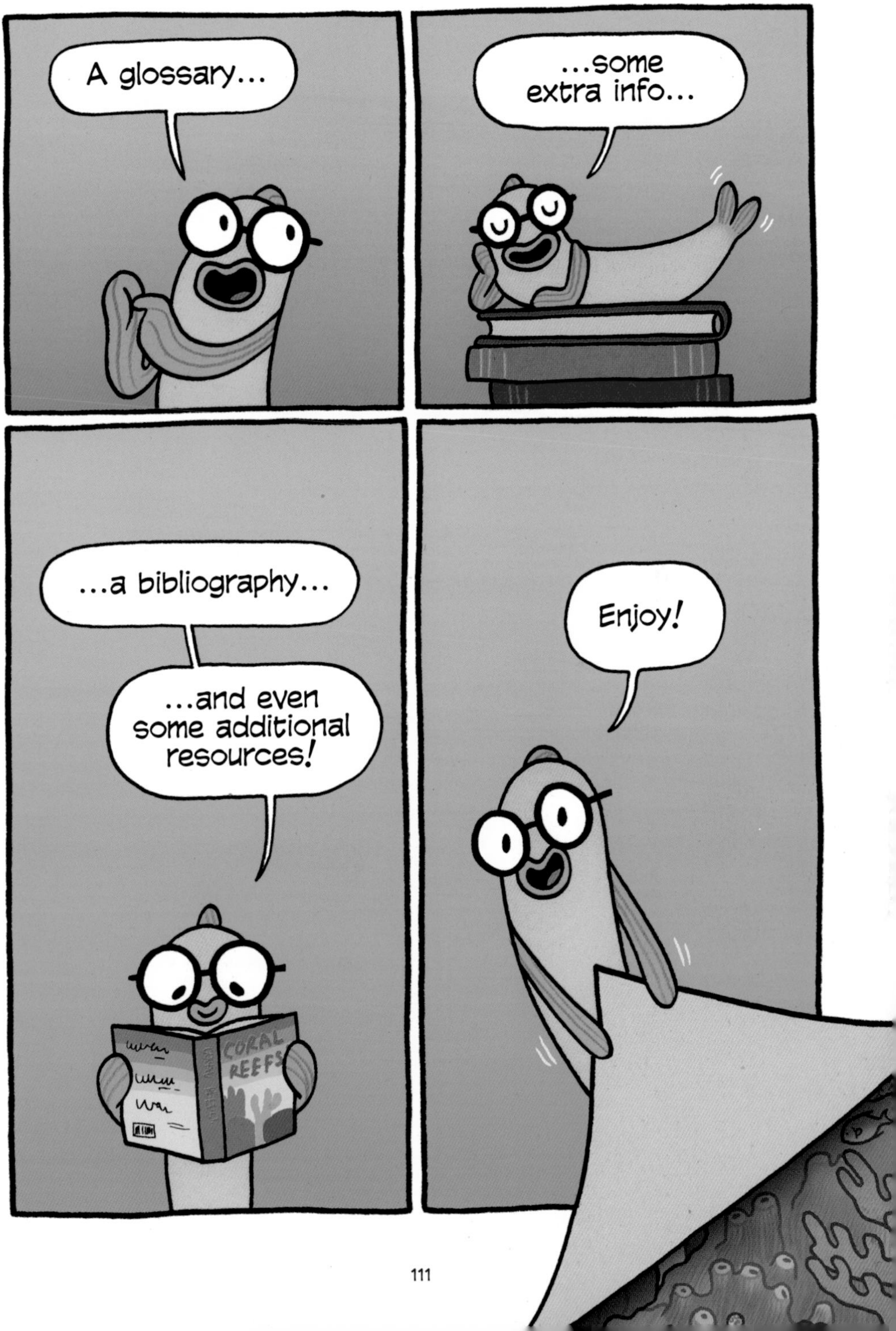
A glossary...
...some extra info...
...a bibliography...
...and even some additional resources!
CORAL REEFS
Enjoy!

—GLOSSARY—

Adaptation
> A change (or process of change) that helps an organism better survive in its habitat

Atom
> The smallest unit of matter

Biodiversity
> The variety of living organisms found in a habitat/ecosystem

Biology
> The study of living organisms

Calcium carbonate
> A molecule that helps form mollusk shells and hard corals

Carbon dioxide
> A gas that is important to plant life when it is at its natural levels; it is also a by-product of industry (factories, cars, buses, trucks, planes)

Climate
> The weather in an area, over a long period of time

Ecology
The study of the interactions of living organisms and their environment over space and time

Ecosystem
A community of organisms and their interaction with their environment

Environment
The surrounding area in which a person, plant, or animal lives

Evolution
The process by which living organisms have developed and changed over time

Exoskeleton
The hard external covering for the body in some invertebrates (like a lobster's shell)

Habitat
The place where an organism lives

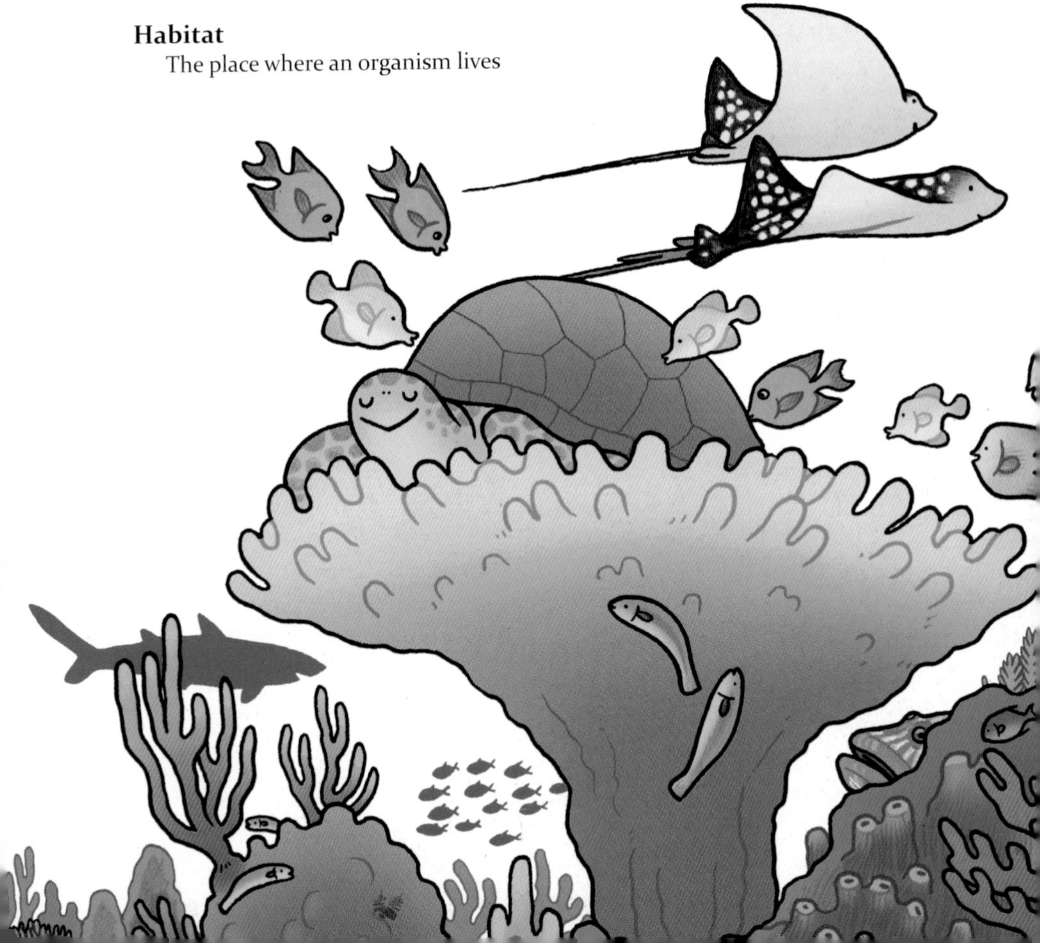

Invertebrate
   An animal that does not have a backbone

Life cycle
   The series of changes in the life of an organism (birth, growth, reproduction, death)

Molecule
   A group of atoms bonded together

Nematocyst
   Specialized stinging cell found in the tentacles of jellies, anemones, and corals

Organism
   A living thing (plant, animal, fungi, bacteria, etc.)

Oxygen
   A gas found in the air that supports most organisms found on Earth

Phytoplankton
   Plant plankton

Plankton
Organisms (often small or microscopic) that drift or float in the open water

Reproduction
The process by which organisms produce offspring

Salinity
The amount of salt in a body of water

Skeleton
An internal or external framework of bone, cartilage, or other hard material that supports or contains the body of a plant or animal

Vertebrate
An animal that has a backbone

Water cycle
The process by which water moves around the earth's oceans, atmosphere, and land

Zooplankton
Animal plankton

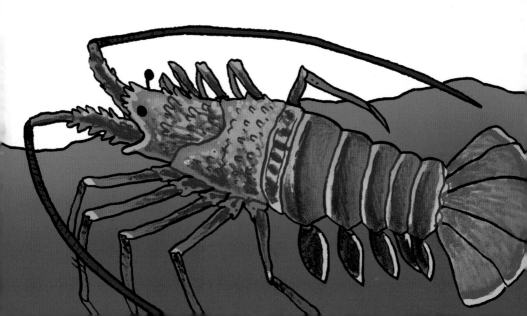

LOOKING INSIDE: A Coral Polyp

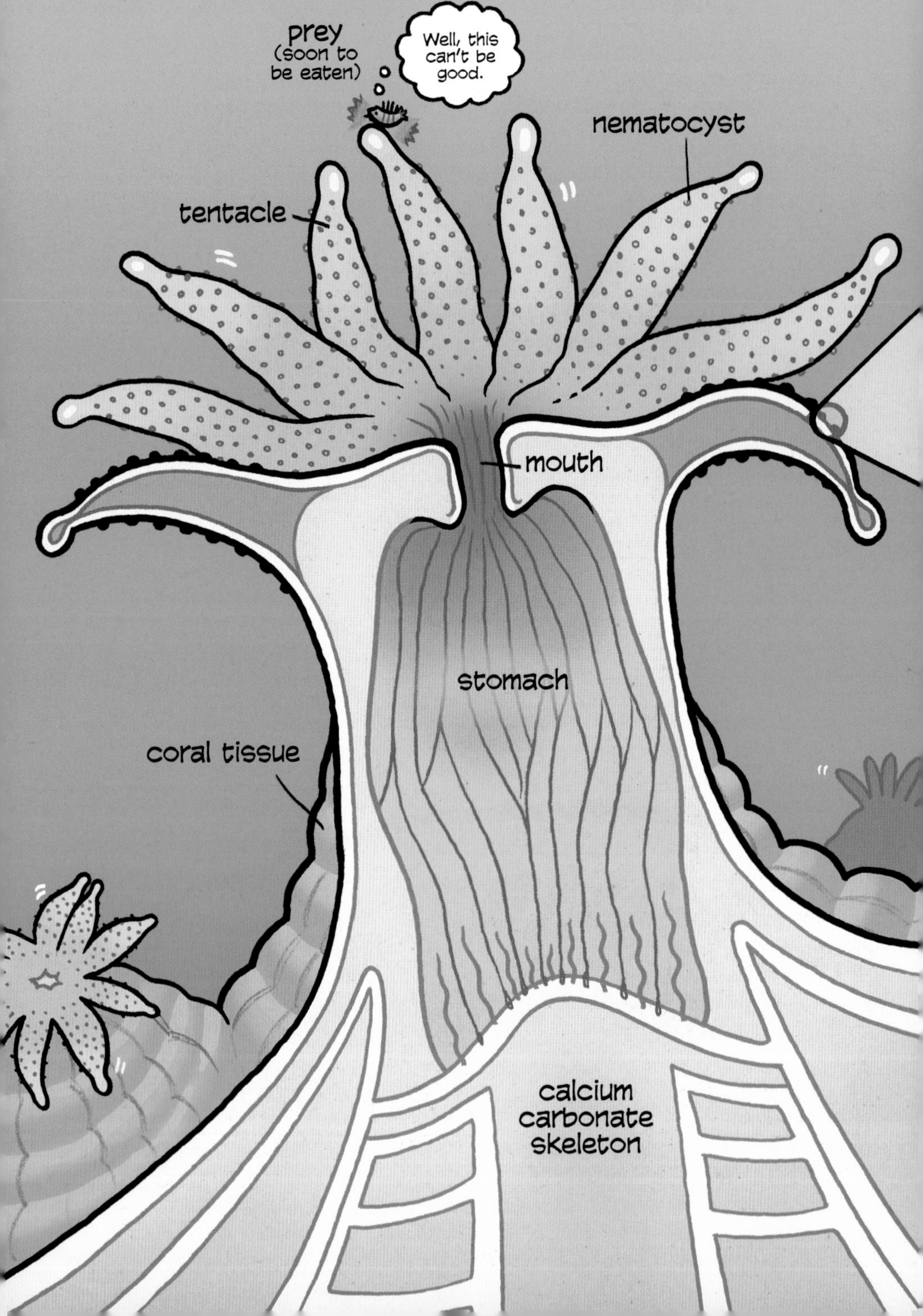
prey
(soon to
be eaten)
Well, this
can't be
good.
nematocyst
tentacle
mouth
stomach
coral tissue
calcium
carbonate
skeleton

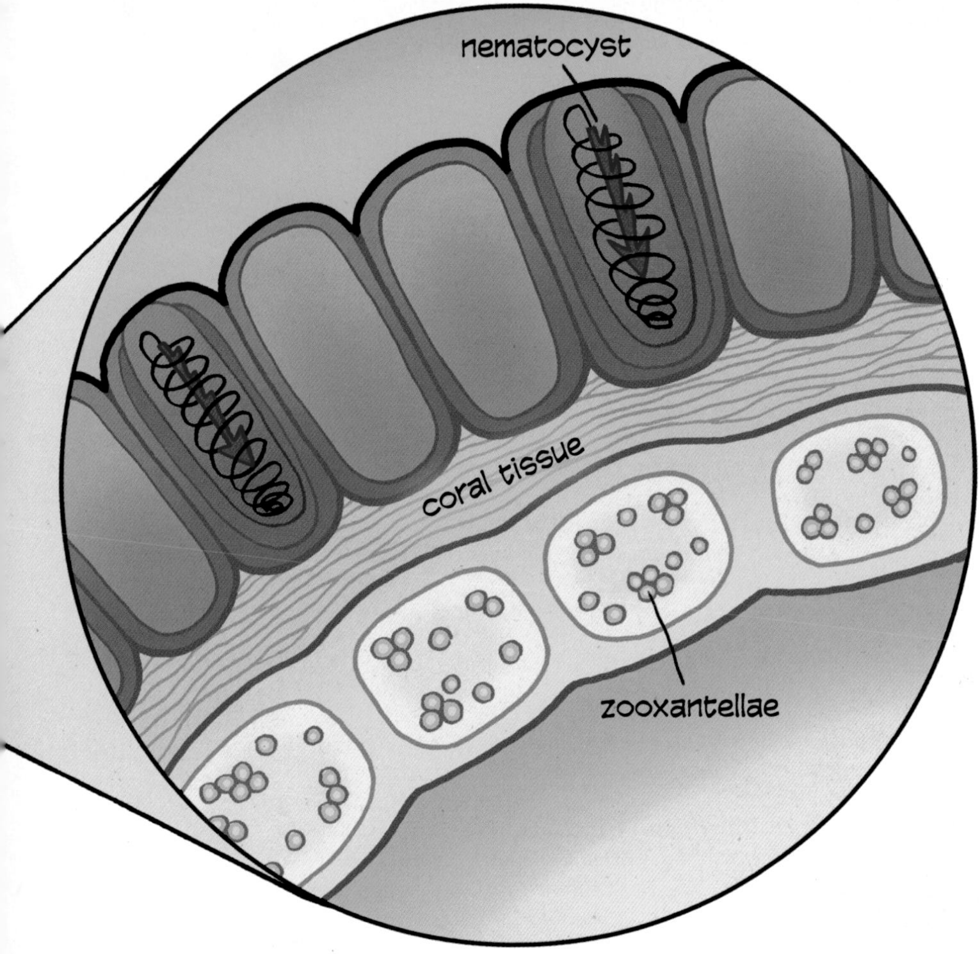
nematocyst
coral tissue
zooxantellae

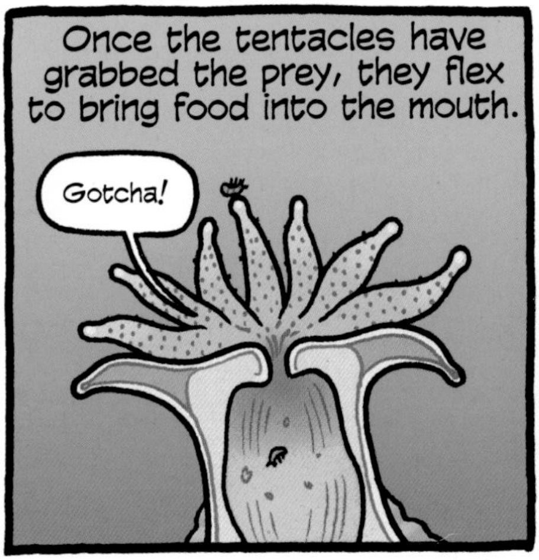
Once the tentacles have grabbed the prey, they flex to bring food into the mouth.
Gotcha!

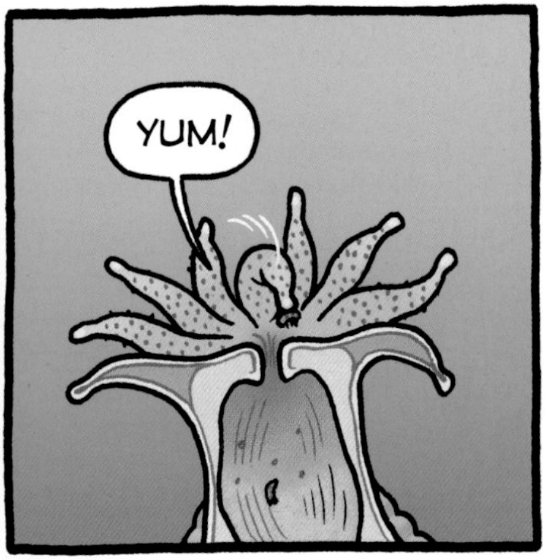
YUM!

—BIBLIOGRAPHY—

General Coral Reef Information

National Oceanic and Atmospheric Administration. "NOAA's Coral Reef Conservation Program." May 7, 2015. coralreef.noaa.gov

United States Environmental Protection Agency. "Coral Reef Protection: What Are Coral Reefs?" May 14, 2015. water.epa.gov/type/oceb/habitat/coral_index.cfm

Woods Hole Oceanographic Institution. "Coral." May 7, 2015. www.whoi.edu/main/topic/coral

Marine Species Identification Portal. May 7, 2015. http://species-identification.org

Conservation and Environmental Statistics

United States Environmental Protection Agency. "Wastes: Resource Conservation: Common Wastes and Materials." May 7, 2015. www.epa.gov/epawaste//conserve/materials/index.htm

United States Environmental Protection Agency. "Climate Change." May 7, 2015. www.epa.gov/climatechange

Pacific Marine Environmental Laboratory. "What Is Ocean Acidification?" May 7, 2015. www.pmel.noaa.gov/co2/story/What+is+Ocean+Acidification

Coral Reef Technology and Innovation

Salazar, Jorge. Earthsky.org. "Brent Constantz Builds Cement Like Corals Do." May 7, 2015. earthsky.org/human-world/brent-constantz-builds-cement-like-coral-do

ETH Zurich. Sepios: Nautical Robot. May 7, 2015. sepios.org

Levins, Nicole. The Nature Conservancy. "Ocean and Coasts: Coral Reefs: Nature's Medicine Cabinet." May 7, 2015. www.nature.org/ourinitiatives/habitats/oceanscoasts/explore/coral-reefs-and-medicine.xml

Quio, Charles Q. Popular Mechanics. "Shark Skin Will Inspire Faster Swimsuits and Airplanes." May 7, 2015. www.popularmechanics.com/science/animals/a10567/shark-skin-will-inspire-faster-swimsuits-and-airplanes-16792156

—ADDITIONAL RESOURCES—

Web

Phoenix Islands Protected Area. phoenixislands.org

Smithsonian Ocean Portal. "Corals and Coral Reefs." ocean.si.edu/corals-and-coral-reefs

Wired.com. "Interactive Coral Reef Panoramas." wired.com/2013/10/coral-reef-panoramas

National Geographic. "10 Things You Can Do To Help Save The Ocean." ocean.nationalgeographic.com/ocean/take-action/10-things-you-can-do-to-save-the-ocean

Books

Coral Reef: 24 Hours. Dorling Kindersley Children. 2005.

Cole, Brandon. *Reef Life: A Guide to Tropical Marine Life.* Firefly Books, 2013.

Knowlton, Nancy. *Citizens of the Sea: Wondrous Creatures From the Census of Marine Life.* National Geographic, 2010.

A great big fishy thanks to Casey, Calista, Danielle, and the rest of the First Second family. Without them, this book wouldn't be possible.

Another great big fishy thanks to the New England Aquarium, and all of my incredible coworkers. And to the wonderful folks at Boston Scuba. I think it's also safe to say that without them, this book wouldn't be possible.

Yet another great big fishy thanks to Rosemary, Sylvia, and (especially) Casey Z.; their feedback helped build the calcium carbonate base of this book.

I hope this book inspires you to get outside and have fun in nature, whether you live right on the beach, or 2,000 miles from one.

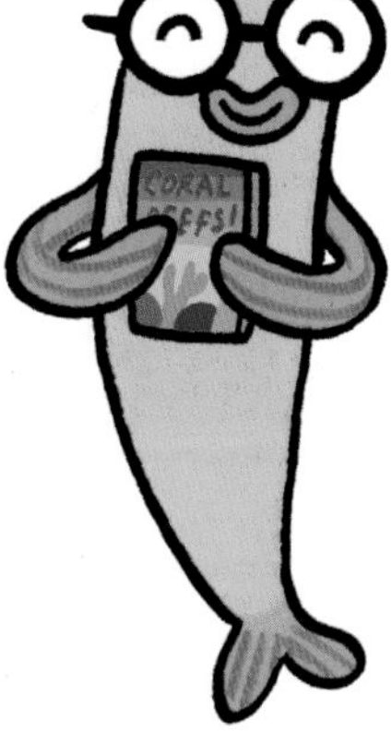
CORAL
REEFS!